A
CALL
AT
4 AM

A
CALL
AT
4 AM

Thirteen Prime Ministers
and the Crucial Decisions
that Shaped Israeli Politics

AMIT SEGAL

A WICKED SON BOOK
An Imprint of Post Hill Press

ISBN: 979-8-89565-202-2
ISBN (eBook): 979-8-89565-203-9

A Call at 4 AM:
Thirteen Prime Ministers and the Crucial Decisions that Shaped Israeli Politics
© 2025 by Amit Segal LTD
All Rights Reserved

Cover design by Jim Villaflores
Interior design and composition by Greg Johnson, Textbook Perfect

This is a work of nonfiction. All people, locations, events, and situations are portrayed to the best of the author's memory.

Post Hill Press
New York • Nashville
wickedsonbooks.com
posthillpress.com

Published in the United States of America
3 4 5 6 7 8 9 10

For Reut, Ivri, Aner,
and Eliana

The translation of this book into English was made possible through the generous support of Genesis Philanthropy Group.

Contents

Prime Minister's Questions

THE PRIME MINISTER SIPPED seltzer from a glass with the emblem of the State of Israel. Behind him was an Israeli flag. Facing him were three people with the national emblem on their uniform lapels—the blue uniforms of the Israel Police.

It was March 2017. Investigators from Lahav 443, the Israel Police's anti-corruption unit, entered the prime minister's residence on Balfour Street in Jerusalem again, bringing heavy boxes with recording equipment through the metal detectors. They had come to question the current tenant under warning, like all his predecessors since 1996. Benjamin Netanyahu was now not only a popular prime minister and admired international leader but also a criminal suspect. The event was broadcast live to the national police headquarters' and the attorney general's offices. In their hands, they now held the fate of a man who was more accustomed to holding other people's fates in his hands.

The detectives were sitting in a small office, a room that had seen historic decisions about war and peace—a backdrop that could hardly be more dramatic or more different from the Israel Police's regular interrogation rooms. Between the officers and the prime minister was a table, and on the table was a jumbled pile of fresh polling data, an envelope marked "Top Secret" containing a report from Mossad agents in Tehran, an old note from the king of Saudi Arabia, a framed photograph of the prime minister's children playing in the snow, and an economics book in English with a bookmark between the pages. The detectives began to bombard Netanyahu with accusations about the illicit benefits that he had allegedly received from a billionaire.

"Do you carry a wallet around, sir?" asked one detective.

"No," replied the prime minister.

"Not even a credit card?"

"Oh, give me a break," snapped the suspect. "I get cash taken out for me in the bank, and I put it in my pocket."

"Mr. Prime Minister," said the chief detective, raising his voice because Netanyahu denied any involvement, "do you really believe what you're saying?"

"Of course I believe it," the prime minister bellowed.

"And I'm telling you—you're lying."

Cue a knock on the door. A note was slipped inside.

"My apologies," said the suspect, suddenly switching back to the role of prime minister. "The president of the United States is looking for me on urgent business."

"Does this happen often?" asked the chief investigator suspiciously.

"Yes," replied the prime minister, shooing the detectives out of the room with a dismissive gesture. "Oh, and if you could please disconnect the recording equipment? This conversation is classified," he added.

After about half an hour of talking about Iran's ballistic missiles program on the telephone, the prime minister put down the red receiver. "Let's continue," he said.

"What color was the champagne you received?" asked the detective.

"Pink," replied Netanyahu.

That night, the prime-time news shows ran two main stories: Netanyahu's troubles with the law—and mysterious airstrikes on Iranian targets.

For any Israeli prime minister, life lurches at dizzying speeds between highs and lows, between cordial conversations with foreign presidents and massive headaches with party operatives, between historic decisions and historic political crises, between red telephones and pink champagne. For the most senior politicians, life is equally uplifting and absurd: standing on the steps of the royal palace in Oslo, where he was awarded the Nobel Peace Prize in 1994, Shimon Peres had to conduct a blitz of phone calls to settle a dispute between hawks in the Labor Party's local branch in Netanya.

When it comes to being prime minister, there is no such thing as "win some, lose some"—it is about winning one minute and losing the next. Whole platoons of journalists, private investigators, and political rivals wake up every morning with one goal in mind: to topple the prime minister. A prime minister's term in office usually begins with a stunning victory and rousing speech, catches few glimpses of glory on the way, and almost always ends very badly. In the meanwhile, the prime minister must be a leader, a manager, and a statesman all in one, and in order to fulfill these roles for as long as possible, the prime minister must first and foremost be a politician. The only way that Israel's leaders have managed to bridge the unfathomable gap between the highs of global diplomacy and the bottomless pits into which they stumbled was simply to play politics—and to do so better than any of their rivals.

Even seasoned observers of Israel struggle to understand it from afar. The Jewish state is a chaotic black box. What triggered the outbreak of war at this particular moment? How did a peace agreement suddenly materialize? Why have there been five national elections in three years? What is Israel: the gay pride parade in Tel Aviv or the tiny religious hilltop outposts? Following the events of October 7 and the subsequent regional conflict that erupted across seven different fronts, the desire to understand Israel has intensified, matched by a growing frustration at the inability to do so.

The reason for this is that the world looks at Israel through an international prism: its relations with the Arab world, how it battles terrorism, its singular alliance with the United States, and its complex history with Europe. However, there remains another Israel, one that outsiders either fail to see or have given up trying to understand: the Israel of domestic politics and its bizarre alliances. How is it that Israel's most socialist parties align with the right-wing bloc? Why are the most enthusiastic supporters of aggressive military action voters of ultra-Orthodox parties who refuse to serve in the army? How is it that in the Israeli left, prominent capitalist billionaires join forces with the communist party and battle-hardened generals collaborate with anti-Zionist Arab parties?

When an Israeli prime minister says to the president of the United States, "That, sir, I cannot do," he speaks not only as a statesman but also as a politician acutely aware of the precarious nature of his position, which is always just a few votes and days away from potential collapse.

When an American president is elected, it is for a full four years. An Israeli prime minister can be ousted at any moment by a no-confidence vote on a Monday afternoon at four o'clock. Consequently, anyone who wants to survive from one Monday to the next must constantly consider the delicate threads that hold their government together. No wonder they can't sleep at night.

So why have I written this book? Well, my late grandparents Shalom and Aviva were very strange people. He was a math teacher; she taught English. In their home office, they had two tables with two chairs, like two neighboring kingdoms with friendly relations but different languages. And they had thousands of books. There was an invisible border running down the middle of the room: my grandfather never read my grandmother's novels and poetry anthologies, and she never leafed through his tomes of math and physics. But they had a wonderful relationship. When she showed him a poem that she had written, he told her, "That's very nice, but I didn't understand a word." And when she had to calculate how much change she would receive at the corner store after buying a loaf of bread and some milk, he was always glad to help her. Despite everything, they shared one common interest: politics—and the understanding that it affects and shapes our lives.

Luckily for me, I have always been interested in both my grandfather's numbers and my grandmother's books. In politics, I found both of them by the bucketload. I have always had an almost perverse fascination about how ballots on Election Day get translated into Knesset seats, and about how the members of the Knesset can turn into a coalition that swears in a new government. The bizarre arithmetical process, whereby millions of votes can change the course of the ship of state, has always struck me as a wonder to be deciphered. The same goes for the funny rumor I once heard about political rivals who keep shouting at each other on TV and later sit down together in the canteen, and the one about ideological allies who look at each other in disgust and can barely say hello.

Take the Bader-Ofer Law, which used a mathematical formula to swindle the smallest parties and give their surplus votes to the Likud and Labor parties. It was named after its two Knesset sponsors: one from the Likud, who spent years sitting on the opposition benches next to Menachem Begin, and the other from Labor, who ended up taking his own life when he was suspected of corruption. "It's a mystery: My whole life, I have only helped as much as I could, and I have never done wrong to anyone, so why did this happen to me?" he cried in one of his last letters. Here is Israeli politics in a nutshell: skullduggery, friendship, corruption, tragedy—and the gulf between the exit polls and the real results. How can anyone not love it? Still, today, when I enter the Knesset or spend long nights waiting for the vote count, I can't believe that my employers pay me for this pleasure. Don't tell them that I would also do it for free.

I have not had the pleasure, of course, of meeting David Ben-Gurion (unless you count visiting the old man's desert hut) or Menachem Begin (although he and his wife, Aliza, went to the movies with my grandparents in Haifa once in the late 1940s). Yitzhak Shamir once visited my elementary school, and even then, I was shocked by how short he was; on TV, politicians always looked larger than life, and yet the prime minister had to look up to speak to sixth graders. I spent dozens of hours with Shimon Peres in the Knesset canteen and even longer with him at the president's residence, as he lounged around in blue jeans, propped his legs up on the sofa, and drank champagne in the middle of the afternoon. ("Raspberry juice" was his code word when he placed an order with his aides.)

This book does not claim to be a biography of all of Israel's prime ministers—there are enough books for that. My aim is to describe the political decisions that they made, just like politicians I knew more closely, under the perpetual specter of the voters' judgment and their desire to make history. The combination of their will to survive and the power of the most important office in the land generates an incredible energy, which has unleashed dramatic changes in Israel. Israel's prime ministers planned to form governments or break up parties, but quite unintentionally, they also changed history.

Nowadays people tend to be nostalgic about the politicians of yesteryear, intellectual giants with a clear sense of purpose. That might be true, but having reported from the Knesset for two decades, I can also remember that politicians from twenty years ago—the ones people miss nowadays—were also described in their time as spineless cynics, pale shadows of those who preceded them twenty years earlier, and so on. So I can't quite shake off a nagging thought: Are there more hidden truths about Israeli politics that it is time to refute?

Oxygen is always in short supply in the Knesset. The building was built before the Six-Day War, when there was still a fear of sniper fire from the Jordanian-occupied Old City of Jerusalem. At the last minute, therefore, the architect decided to change the Knesset building's orientation from east to west, with its back to the prevailing winds. As a result, no air comes through the windows and where there should be air—there are no windows. I learned this from the late writer Amnon Dankner, whose conclusion was stark: "Don't spend too long in the Knesset—it'll do irreversible damage to your brain."

If this book contains bits of nonsense here and there, it is because, against Dankner's recommendations, I ended up spending twenty years in the Knesset. In this time, I have learned a thing or two about politicians: For example, they tend to forgive you quite easily if you tell a lie about them, but some of them will never forgive you if you report an unflattering truth. Or that being a professional politician requires two different skill sets: the ability to wage guerrilla warfare in the hallways of power, committees, and the plenary and the ability to get elected, to get the public to follow your lead. Few people have complete command of both. What the vast majority of Israel's prime ministers had in common was that they knew their way around both Israel's streets and its long hallways of power; they felt at home both in smoke-filled rooms and in crowded squares. The people who have led Israel since 1948 have shaped, through their decisions, how Israelis elect their leaders, how those leaders form governments, how the public views *Haredim* (ultra-Orthodox Jews) or Arabs, and the worth of a politician's word. They shaped Israel itself.

This book contains eleven chapters about eleven key political decisions made by Israeli prime ministers: from the establishment of the Likud to the collapse of the left; from the moment that Israel was lumbered with an electoral system that has trapped it in endless cycles of elections to the invention of the "rotation" arrangement, an innovative Israeli solution to paralysis; and from the foundation of the right until the birth of the Israeli political center. All this against the dramatic backdrop of wars and peace agreements and of motorcades that keep getting longer and security cordons that keep getting tighter.

Why specifically these decisions? Because if you understand them, you will understand Israel's politics. Moreover, these decisions were born out of political necessity, but their impact is felt far beyond the Knesset's walls. Israelis tend to fail to appreciate how unusual it is that they vote based on the country's security situation much more than their own economic situation, and that all this began with a phone call that Golda Meir received at 4:00 a.m. They also tend not to understand the massive influence on their lives, from cradle to grave, of Ben-Gurion's choice of Israel's electoral system, which empowered tiny parties, or how Begin's Jewish identity shaped how TV networks still divide the electoral pie on election night. Or how, in their drab and quiet ways, Levi Eshkol and Yitzhak Shamir formed unity governments that cooled passions and led Israel to major achievements. The eleven decisions in this book represent, therefore, an alternative biography of the State of Israel.

—*Amit Segal*

CHAPTER 1

"A Cancer in the Body of the Nation"

Ben-Gurion's Decision— A World-Exclusive Electoral System

THREE WORDS, IF SPOKEN on the radio during rush hour, can trigger a worrying spike in road accidents: "the electoral system." Listeners yawn, drivers start dozing off at the wheel, and cars inexplicably veer from their lanes. Polls in Israel show that only 1 percent of respondents believe that this subject is important, with a margin of error of 4 percent. Mathematically, this means that the true level of interest might even be less than zero. If you ever want to get rid of Israeli guests after a dinner party that has gone on for too long, just say, "Hey, let's talk about the electoral system," and you will be pleasantly surprised by how quickly they grab their coats and disappear off to their cars.

It is only natural, therefore, for this book to begin with a long chapter about Israel's electoral system. I can only imagine my non-existent literary agent threatening to quit now. *Don't you dare use those three words,* she's warning me, wagging a finger. *You promised me stories about Sara Netanyahu? What about a bit of juicy gossip from the Knesset canteen? The book market is brutal enough as it is. Do you seriously expect to sell books like this?*

Call me a weirdo, or don't read my book, but there is nothing that captivates me, day and night, more than looking into the strange and mysterious ways in which citizens elect their rulers. "Espionage," John le Carré once wrote, "is the secret theater of our society." Allow me to propose another possibility: The depth of a nation's soul is reflected not only in its spy agencies but also in the system of government that it has chosen. Only at first glance does this seem like a matter of technical details, such as the electoral threshold, party list voting, or electors. Behind all these lurk nations' fears, traumas, and historical memories.

Take the United Kingdom, for example. The British political system reflects the two most sacred values in the eyes of the Queen's subjects (and I am not referring to English breakfast tea and the revolting sauce that they call HP, which tastes like printer toner): stability and tradition.

At the start of 2021, when this book was written, an elderly woman woke up in Buckingham Palace. A servant pulled open the curtains and served her a glass of gin, the first of four that day; then, documents were brought into the room in a red box embossed with the royal insignia. Thus began the 348,575th day of an almost uninterrupted monarchy. William the Conqueror became king of England in 1066, and ever since, spanning eleven centuries and two millennia, his direct descendants have reigned over this rainy island. The kings and queens of England have been cruel and kindhearted, wicked and righteous, young and old, popular and despised—but the sacred continuity has continued. Only once, in 1649, did English subjects rebel and kill their king, the miserable Charles I. This was a supremely un-English moment. Just a few years later, they wised up, looked at each other as if to say, "What have we done?!" and quickly returned the crown to his son's head and asked for forgiveness. They also decided to execute the chief rebel, Oliver Cromwell. It made no difference to them that Mr. Cromwell was already quite dead. His corpse was exhumed, hanged in public view, and beheaded—just to be extra sure that he was definitely dead.

That is what stability looks like. What about tradition? Once a year, at the official state opening of Parliament, the British hold a symbolic ceremony that exemplifies the supremacy of the House of Commons over the monarch, whose job has become largely symbolic over time. The door of the chamber is slammed shut in the face of the Queen's representative, who then taps on it three times with a black rod topped with a miniature golden lion. Since 1642, the same black rod has been struck on the same door every year in the name of the same crown. If you ever ask, "Siri, what's tradition?" your iPhone might give you a picture of the dent on the door caused by 1,134 knocks, three a year.

Countries that place their faith in tradition are unafraid to create political systems that impose and guarantee stability. The British electoral system is called "first past the post." The United Kingdom is divided into 650 electoral constituencies. The candidate who wins the most votes in the London neighborhood of Islington, for example, gets elected to Parliament, even if there were seven candidates and the winner only gained a small percentage of votes. This system almost always guarantees a parliamentary majority for the ruling party, even if it only wins as few as one-third of the votes. A party whose national vote share is only a few percentage points lower, meanwhile, might end up without a single seat. When, once in a generation, no party wins an absolute majority, raising the need for a coalition government, British pundits discuss the prospect with horror, as if the Queen had just been asked to leave her spacious palace and move into a shoebox apartment with roommates.

In Britain, a Conservative voter can live in a left-wing constituency and never in their whole life have the pleasure that Israelis regularly enjoy: to be represented in the legislature. In places with a warmer climate, this would have already sparked a revolution; but in Britain, the losers make do with downing a pint of Guinness and saying, "Things could have worked out better, don't you think?"

The American political system also teaches us a great deal about the most powerful nation in history. When the United States was born, its Founding Fathers were suffering post-traumatic stress disorder, still reeling from the Boston Tea Party. The stubborn King George III had given his assent to discrimination against American tea merchants in favor of their British competitors in order to line his kingdom's coffers. The British cared deeply about tea; the Americans, about liberty. They chucked crates of tea from British ships into the waters of Boston Harbor, paving a short road to the Declaration of Independence in 1776.

The young United States of America drew two lessons from the events in Boston: Never leave too much power in the hands of a single ruler—because they might become a tyrant—and always prioritize the individual and their interests over the collective. The American electoral system puts both of these lessons into practice: the United States does not have a king but a president—an innovative institution at the time of its creation, designed to make the head of state a kind of symbolic "director of the board" and not the powerful leader that he has since become. One thing that has not changed since the dawn of American political history is the principle of checks and balances: Congress is usually controlled by the rival party to the president. The president of the United States is usually considered the most powerful person in the world, but most of the time, he is probably not even the most powerful person in Washington. America, the Founding Fathers promised, would never see a dictator.

No less importantly, Americans do not vote for political parties but for specific people. In principle, one can be elected president without belonging to any political movement. Americans go to the polls with alarming frequency and always vote for individuals: Each citizen casts a vote for president, senators, members of Congress, governor, and sometimes also judges, attorneys general, and sheriffs. That's America: a country of 330 million individuals.

Americans become deeply suspicious when they encounter powerful organizations in which individuals might disappear completely, and they are also deeply suspicious of central government. If they can buy a fridge from a hundred different brands, why should their roads always be paved by the same government? Federalism, the decentralization of power into fifty different states, was designed to open up to competition something that in Israel is a greasy and inefficient monopoly: government. If I am disappointed with my fridge, I can always switch to Samsung, Bosch, or Siemens. But what if I am fed up with getting so little back for my tax dollars? In theory, as an Israeli, I can always choose to emigrate—but what if I am a proud patriot or simply love the vibe in Tel Aviv? The federal system invites citizens to treat government as a service and the state as a service provider, which is exposed to competition. If California hikes up taxes and provides them with power cuts and megafires in return, Californians can always move to Texas. But in tiny Israel, as anyone who has ever tried dealing with tax authorities knows, a culture of service is hardly the state's strong suit. It is hard to be the realization of a millennia-old dream while at the same time also fretting about improving sanitation infrastructure.

Modern Germany was founded atop the rubble of the terrifying Nazi regime, and the people who designed its political system live in the same square mile that spawned the absolute evil that murdered tens of millions of people. The architects of the new federal republic, determined to stop another monster from seizing power by democratic means, decided to do everything exactly the opposite from before. If the Führer laid waste to Europe from his smoke-filled underground bunker, the new chancellor's office would be made of glass, so that anyone strolling through the Tiergarten could see Angela Merkel at work.[i] If Adolf Hitler rose to power on the back of a dictatorial party, in Germany, any political party without internal democracy and primaries would be shut down, disbanded, and banned. Israelis might joke about Avigdor Lieberman or Yair Lapid's one-man rule, but if they were German, agents from the Federal Office for the Protection of the Constitution would have shown up at their doors with an arrest warrant long ago.

So what does Israel's electoral system say about it? Well, first and foremost, it reflects the most sacred Israeli value of all, the rock of Israel's existence: slapdashery. Ben-Gurion's many biographies hardly mention the consequential debate that shaped how, for the first time in history, the Jewish people would elect its leaders. That's no coincidence. Appropriately for a country that was dreamed about for two thousand years but built in a fit of absentmindedness, the meeting that decided how Israel would elect its leadership, in late 1948, was not particularly long. Only three people took part in it: Israel's first prime minister, David Ben-Gurion, Interior Minister Yitzhak Gruenbaum, and Justice Minister Pinchas Rosen. Their sense of urgency was understandable: They had to choose a state emblem, bring over tens of thousands of immigrants on chartered flights and rickety boats, force open the road to Jerusalem, drive back the Arab invasion—and all this before lunch.

They were short on time and drowning in work. Any debate on the choice of a political and electoral system requires decisions on three fateful questions: First, how much power do you want to give a rival leader, whose personality and policies you completely oppose? Second, should politics be a story about people or about ideology? And third, what is more important: to let elected officials get on with governing or to give the voters maximum representation?

---

[i] Owing to its appearance, Berliners sarcastically call one of the transparent, rounded wings of the Bundestag *die Bundeswaschmaschine*: "the federal washing machine."

The first question concerns the nature of the political regime: presidential or parliamentary. Presidents are directly elected by the people for fixed terms. Prime ministers, in contrast, are elected by their countries' parliaments. They are appointed and ousted not by the voters, but by fellow politicians. If they ignore them, belittle them, or even worse, not answer their phone calls, they will find the movers outside their official residence sooner than expected.

The second question is more philosophical than political: Should we place our faith in ideas or individuals? Should politicians win the public's confidence by force of personality, or should they simply be the faceless messengers of a great idea? Direct elections presuppose that politicians are more important than their parties or principles. Proportional representation, meanwhile, encourages people to coalesce around a shared platform, band together as a political party, and go hunting for votes as a team.

The third question is about the supreme value in a democracy: representation or governance? If all we care about is governance, then maybe one person should receive all the power—and all 120 seats in the Knesset. But this, of course, would swiftly become a dictatorship, silencing the voices of millions of voters. On the other hand, if what matters most is representation, then perhaps we should simply abolish parliaments and hold referenda on everything, from deciding to go to war to raising VAT (value-added tax). This would also not be particularly successful: Democracy is a wonderful thing, but too much of it can be lethal. We pay politicians' salaries so that they can make unpopular decisions, for which we will hate them and ultimately boot them from power.

The right model, therefore, must be something in the middle. And the debate is about the purpose of the imposing concrete structure known as the Knesset: Is it a place where arguments are conducted or decisions are made?

The State of Israel made this historic decision, one that would shape Israelis' fate for generations, in little more than an hour: It opted for prime minister, not president; ideas, not individuals; arguments, not decisions.

Let's step out of the cloistered room where Ben-Gurion chose Israel's electoral system for a moment and look at the young country from the outside: Israel was a society in which the most vulgar word that anyone could say was "me." It was a culture that sanctified modesty and glorified the Palmach paramilitary and pioneers—not small business owners and city dwellers. It was a country whose greatest ideal was the world-beating invention of the kibbutz, which aimed to subordinate any sign of individuality to the great socialist vision of collectivism and equality. Kibbutz members fought with one hand against seven Arab armies and with another against egoism and bourgeois values.

The first Israelis admired the kibbutzniks. They elected no fewer than twenty-six of them to the First Knesset.[1] The kibbutzim of Mishmar HaEmek and Ein Harod each sent five representatives to the legislature. In 1978, Aharon Yadlin, one of the most popular officials in the left-wing Alignment, announced his surprise resignation from the Knesset. The reason quickly came to light: The members of his kibbutz, Hatzerim, had demanded that he quit public life and go back to working on the farm. They intended for this former education minister to become their duty dishwater; after three months, he would be promoted to the role of "integration coordinator"; and if he proved his worth, he would be appointed secretary of the kibbutz. The press ran photos of Yadlin standing behind massive dirty pots in the communal canteen of the kibbutz.[2]

It was a time when the "will of the movement" was not an empty excuse for self-justifying politicians but a genuine reason for their actions. Politicians had their own desires back then, of course, but they avoided publicizing their hunger for power in order not to turn off the voters. When Israel's third prime minister, Levi Eshkol, died in office, Golda Meir was horrified to read a report in the newspaper that she wanted to succeed him. Back then, the best way to thwart an Israeli politician's promotion was to prove that they wanted it.[3] "I have never been asked something so cruel," she said, wringing her hands, when asked to head the government.[4] In the end, she obliged, nonetheless.

If we jump back to Ben-Gurion's office, hoping that we haven't missed the big decision, it is no surprise that the young country was about to adopt one of the most extreme electoral systems anywhere on earth: Israel, it was decided, would never elect a person, only an idea. The movement is more important than the man; the party, more important than the individual.[ii] Since then, when Israelis step into the voting

---

ii It helped that the famous United Nations General Assembly resolution of November 29, 1947, called for the legislature of the young Jewish state to be elected "on the basis of proportional representation."

booth, they are faced only with the names of parties, not of individual candidates. They might think that they are voting against Netanyahu as prime minister but end up electing the twenty-ninth candidate on his party's list, whose name they have never heard before. Israeli electoral law gives no particular advantage to the first person on a party's list, even if they lead their party to winning all 120 seats in the Knesset. The day after the elections, even the most anonymous backbencher can form a government.

The first rule of shopping at a market is never to buy strawberries in a box, only in bulk—one by one. Otherwise, the stallholder will slip you the rotten ones at the bottom. In politics, the rule is completely different: The rotten ones usually rise to the top, but as a voter, you have to take the whole box.

The power given to Israeli political parties has given rise to an eye-popping paradox: In the holy of holies of Israeli democracy, the Knesset plenary, lawmakers are prevented from exercising their democratic right to vote as they see fit. They are obligated by factional and coalitional discipline. Meir Ariel, the popular Israeli folk singer, sang about this once: "I've noticed that members of Knesset sometimes / get permission to vote according to their conscience, / which means that most of the time, / members of Knesset are voting against their conscience."[5]

The party list system means that one can only enter the Knesset by public transport, so to speak: on party buses, not in private vehicles. Of the 194 countries in the world, only the Netherlands and Slovakia have similar electoral systems.

Look at Israel in the eighth decade of independence: at the glistening skyscrapers of Tel Aviv, the narcissistic outbursts on social media, the politicians who remember to say "we" only when they discover a need to share the heavy burden of failure. Look at the privatized kibbutzim. One day, in 2015, Israel woke up to discover that not a single kibbutznik remained in the Knesset. Only Israel's electoral system has remained loyal to kibbutz values.

Ben-Gurion's second decision was about the electoral threshold. Imagine the electoral threshold as a barrier outside the Knesset building, where the guards check the trunk of every car. Only parties that have crammed enough votes inside can drive through the gates of the legislature. How strict should the security check be? If the bar is too high, only a few parties will be able to enter. In this scenario, it would be quite easy to govern inside, but the outside would be swarming with disgruntled crowds. If the number of required votes is lowered, in contrast, only a few disappointed souls will be left outside—but the inside will be a cacophonous mess and extremely difficult to govern.

Here too, Israel's Founding Fathers made a highly unusual choice: At the entrance of the old Knesset building, they decided that there would be no barrier at all. Any party that won enough votes for a single seat would be represented in the Israeli parliament. And thus, the First Knesset contained one representative from the Yemenite Association; one from WIZO, the Women's International Zionist Organization (a sixty-year-old housekeeper from Haifa); one farmer and one lawyer from a small local party in Nazareth; and even a single representative from the small Lehi paramilitary group. Three thousand votes were all one needed to serve in the world's first Jewish legislature.

Why did Ben-Gurion avoid raising the electoral threshold, which might have reduced the number of parties from twelve to three or four? Here too, he was giving expression to the soul of the nation. Biblical Judaism featured hugely powerful monarchs, but the rabbinical Judaism that followed the destruction of the Second Temple in 70 CE exalted and glorified arguments. Every morning, the *beit midrash*—the Jewish study hall—hosted a noisy debate club. "These and these are the words of the living God," declared nobody other than the Almighty himself, according to one popular Talmudic story. Students of the Talmud often find themselves at their wits' end after reading arguments that go on for pages and pages and then end suddenly without a resolution. It is as if the editor of the Talmud was so engrossed by this breathtaking battle of brains that he forgot that in the end there had to be a real decision.

The fact of argumentation as the way of life is also a natural consequence of Jewish history: After two thousand years without central leadership or elected institutions, it was impossible for any particular group to impose its will on others by means of law, guns, or the police. All they had was their words.

Throughout the ages, rabbinical Jews clashed with Karaites and the rabbi Maimonides with other contemporary luminaries. The scholarly Misnagdim went head-to-head with Hasidic Jews; Reform Jews clashed with Orthodox Jews. And for the most part, Jews waged these battles with the most lethal weapon at their disposal: their sharp tongues. During the long, cold years of the Jews' dispersion, they kept themselves warm through words. Lots of words. The word "parliament"—from the French *parler*, meaning "to speak"—could have been coined for the chosen people. When the sun rose on Zionism at the famous conference in Basel in 1897, the Jews were already squabbling with each other as factions. In a famous song, Yoram Taharlev wondered whether this was what killed the Jewish state's founding visionary, Theodor Herzl: "One demands revolution, the other equality / one demands the whole of Zion / and Herzl, who had nothing left in his life / gave them his heart and shut his eyes."[6]

There was also another reason: In its first few years, Israel absorbed immigrants from dozens of Jewish communities around the world, almost all from countries without a tradition of democracy. The conflict between pre-state Israel's two major paramilitary groups over the authority to use arms within the borders of the new state had ended a few months earlier with Israel Defense Forces (IDF) artillery shelling the *Altalena*, a ship ferrying arms for the rival Irgun militia. Nineteen Jews were killed, and Menachem Begin, the incoming leader of the opposition, was nearly the twentieth casualty. In an act symbolizing Israel's admission into the Middle East, government cannons took potshots at the future opposition leader. He jumped into the water and swam ashore to Tel Aviv, shivering with cold and fury. The young State of Israel took advantage of the first ceasefire in the war against the Arabs for a brief war between the Jews.

So many years later, it is hard to grasp the reality in which the Arabs of Israel, citizens of the young state, went to the polls just a few months after some of them waged a battle of life and death against the same Jewish state. Many Arabs had been killed, many had been expelled, and the minority who remained soon received voting cards embossed with the reviled Star of David.

It is easy to understand, therefore, why Israel decided to adopt a system that would give almost every citizen their own representative in the Knesset. In the absence of a democratic tradition and under the specter of a deadly national conflict, there was a genuine fear that any minority who felt unrepresented would try to storm the parliament building with tanks.

This fear has subsided over the years. In the 1950s, stones were thrown at the Knesset during a protest against the reparations deal with West Germany, and a prime minister was murdered in the heart of Tel Aviv because of a bitter dispute over the state's borders, but the overall score for Israeli democracy is "very good." As of 2021, a total of 2,322,099 votes have been wasted under the electoral threshold. But nobody has tried to storm the Knesset building. Even on the Knesset's stormiest days, it is worth remembering that the opposition leader in Egypt is in jail, the opposition leader in Syria drives around in an armored personnel carrier, the opposition leader in Lebanon lies six feet under, and the opposition leader in Israel meets the prime minister once a month for a friendly conversation over coffee and bagels.

One thing that could have strengthened the connection between voters and their representatives, which even then looked quite flimsy, would have been regional elections. Ben-Gurion considered this briefly before deciding against it: There was still a war raging over the nation's borders. So many soldiers were stuck in the freezing cold, miles from their homes, unable to return to vote. One in one hundred citizens would be killed throughout Israel's War of Independence, and many of the men were still fighting on the front. With the country's borders fluctuating day by day, there was no point dividing the country into electoral constituencies. Israel was fated to be a state without voting districts.

One of the immediate results of this decision was that the inescapably sour aftertaste that lingers in every democracy would be especially sour for Israel's citizens: the feeling that public representatives are disconnected. The reason is, indeed, that they really are disconnected. This is worth repeating: In Israel, citizens do not elect members of the Knesset. They elect parties, which elect members of the Knesset, who elect the prime minister, who nominates ministers.

This is all connected to the absence of constituencies—another word that does not exist in Hebrew because there has never been a need for it. The word "constituency" describes not just a voting district, but the sacred relationship between members of parliament and the inhabitants of the districts who elected them as their representatives. In most of the world, nothing is dearer or more sacred to politicians than the satisfaction of their voters, far away at home. If the representative for Iowa's Third Congressional District has the president of the United States waiting on the phone, but on the other line has an activist for the local beef industry also waiting, it is anyone's guess which person the Iowan congressman will answer first. In Britain, the foreign secretary can schmooze with the world's rich and powerful during the week, but every Friday he or she must listen attentively as local residents complain about municipal taxes or garbage collections, and the same goes for every other member of the British Parliament.

Even the short working week of just three days and the long recesses— one month in the summer, two in the spring—were designed to enable politicians to return from the capital and visit their constituents in the days before telephones, computers, and airplanes. In the nineteenth century, a senator from Florida had to travel back home for weeks from Washington, DC, in a horse-drawn wagon in order to meet the people who had sent him there, hear their petitions, and tell them about his work on their behalf. Most members of the Knesset are just an hour from home and a click of a button from their voters, but they still enjoy nearly one hundred days of vacation a year.[iii]

The Israeli electoral system, like matzah, is only half-baked. The people who came up with it kneaded it into Israel's national ethos, the Jewish character, their deep worry for the young country's stability, and short-term practical concerns. *Never mind*, they consoled themselves, *we'll try it out once, and if it doesn't work—we'll just change it!* This is probably also what the Israelites thought when they escaped from Egypt, but we are still eating their matzah recipe over three thousand years later. Ben-Gurion, eat your heart out.

The Israeli electoral system fits Israel like your high school jeans fit you in your middle age. It used to suit Israel perfectly. But with more "me" and less "us," in the absence of fears of a civil war, in a feverish

---

iii Nevertheless, the absence of constituencies from Israel's political system is not completely regrettable: The dark side of the close link between elected officials and their constituencies is the narrow thinking and use of legislation for political bribery at taxpayers' expense. Felipe González, Spain's prime minister from 1982 to 1996, was a resident of Seville. In order to placate his constituents, he decided, contrary to all logic, that Spain's first high-speed railway line would not connect its two biggest cities, Madrid and Barcelona, but his beloved hometown and the capital Madrid. When I took this train in 2010, I enjoyed the silence and solitude of a totally empty carriage, without knowing why it was empty. This kind of provincial politics is known as "pork barrel politics" because US congressmen in the nineteenth century made sure that pork was purchased in barrels from their specific constituencies.

world that prefers snap judgments over never-ending debates—Israel's electoral system no longer fits the new generation of Israelis.

Ben-Gurion was not thrilled with the scheme to begin with. He favored regional elections, with directly elected members of the Knesset, but somewhat out of character, he was not particularly insistent. If there was one person in Israel who could have comfortably said, "L'État, c'est moi," it was Ben-Gurion. With his signature combination of prophetic vision and sharp-elbowed politicking, he did everything to shape the State of Israel exactly as he envisaged it. When needed, he did not hesitate to use the security services to eavesdrop on political rivals. He doggedly persecuted rival paramilitary groups during the *Saison* (the crackdown on the Irgun insurgency against the British authorities), forcefully dismantled the Palmach, volunteered helpless Jewish immigrants from Arab countries to settle the desert, and forced IDF generals to adopt new surnames because he believed that proper Hebrew soldiers should be commanded by officers with proper Hebrew names. He intervened in everything in obsessive detail, from Israel's nuclear program to the flag design. Even *ptitim*, the toasted pasta ball dish that became a staple of Israeli cuisine for decades, was invented on his orders as a substitute for rice. His political enemies, of whom there was no shortage, came up repeatedly against an iron fist. The State of Israel would be made in the image of one man alone.

So how was it possible that it was *this* leader who suddenly accepted, with such equanimity, an electoral system that would constrain his power? The biblical hero Samson was shorn of his hair and stripped of his strength because he succumbed to the dark charms of a philistine beauty, but Ben-Gurion surrendered his political powers of his own free will. There was no Delilah to make him imprison his party and himself in the chains of a coalition. He was a genius and a cruel man, but nobody ever accused him of generosity.

We shall probably never know the answer: Ben-Gurion's biographies are too stingy on the details. Perhaps he felt that this was one battle too many, or perhaps he was just a bit complacent. His party, Mapai, in any case, enjoyed clear primacy and a perfect place in the center of the political map.

Ben-Gurion would live to regret his decision bitterly. When the ballots were counted for the Constituent Assembly soon after independence,

Mapai was disappointed to discover that it had won only a third of the votes: The party won forty-four seats in the 120-seat assembly, with a huge lead over every other party, but not enough to govern by itself. Its leader would soon discover that he had been stripped of his powers to shape the State of Israel in his image: He wanted a constitution but gave in to the religious parties' aversion to the principle of equality. He wanted universal conscription, but the ultra-Orthodox representatives put up a fight, and he found that he had been outmatched.

Ben-Gurion would also pay an even heavier price: Over the years, he resigned as prime minister no fewer than seven times because of political crises inflicted on him by Israel's electoral system. The statist leader who crafted Israel in his own image would keep banging his head against the wall in frustration at the system that granted so much power to the most fringe parties. But the wall on which he kept banging his head never fell down.

It is easy to understand why Ben-Gurion wanted a majoritarian system of constituency-based elections: It would allow any party that won widespread support across most of the country to govern with an alarming amount of power. In 1969, the Alignment (the successor of Ben-Gurion's Mapai) won fifty-six seats, compared to the twenty-six for Menachem Begin's Gahal party. But if the elections had been held on a regional basis, the Alignment would have mustered an astonishing 103 seats.[8] On the other hand, Ben-Gurion, who despised Begin, would have been horrified to know that in 2020, his original choice of electoral system would have given Netanyahu's Likud not thirty-six seats but ninety-two.

Israel's founding father set about fighting the golem that he had created with his own bare hands in the only way that he knew: stubbornness, with a splash of obsession. The inventor of the Israeli melting pot claimed that the electoral system was fostering divisions between the country's ethnic groups, between native-born Israelis and new immigrants, and between different cultures.[9] He even called it "a cancer in the body of the nation." But none of the treatments to excise this tumor worked.

With the formation of Israel's fourth government, it was agreed to raise the electoral threshold to 10 percent, which would sweep the fragments of splinter parties out of the Knesset once and for all.[10] But it was then that the absurd power of these fragments proved itself: Although two parties in the coalition enjoyed an absolute majority in the Knesset, they had to make more and more concessions—from 10 to 5 percent, then from 5 to 4, and by the time they dropped to 2 percent, Ben-Gurion had lost interest. Even after seventy years of superhuman efforts on the part of the major parties, the electoral threshold remains much lower than they wanted, at just 3.25 percent.[iv]

From this point, everything went downhill. Instead of focusing on his own party's election campaign, Ben-Gurion spent the campaign for the Third Knesset sponsoring a satellite party that supported changing the electoral system, but this party failed to take off and quit the race. In the run-up to the elections for the Fifth Knesset, Ben-Gurion demanded that the Mapai's platform contain just a single promise: a new electoral system.[11] The rejection of his proposal marked the end of the road for Israel's first prime minister in the movement that he had helped to found back in 1948.

Here we have the answer to an ancient philosophical riddle: Ben-Gurion *did* create a rock that was too heavy—even for him—to lift.

It is easier to grasp the drawbacks of Israel's system if we look at its political calendar and divide it into two periods: one, when Israel has a transitional government because of elections or coalition negotiations and the other, with a full-time, functioning government. In economic terms, the first period is the investment stage, and the second is the payback: The country invests time and money in the hope of receiving a yield in the form of many days of stability.

Any investment adviser who looks at the data from Israel's electoral system would tell you: Run away as fast as you can!

---

iv This compromise might have inadvertently only caused more instability: Israelis tend to look with astonishment at the bizarre American electoral system, which sometimes awards victory to the presidential candidate with fewer votes. But this is exactly what happens right under Israelis' noses: What the Electoral College has done to the American left is what the electoral threshold has done to the Israeli right. In both cases, the side that has won the most votes over the past generation has lost time and again because of the electoral system: Since 1992, Democrats have won the popular vote in seven out of eight presidential elections, but only five times have they managed to reach the White House. In Israel, the right won a slender majority in 1992 but lost power to Yitzhak Rabin because the small parties crashed below the electoral threshold; in 2019, Israel was thrown into repeated elections because of Naftali Bennett and Moshe Feiglin's failures; and in 2003–2020, the right cumulatively lost ten seats, which would have stabilized its rule.

In Britain, the process of government formation starts and ends with a polite bow before the Queen. In a wonderfully British combination of misanthropy and sportsmanship, at six o'clock in the morning after an electoral upheaval, a moving van pulls up in front of 10 Downing Street. In Israel, the process can easily take two months and often collapses on the way. When, in Britain in 2010, forty-eight hours had passed since the polls closed without the formation of a new government, newspaper headlines in London cried that the situation was intolerable. In the United States, presidential terms are limited to four years and the transition period, just ten weeks. Since the Second World War, Britain and the United States have each invested around two years of transitions in order to create seventy years of continuous government.

But in Israel? Election campaigns are getting longer, terms in office are getting shorter, and the results are accordingly shocking: In its first seventy-two years of independence, Israel has frittered away no less than eleven years, two months, and four days on elections and coalition talks. Israel's prime ministers are supposed to build the Jewish national home, but instead, they waste much of their time on sealing the roof, fixing leaks, and collecting maintenance fees.

Even once a government is finally sworn in, power gets handed to the small- and medium-sized parties. Only to Israelis does it seem natural that a party with just a handful of seats, such as Shas, keeps winning plenty of ministerial portfolios and budgets, while a party that wins three or four times as many seats spends years rotting in the opposition. Just like in the United States, where presidential candidates invest so much more in tiny Iowa than in California or Texas, in Israel, all voters are equal, but some are more equal than others.

The most striking consequence of Israel's electoral system is the massive gulf between public opinion on matters of religion and state and government policy. While Israelis have been increasingly drifting toward liberal positions in recent decades, their governments have been chained to the ultra-Orthodox monolith. Most Israeli citizens support civil marriage, equal rights for same-sex couples, the smashing of the chief rabbinate's monopoly on kashrut certification, and less stringent conversion standards. But in the present system, in which everyone depends on Shas and United Torah Judaism (UTJ), the target date for all these reforms is...never (and maybe, if Israel were to lie down on

Sigmund Freud's couch, it might admit that its national subconscious has also played a role here: After all, Israel was never going to be a country where Shabbat is just a normal weekend like in other countries, even if there might occasionally be a majority for it).

A government that is but the sum of the pressures applied by its members will never be able to fully implement the manifesto of any constituent party. Israelis can vote for a Likud party that promises to move mountains to roll back judicial activism or lower food prices, but in order to form a government, the party ends up selling the justice portfolio to a left-wing party and the economics portfolio to a socialist. And most outrageously, there is nobody to blame. The damage is inflicted on the parties' credibility: They can promise heaven and earth and then explain that in order to form a coalition, their hands were tied. And the result is that Israeli parties do not bother to write manifestos anymore. There are no manifestos, because nobody has any expectations.

* * *

Yitzhak Shamir, Israel's seventh prime minister, wrote in the 1990s: "I have a rule that I never break. I never fight for any role. Till today, I have never gotten used to the American approach of politicians running for a specific office."[12] But his successors got used to it very quickly. When Benjamin Netanyahu ran for the leadership of the Likud in 1993, he held a televised debate with his challengers: David Levy, Moshe Katsav, and Benny Begin. Compared to him, they looked like a wandering herd of unshepherded dinosaurs. "I am the only one who can restore the Likud to power!" claimed Netanyahu, ignoring Levy's astonished cries of "Napoleon!" Begin, appalled, reprimanded him: "I don't recall that in the Likud's greatest days, any of its leaders imagined themselves to be the only man who could get things done. In any case, an odd style."[13] But by now, Begin was the one who looked odd. The American style that Netanyahu imported included the intensive use of the first-person singular, telegenic skills, and even a live televised admission of an affair.

The massive earthquake in Israeli politics had begun to rumble three years earlier, in 1990, in the most un-American place in the country: the cowshed of the moshav of Yad Binyamin. The State of Israel was governed at the time by a mammoth unity government containing both the

Likud and Labor parties, headed by Prime Minister Yitzhak Shamir and his deputy, Shimon Peres.

Two years after the 1988 election, Peres grew tired of his partnership with Shamir, whom he considered a man of the past: Peres was pushing for a peace deal with the Palestinians, while Shamir was personally calling journalists to nag them to stop writing on the subject. "The Palestinians are a passing phase, like men's earrings," he fumed. Peres spotted an opportunity to form an alternative government: He forged a secret alliance with two religious parties, Agudat Yisrael and Shas, and in a dramatic no-confidence vote, for the only time in Israeli history, he managed to bring down the government.

But it quickly became clear that it is much harder to build a government than to demolish one. On the morning of the fateful confidence motion for the new government, after signing a coalition deal with Agudat Yisrael, Peres discovered that two ultra-Orthodox legislators—Eliezer Mizrachi and Avraham Verdiger—had disappeared, as if the earth had swallowed them whole. His fears intensified when he looked over the coalition deal and noticed that Verdiger's signature was not even on the document. Peres's staff ran to the archives of Israel's only TV channel, rewatched the tape of the news report, and realized that the smarmy Verdiger had only waved his pen over the agreement, without actually signing it.

Never since the infamous abduction of a child by his grandparents in the 1960s had a Haredi citizen been the subject of such a massive national manhunt. In the end, the pair were tracked down: Mizrachi was hiding in an orchard near Rehovot, and Verdiger—in a cowshed. Peres's big day ended, and not for the first time, in sadness. Israel's now-former "next prime minister" burst into tears and collapsed into the arms of President Chaim Herzog. The First Lady had to feed him hot soup to bring him back to his senses because the Knesset canteen was closed for Passover. The "stinking maneuver," as Yitzhak Rabin called the episode with evident glee, indeed ended with the strong whiff of cow dung.

The foul stench of three months of crisis, characterized by shameless political extortion and undisguised bribery, spread across Israel. Anonymous backbenchers, whom nobody had ever heard of, suddenly came to hold the country's fate in their hands. In order to end the crisis, one had to be bribed with the role of tourism minister, a second with ambassadorship to Georgia, and a third with the deputy minister position for Jerusalem (a city that had gotten along just fine for three thousand years without a deputy minister). One day, Shamir was astonished to discover that one member of the Knesset was demanding, as a condition for his support, a bank guarantee that he would honor their agreement: $10 million, which he demanded that the Likud deposit in a trust account.[14] His rationale was understandable: The previous agreement that Shamir had signed, with the right-wing Tehiya party, had been rudely violated two years earlier. When its astonished party leader asked Shamir what he was supposed to do with their agreement now, Shamir dryly replied: "I guess you can frame it on the wall."

Israel's summer anthem that year was a song by the rock band T-Slam about a generic politician: "The conversation was clear, he was promised stuff, / for years, he hasn't represented the voters / He looks at the landscape of the country he loved / So what if on the way he lied and stole? / His face is reflected in the window in the corner / His face is the face of the country."

Tens of thousands of Israelis took part in a massive rally in Kings of Israel Square in Tel Aviv, demanding electoral reform. They also had a proposal: direct elections for prime minister, giving him untrammeled power and protection from the blackmail that had embittered the lives of so many Israeli premiers, and which had appreciated at a dizzying rate of inflation. Ben-Gurion had distributed ministerial jobs on the basis of one for every six members of the Knesset; Shamir was forced to give one ministerial portfolio for every three members. The audacity and political appetite of Israel's politicians were at an all-time high, and the public was fed up with the perceived corruption. In their imagination, Israelis hoped to vote for a strong and popular leader—not another gray apparatchik or "first among equals," but someone who could govern with a heavy hand, without the annoying need to keep appeasing coalition partners.

Israel was already being transformed by the winds of change: The Israeli textile and manufacturing industries were clearing the way to high tech, which was taking its first steps and transforming young millionaires into cultural icons. New values and lifestyles were imported from the United States through cable TV (albeit with several months' delay after the original broadcast). At the height of the stinking maneuver, and as a direct consequence of it, forty-five thousand soccer fans were shocked when three of Israel's greatest soccer stars—Ronny Rosenthal, Eli Ohana, and Shalom Tikva—back in Israel after playing for their European teams, refused to play against the Soviet national team because the Israeli national club had not taken out injury insurance for them. Angry fans booed the team during the Israeli national anthem and spent the whole game cheering on the baffled Soviet players. The three musketeers taught the crowd the hard way that even in sports, the "me" was more important than the "us," and that their legs' well-being was no less important than the nation's morale.

Slowly but surely, modernity snuck into Israel's fossilized and inflexible parties. Until the late 1970s, almost every party selected its Knesset list using a party committee. These committees all looked the same: They were small groups of middle-aged Ashkenazi men (with the odd token woman or Mizrahi man thrown in), meeting in closed, smoke-filled rooms in a world that had yet to discover the dangers of secondhand smoking. They went through names one by one, almost all of them middle-aged men with graying hair, until white smoke came out, and the party announced the composition of its list without any explanation.

In 1977, the Likud started selecting its Knesset candidates in a process called "the sevens," which shifted deliberations to a slightly larger and better aerated room. Members of the Likud central committee elected seven representatives at once in a process that, like early computers, now looks clunky and cumbersome but at the time looked like the height of innovation. The result was a young and attractive list, with diverse representation. The nomination process helped the Likud to pitch itself as modern and in touch with the people, and thus to pull off the great electoral upset that ousted the left from power.

Fifteen years later, ahead of the 1992 election, Labor elected its leader in party primaries for the first time, with tens of thousands of members voting. For the four previous elections, the party's wheelers and dealers had picked Shimon Peres, but the masses gave their backing to Yitzhak Rabin, who proved to be more popular, and he pulled off a victory. The conclusion was clear: The road to power ran through opening up a party's ranks and paying special attention to candidates, not just positions. Ben-Gurion's name never appeared on Mapai's ballot, but in the election for the Thirteenth Knesset, the Labor Party ballot read: "Labor, headed by Rabin." The party's name disappeared from its catchy jingle, its other candidates were hidden away, and the tired sheaves of wheat in the party's logo were trashed in favor of a headshot of the prime minister-to-be.

Local authorities had long since started holding direct elections for mayor, and the country was awash with popular local leaders, from Tel Aviv's Shlomo Lahat to Jerusalem's Teddy Kollek. And if direct elections had worked at the municipal level and the party level, then why not at the national level? In 1990, lawmakers from most parties in the Knesset started pushing for change, to bring Israel into the new millennium with a brand-new electoral system.

But by the time the bill came up for a final vote in the Knesset two years later, it looked like the old joke about a camel being a horse designed by committee. An amendment submitted at 1:15 a.m. suddenly gave the Knesset back the power to accept or reject the prime minister–elect's new government and the ability to express no confidence in it. Members of the Knesset were presented a strange, two-headed creature—one without parallel anywhere on earth: a directly elected prime minister who still needed the legislature's approval for his coalition; a leader elected by millions of citizens, who could still be ousted by sixty-one members of the Knesset. He would have to rally the support of Israeli voters once every four years while also fending off no-confidence motions once a week.

When Israelis went to the polls in 1996, for the first time they cast two ballots: a yellow ballot for prime minister and a white ballot for a party for the Knesset. The lamentable result soon became clear: The voters had decided to split their votes, responding to the new Third Way party's message that voting for both Rabin and Labor was like voting for "bread inside pita." After fulfilling their civil duty by voting for a prime minister from the major parties, Israelis had pampered themselves by voting for a range of small, one-off boutique parties, which were suddenly not quite so small.

The two major parties were dramatically weakened, and for the first time since Israel's independence, they lost their absolute majority in the Knesset. Three years later, the two parties collapsed to just forty-two seats combined. The Knesset's center of gravity could no longer hold its own weight. Instead of reducing the small parties' blackmail power, the new electoral system only intensified it. Israel no longer had large parties, nor did it really have any small ones. Instead, the Knesset was littered with many medium-sized parties.

The governments that served after this electoral reform were short-lived and miserable: Netanyahu was elected by 1.5 million citizens in 1996, and two and a half years later came the final death knell for his government, which in misty memory looked like one long coalition crisis. His successor, Ehud Barak, was elected by a landslide—only to tumble within a year and a half into the most crushing defeat in Israeli political history. For a month, he found himself navigating a political crisis that was bizarre even by Israeli standards: the question of when to transport a large turbine belonging to the national electricity company. In the end, the turbine was moved on Shabbat—the holy day of rest—and UTJ quit the government. The man who defeated Barak in the subsequent election, Ariel Sharon, knew what his first step would be: On his first day in office, in the winter of 2001, he revoked the direct elections law. Out of breath and licking its wounds, Israel fell back into the arms of the electoral system that it had scrapped nine years earlier without intending to return.

Years later, Israel's major parties are still struggling to recover from this setback. Between Israel's independence in 1948 and the direct elections reform, the ruling party had always won at least forty seats in every election. Yet, never since this reform has any party won at least forty seats. Israelis became enamored with voting for boutique parties that reflected their opinions to a tee. The era in which the large majority of Israelis voted for the two major parties was an era of limited choice both on television and in supermarkets: In the 1980s, Israelis had only one channel and could choose, at best, between skimmed and semi-skimmed milk. But nowadays there is a mind-boggling array of channels on TV, and supermarkets sell soy milk, rice milk, low-lactose milk, lactose-free milk, and many other options. No wonder that Israelis have also become fussy eaters in politics: Two Sephardic ultra-Orthodox parties ran in 2015, and in 2019, there were no fewer than three national-religious parties.

Political extortion also increased accordingly. Barak, who had complained bitterly during his premiership about the extortionate price that he was forced to pay his partners, a decade later extorted Netanyahu for the eye-watering price of four ministries for his five-person party,

Independence. The Netanyahu-Benny Gantz rotation government contained thirty-five ministers for seventy-two lawmakers, almost a ratio of one to two. A Knesset seat, once a life's goal in its own right, had become—in the minds of Israel's politicians—a mere pit stop, as short as possible, on the way to their real destination: the government. Ehud Olmert served in the Knesset for fourteen years before being appointed a minister, and he never complained. In the past decade, members of the Likud and the Blue and White party who were not given a ministerial position in their first year banged their fists on the table and threatened to quit.

Worst of all: A nation still suffering from post-traumatic stress disorder after electoral reform thirty years ago is finding it extremely difficult to muster the courage for another, more successful attempt at reform. And thus, roughly once a week, members of the Knesset take turns to strut up to the prime minister's bureau and exploit a brief moment of power to rattle off demands. On the right-hand side of the door is a portrait of David Ben-Gurion, and if you look closely, you might just catch a glimpse of his seething fury.

CHAPTER 2

The 4 AM Phone Call

Golda Meir's Decision—Not Going to War

T HE PHONE RANG, SHREDDING through the night's silence. Then another machine came to life, and then another. The telephones had been installed in every corner of the large, empty apartment and all started ringing at once, but nobody answered. The elderly woman living in the apartment knew exactly what the sound of the phone ringing meant, and she was afraid to pick up.

Then she woke up with a jolt.

She sat up in bed, covered in a cold sweat. It was 4:00 a.m., and Golda Meir could not get back to sleep. "It was the same nightmare, repeating itself," Israel's fourth prime minister told a close friend in the morning.[1] Together, they tried to work out what her subconscious was trying to say. It was the summer of 1973, and Israel's situation, or so people thought, had never been better.

Golda Meir was a sharp-tongued and active politician, especially in the field of social policy. Until her dying day, she never forgot the darkest days of her life, as a young, penniless woman in Jerusalem. She had to wash the dirty laundry of all the children at her local kindergarten just so that her daughter could go there too. The experience remained etched in her memory, all the way to the top. Driven by this memory, she smashed what we now call the glass ceiling, becoming the lone female portrait in a long row of white-haired men while fending off chauvinism and distrust. "Kudos to this clever, energetic woman," declared the newspaper of the religious Zionist community when her promotion to the government came on the agenda, "but she cannot be placed at the top of one of the most important mechanisms of the Jewish people. There is a law as natural as the laws of nature, the eternal body of Jewish law. There are limits, and each sex must know its own limits."[2]

When Golda Meir was nevertheless appointed a minister, she built the National Insurance Institute with her own bare hands—saving millions of Israelis from dire poverty—forced the state to pay reserve soldiers, passed labor regulations protecting young people, instituted an annual holiday and severance packages for workers, and worked to narrow the gender pay gap. She also paved roads to poor towns and did everything in her power to fight the blatant discrimination in relations between Ashkenazi Jews and those of Middle Eastern descent.

But now, as prime minister, she knew that none of this would be remembered to her credit if, God forbid, fighting were to resume with the enemy states on Israel's borders. In the debate in which the Knesset voted to make her prime minister, an Agudat Yisrael lawmaker warned: "Many people around the world, Jews and non-Jews, will surely express their astonishment that now, of all times, it was deemed appropriate to make a woman prime minister. Nor am I convinced that this will deter the Arabs."

"Only people who hate and fear war should be entrusted with the conduct of war," Golda Meir once said.[3] Golda, as she was popularly known, hated and feared war, and now the country was in her hands. Her daily intelligence briefings every morning brought fresh and disturbing pieces of information, but the lines connecting the dots were not quite clear to her. Not long earlier, ahead of the 1973 elections, she had decided to volunteer herself for one last term as prime minister, her third overall. She was secretly hoping that her last term in office would usher in a social revolution.

* * *

The number one rule of investment states, "Diversify risk." Never put all your eggs in one basket and all your money in one place. Put some in the local stock market and some on Wall Street, some in dollars and some in bonds, some in gold and some in Bitcoin. If your investment adviser ever advises you to dissolve all your savings, sell your house, break open your mutual funds, and put all your money in a single stock—you should demand his dismissal.

But that is exactly what happens in politics. The only thing that makes modern-day Israelis different from previous generations or neighboring countries is the fact that they can replace their leaders at the ballot box. But in modern democracies, voters only cast one ballot, once every four years (or every four months in Israel's case, but let's put that to one side). All of Israel's hopes, beliefs, prayers, and hidden fears get funneled into a single vote—or, in economic terms, into a single long-term investment in a blind trust. Did you vote for Benny Gantz in 2020 because he promised "just not Netanyahu" about a week before jumping into Netanyahu's arms? As the kids say, "That's life." Did you vote Likud in 2003 in order to prevent unilateral territorial withdrawals, only for Sharon to mastermind the Gaza disengagement about a month later? In chess, that's called the "touch-move rule." Did you vote for a party that promised to lower taxes and ended up hiking them? Imagine a sign: "If you break it, you buy it."

There is no point calling the Central Elections Committee and demanding a new voting slip, because unlike your local department store, the returns policy here is extremely strict: no returns. Since you only get one vote, only one consideration truly matters when you cast your vote. The second-most important consideration is not really second: it is simply not important.

All around the world, voters' main consideration is money. The word "politics" comes from the Greek *polis*, meaning "city." Imagine being a citizen of Athens 2,500 years ago. You have just discovered that the fearsome Persian army is advancing on the city. There is only one small problem: The city is unwalled. Actually, there is another problem—just a teensy-tiny one: The city's treasury is empty. "There is no such thing as public money," said British Prime Minister Margaret Thatcher two and a half millennia later, "there is only taxpayers' money." But now the city needs to urgently raise money from its citizens in order to defend itself.

At that exact moment, politics was born. It raised several questions: Should a family with ten children be taxed the same amount as an aging bachelor? Should the rich be taxed more heavily than the poor? Should residents of the rural periphery be taxed more than the relatively safe metropolis? And if the city is already building a wall, then why not seize this festive occasion to open a school for Athenian children? In sum, how much money should the state take from me, and what should it give me in return?

At the far-left extreme is the former Soviet Union or the old Israeli kibbutz, which followed the rule from Karl Marx: "From each according to his abilities, to each according to his needs"—in other words, 100 percent income tax. The treasury would take the fruits of your labor, but in return it would be expected to provide you food, housing, education, and healthcare. This unprecedented experiment on human beings ended in a searing failure, and nobody wants to go back to it.

On the right-wing end of the scale is the United States of America, or at least what it used to be: the land of unlimited opportunity. It was a country where a penniless immigrant could step off a ship at Ellis Island and become a millionaire within a couple of years, simply because the state did not push its grubby hands into his pockets and took basically no income tax. But the dark side of America is that it is also a land of impossible limitations: At the feet of its colossal steel and glass skyscrapers, countless homeless people go to sleep every night covered only in newspaper sheets. That's America in a single snapshot. This miserable reality was on clear display during the 2020 COVID-19 coronavirus pandemic, when the most economically powerful empire in history revealed itself to be a third-world country when it came to public health, at least for those who could not afford to buy their own health insurance.

Everywhere in the world, politics is conducted between these two poles, and the main question is, "To what extent do I trust the state and want it to use my hard-earned money to supply the public good known as 'equality'?" This is the situation *almost* everywhere in the world. Because in one country, a Hebrew-speaking land, things work a little differently.

Like people anywhere else, Israelis also care about their financial situation and want affordable housing and functioning public transport. They too are fed up with being stuck in traffic for hours, and they too wrestle with questions about the free market versus social solidarity. But most Israelis, for most of Israel's history, have been worried about something much greater than their quality of life: life itself. In the professional lingo, we call that "security." A more precise definition would be "*insecurity*." But if we are being honest—the right word is "fear."

If you are in Israel, it doesn't matter where you might be reading this book, even if you are in a Scandinavian-style apartment and sipping a cocktail. A ninety-minute drive, at most, is all that stands between you and someone who wants to kill you with a knife, gun, rocket-propelled grenade launcher, or surface-to-surface missile. Yes, you. Hamas's terror tunnel squads in Gaza, the Islamic State's armed militias in Sinai, Hezbollah's elite forces training in Lebanon to conquer Israeli border villages, and Iran's Revolutionary Guards in the Syrian Golan Heights—none of these are more than half a tank of gas away. Israelis might imagine themselves part of the West, but in the end, they are in the Middle East.

Israeli parents want their children to speak native-level English, but all around them are people who speak a range of Arabic dialects. I shall never forget listening to the IDF Army Radio in the summer of 2014, during the conflict with Hamas known as Operation Protective Edge. "Next up, Beyoncé's new hit single," said the presenter. "But first, an update: There's heavy traffic on Route 6 heading south because of convoys of tank transporters." Israel in a nutshell.

In nearly every poll over the past generation, at least since the social justice protests that filled the streets in 2011, Israeli voters have said that their financial situation is the most important consideration behind how they vote.[4] The Talmud had something romantic to say about this: "The heart does not always tell the mouth what's on its mind." Or to translate this Aramaic maxim into Freudian terms: "Nations also have a subconscious." Beneath Israelis' Western exterior lurks a terrible fear: One morning they will wake up and discover that Israel suddenly stopped existing overnight. There are historical reasons for this, of course. The sovereign State of Israel was built as a safe haven to put an end to two thousand years of anti-Semitic persecution, massacres, and pogroms. Less than eighty years, the blink of an eye in historic terms, have gone by since the fires of the Auschwitz crematoria. Holocaust survivors still live among us today, bearing the blue numbers tattooed onto their forearms by the Nazis. There is not a single Israeli who is not a descendant of Holocaust survivors, personally acquainted with Holocaust survivors, or at least educated about them in school.

Nearly three thousand people were murdered on September 11, 2001, in the biggest terror attack in human history. There is not a single American who does not still get goosebumps from looking at images of airplanes full of passengers and jet fuel obliterating New York's skyline. But no American went to sleep that night fearing that the United States of America might cease to exist. Over the past decade, the Islamic State and its acolytes massacred French people in a series of gruesome attacks, but the French feared only for their own lives, not the life of the Republic. But in a country living on the edge, post-traumatic stress disorder is a contagious condition; it afflicts every generation and lurks around every corner. So much of what is strange about Israel makes sense when looked at through the kaleidoscope of raw fear.

In 2010, I moved to London for studies. As a cash-strapped student, I chose not to eat out on my first night and went to the supermarket to buy some ingredients for dinner, and most importantly—tomatoes for a salad. British cashiers are the most impeccably polite species known to nature, but when the woman at the till saw a twenty-seven-year-old student holding a bag full of eleven beautiful, red tomatoes, she could not hold back and asked, "Are you expecting guests tonight, sir?"

I mulled this over on the way home. Ordinary people go to the supermarket to stock up for dinner: two tomatoes, a sausage, a baguette, and a half-dozen eggs. Israelis go to the supermarket subconsciously assuming that it might be their last time. Tomorrow will surely bring a nuclear apocalypse or a war of annihilation, and they will all have to huddle in bomb shelters—so they should at least have enough tomatoes. That is why one-third of all food in Israel goes to waste; that is why Israeli shoppers often throw food in their trolleys and mutter, "Just in case." They buy things they don't need, just in case they do.

Israeli shopping habits are not the only thing on a permanent war footing: So is Israeli rhetoric. When the Environment Ministry found itself starved of funds and attention, it renamed itself the Environmental Protection Ministry, as if its job were to equip rare flowers with bulletproof flak jackets. Israel's firefighters recently rebranded themselves "fire warriors." And the "war against the virus," as the Sisyphean civilian effort to contain COVID-19 was called in the winter of 2021, was waged by the "coronavirus cabinet" (in Israel, the "cabinet" is the shorthand name for the security cabinet). The name was likely chosen because a plain old ministerial committee would probably not scare the virus, but when faced with such an impressive-sounding body, it would surely panic and retreat at once.

Israel's national obsession with news is also linked to its primordial fears. In 2020, for example, the seven most-watched television broadcasts were all current affairs shows. No country in the world broadcasts news at prime time. Every Israeli knows that the late Roni Daniel was Channel 12's military correspondent, but far fewer can name the head of IDF Central Command. And who gets stopped more often for a selfie in the street: Channel 12's police correspondent or the police commissioner himself? The reason is that in Israel, unlike in Europe and the United States, the news and reality are one and the same. The United States fought two world wars against Germany, but no German stormtrooper has ever been seen goose-stepping through Philadelphia.

In Israel's case, however, the assassination of a nuclear scientist in Tehran can turn into blaring rocket sirens in northern Israel in less than a day. This is also why the hallways of the Knesset are flooded with reporters, even though the image of professional journalism in Israel is declining. In early 2021, a majority of US senators (fifty-one out of one hundred) were lawyers by trade, serving alongside just one journalist. In Israel's elections in early 2021, four journalists headed party lists. When Yair Lapid wanted to kickstart his political career, his first stage was to pivot from hosting a chat show in a black T-shirt to anchoring a hard news show. "I am Yair Lapid, and I have a tie," he announced during the opening of his first broadcast. Because in Israelis' subconscious, if you have spent long enough talking about policy and security on TV, your words will carry greater weight when you want to address the same subjects as a politician.

Israelis' existential fears shape not only their shopping and viewing habits but also their voting behavior. They can always tell themselves small, white lies about wanting cleaner politics, greater attentiveness to their day-to-day needs, and efficient and technocratic politicians, like those in Scandinavia. But inside the voting booth, hidden from view, most Israelis, most of the time, vote on the basis of a single question: *When the red telephone rings at 4:00 a.m., who should answer?* Who should pick up the receiver and make the fateful decisions that will keep the State of Israel alive? That's the question, and there is no other. Everything else is usually pushed aside. If Israel is indeed a "villa in the jungle," as Ehud Barak memorably put it, then the fear of nasty beasts in the jungle trumps questions about the villa's electricity bills and local taxes.

From the moment of Israel's independence, it was clear to its citizens who would have to provide security. The army of the young state was built on the scaffolding of the pre-state Haganah, the military arm of Mapai. This fact was hinted at strongly in its name: the Israel Defense (Haganah) Forces. Veterans of the rival Irgun and Lehi were conscripted into the new IDF but almost completely blocked from scaling its ranks. The only place in the security forces where they could make their way up with relative ease was the Mossad spy agency, but serving there fated them to anonymity. This was a time when officers were categorized, almost openly, by their political affiliations. The army was the key to integration in Israeli society; the General Staff, to politics.

Mapai leveraged its battlefield glory from the War of Independence to bolster its standing. On its First Knesset list, it fielded two high-ranking officers: Lt. Col. Moshe Dayan in tenth place, followed immediately by the future head of the IDF Southern Command, Asaf Simhoni. Dayan attended election rallies wearing full uniform and an eyepatch. Back then, the "cooling-off" period that officers must take nowadays before jumping into politics was not even a distant rumor. Mapai was a party with its own state, and the whole nation was its army.

Israel's ruling party led the country to victory after victory in the battlefield: Under its leadership, Israel's borders were expanded beyond recognition in the War of Independence. Eight years later, the IDF, under its command, conquered Gaza and the Sinai Peninsula in a combined operation with France and Britain. It reached the height of its glory, of course, in the Six-Day War. This stunning victory over the whole Arab world turned the IDF's commanders into celebrities, but Mapai's leadership also reaped the dividends. Defense Minister Moshe Dayan marched through the Lions' Gate of the Old City of Jerusalem next to IDF Chief of Staff Yitzhak Rabin, in khakis. Could anyone imagine Benny Gantz marching into Gaza in combat uniform?

The first eight generals who entered Israeli politics all parachuted into the ruling camp. And Menachem Begin? He was a private in the Free Polish Army. Irgun and Lehi officers staged daring operations against the British and later during the War of Independence. But their role was erased from the curriculum by the government—and in any case, this was already distant history, almost as much as the Crimean

War. In elections, there is no point wasting time and money on fruitless persuasion efforts. Security was the ruling party's monopoly.

That is why even in the 1973 elections, as in the seven previous elections, the Likud hardly saw any point in campaigning on security issues. The calm that had prevailed for the past three years along the borders of a newly expanded Israel, from the Suez Canal in the south to Mount Hermon in the north, was fully credited to the Alignment (the successor of Ben-Gurion's Mapai). Golda Meir was the "only man in the government," as Ben-Gurion put it. Moshe Dayan was busy stealing antiquities, with nobody to tweet about it. And the Likud, the main opposition party, had nothing to offer yet on security.

Not that Begin did not try. In December 1969, the Likud's first general—former Israeli Air Force commander Maj. Gen. Ezer Weizman—parachuted right into his turf upon learning that he would not be appointed chief of staff. He quit the army and handed back his uniform the very same day. By evening, to everyone's astonishment, he was already sworn in as a minister in the unity government, representing Begin's faction. The Likud's latest acquisition was especially attractive in light of his biography: He was the nephew of Israel's first president, Chaim Weizmann; the son of a solid Mapai family; and a Haganah hero.

In 1973, Begin was joined by another former Mapai member, a reserves major general by the name of Ariel Sharon. Suddenly the Likud could also boast military ranks. By now, Begin had already quit the unity government. It happened after Golda Meir caved under heavy American pressure and adopted the Rogers Plan to end the War of Attrition in western Sinai, which included an Egyptian commitment to the military status quo. That very night, the Egyptians violated the deal and pushed advanced antiaircraft missile batteries toward the Suez Canal. The timing soon proved especially chilling: The ceasefire was imposed 1,162 days after the end of the Six-Day War and exactly 1,162 days before the outbreak of the Yom Kippur War. The countdown toward war had begun and so had the countdown to a great electoral upheaval.

But the Likud was focused back then, quite rightly in its view, on economic issues. In early October 1973, the Likud announced that the Alignment was responsible for poverty. Just one day before the outbreak of hostilities, a Likud advertisement promised war—but against "the rule of bureaucrats and nepotists."[5] There was no point arguing about the territories captured in 1967, because nobody was planning on withdrawing from them. The Alignment devoted just one election poster to military-diplomatic issues: "On the banks of the Suez Canal, calm prevails, as in the Sinai Desert and the Golan Heights…settlements are being built. Our diplomatic standing is strong. This is the result of a level-headed and daring policy. This is proof of the short-sightedness of the leaders of Gahal [the Likud]." The summer before the war, the government had decided to shorten mandatory military service by three months. The change was supposed to enter into effect in late 1973.[6]

Of all the intelligence pouring in, the report that would finally alert Israel that a terrible war was on its way was about pita bread: the IDF Military Intelligence Directorate discovered that the Syrian army had ordered tens of thousands of pitas from a bakery in the middle of nowhere.[7] There is no point recounting for the millionth time how Israel sleepwalked into the war; it is enough to note that at the age of seventy-five, and with absolutely no security experience, Golda Meir had good enough instincts to sense that something was not quite right, but she lacked the courage to bang her fist on the table in front of her generals and say, "Guys, there's about to be a war." When she tucked herself into bed, exhausted, there were no more telephones ringing in her dreams. Israel was getting younger, but its government was aging: The average age of Golda Meir's ministers was sixty-three.[8]

At 4:00 a.m., on October 6, 1973—Yom Kippur, the holiest day in the Jewish calendar—the phone rang. For real this time, not in a dream. "There's going to be a war today," said a voice over the line. "I knew it," said Golda and hung up. "Apart from me," she later complained, "they were all men, used to military affairs, but nobody thought otherwise. Nobody got up and said, 'Something's different.' And I, the civilian who did not quite know what a platoon was, had to make a decision. I agonize about this, till today."

In her old age, Golda was reminded of the trauma that pushed her to become a Zionist in the first place: As a young girl in Kyiv, she heard one day, with the rest of her community, that anti-Semitic gangs were on their way to launch a pogrom against the city's Jews. Her whole life, she remembered her anger at her father, a carpenter, who, instead of preparing knives and pitchforks to return war, only sealed the windows and reinforced the doors. She had sworn to always favor preemptive action and never be on the back foot, and yet seventy years later, she too could only wait in horror, behind a locked door, for an attack on the Jewish state. Something inside her died when she heard the first siren. "I am only an old woman," she later lamented. "What could I have done?" She later told a senior general a terrible secret: In the darkest days of the start of the war, she had seriously contemplated taking her own life.[9]

Little did she know at the time, but Israel's military fortifications were not the only defenses that were about to collapse within a few hours: so were the defenses of the Alignment's grip on power, which had lasted twenty-five years. Golda's failure to address the Egyptian and Syrian war plans would also prove to be her most important political decision: Had she landed a pre-emptive blow in 1973, perhaps the Likud would not have surged to power in 1977.

There had never been a war like it in Israel's history. In the middle of the election campaign, candidates from the major parties found themselves changing into uniform and rushing to Sinai to save the country. The Alignment's industry and trade minister, Haim Bar-Lev, was appointed commander of the southern front. Under him served Maj. Gen. Ariel Sharon, a senior candidate on the rival Likud list, as a division commander. The wars of the generals were also wars between politicians. On the eighth day of the war, in the army's command bunker, Major General Sharon launched himself at southern front commander Lieutenant General Bar-Lev and nearly hit him on the head. Only at the last second did he hold himself back and avoid punching his commander.[10] "Soldiers on the southern front," the newspapers reported, "are talking about a Likud division and an Alignment division."[11]

The video camera that recorded Golda visiting soldiers on the western side of the canal, shortly after the ceasefire, did not catch any unusual signs of protest. On the contrary, the prime minister still attracted respect, even admiration. Her victory in the subsequent elections also showed that it would take time for the public to digest the news. But when the soldiers' votes were counted, they revealed something dramatic: Israeli soldiers had flocked to the polls—stationed for the first time in Israel's history from the soil of Africa to the outskirts of Damascus—and, for the first time, had swung toward the Likud. Having witnessed the disaster of the war up close, they would soon return home and infect their families and friends with the same sense of outrage, which would end the rule of the old regime. The Israeli public had gone to sleep peace-fully, having entrusted the Alignment with safeguarding their security, only to discover that the guards had fallen asleep on duty. Forget about corruption and economic failures: This is the only sin for which there is no atonement in Israel. The Labor Party has been carrying out its painful sentence ever since. The electoral upheaval of 1977 represented, first and foremost, the transfer of the role of national guardian from the Labor movement to the Likud.

Luckily for opposition leader Menachem Begin, only the archives would remember his bombastic statement shortly before the war: "I can announce that the Egyptian army cannot cross the canal. If it launches an attack, it can expect a greater defeat than in the Six-Day War."[12] But many Israelis identified with his cry in the Knesset immediately after the war: "In the name of God, why didn't you send the troops to the front?" Once again, this proved the truth of an old rule of politics: When you are in the opposition—talk is free. Yet despite his past experience as the commander of the Irgun, Begin was never seen as an authority on security. But politics is a game of alternatives. For extra security, pun intended, Begin armed himself with a few more retired officers ahead of the 1977 elections. "We'll have five generals," he confided to a friend, his eyes glistening.[13]

Since 1977, peace deals have come to life and gone to their graves; the IDF has staged withdrawals and conquests. But the Likud's winning message has remained the same. It can be defined in two words: cautious pessimism. The pessimism is based on the sober assessment that Israelis are forever fated to live by the sword (or, at least, *with* the sword); the skepticism about the honesty and peaceful intentions of Israel's neigh-bors; a fear that moderate neighbors will be ousted by extremist Islamist forces; and a belief that withdrawals must be executed, if at all, with utmost caution. Over the years, the Likud has uprooted dozens of settle-ments and embarked on military operations in Gaza, Judea, Samaria, and Lebanon, which, combined, claimed the lives of hundreds of sol-diers. In most cases, the public has been glad to give it the credit—both for peace and war.

Security incidents have shaped the results of most Israeli elections to date: In 1981, the bombing of Iraq's nuclear reactor helped the Likud cruise to victory against all odds and all the polls. On the eve of the 1988 elections, a mother and her three children were killed when a terrorist chucked a Molotov cocktail at a bus near Jericho; the Labor candidate, Shimon Peres, claimed that the incident cost him "two to four seats" and thus handed victory to the Likud with a lead of a single seat. In 1992, a wave of stabbings by terrorists from Gaza weakened Prime Minister Yitzhak Shamir's position on the eve of the national election and contributed to his defeat.

Netanyahu closed the gap with Peres four years later after a wave of suicide bombings butchered dozens of Israelis and shook their belief that the Oslo Accords were paying off. Ehud Barak, who soon defeated Netanyahu, was forced to call an early election in 2001 because of the Second Intifada. Moshe Arens, the Likud's esteemed defense minister, summarized it well: "Security is the beating heart of Israeli politics, and until the Labor Party can give the public better answers than the Likud, or until the Likud, God forbid, makes a serious mistake on this front—the Likud will presumably remain in power."[14]

This assessment has held firm in most elections since Menachem Begin kissed his wife Aliza on that dramatic night in May 1977.

The most absurd thing is that after the fiasco of the Yom Kippur War, the number of generals in Israeli politics skyrocketed. Perhaps it was because of the soldiers' bravery, compensating for the politicians' mistakes; or maybe it was because, as Meir Ariel sang, "People cry out for what they're missing. They're missing security? They shout security." Infantry officers were marched into political parties, and paratroopers were parachuted into party lists. Sixty-five officers have sauntered into the Knesset over the years. Maybe this is also why no woman has ever served as prime minister since the Yom Kippur War: If the main breeding ground for politicians—the top brass of combat officers—has been populated exclusively by men, what hope is there for a woman who has never commanded the Israeli military, or even a single combat unit?

Kadima's 2009 election broadcasts reminded voters that Tzipi Livni had been an officer, a Mossad agent, and a member of the security cabinet for years, but in the polls, Kadima's candidate for prime minister was thought to have far less military experience than Netanyahu and Barak. Golda Meir remains the only female prime minister in Israeli history—a title that will not be wrested from her anytime soon.

But even for the most senior retired generals, life in the Knesset has proven extremely frustrating.

A rabbi, a professor, and a general walk into the Knesset. It sounds like the start of a joke, and history shows that it often ends up as a joke as well. What all three professions have in common is that they enjoy captive audiences: Commanders must be obeyed if their soldiers want to avoid prison; professors must be listened to if their students want to pass their exams; and rabbis must be respected if their disciples know what is good for them. But then they reach the Knesset and suddenly a general and a private are on equal footing.

In politics, there are no captive audiences; nobody takes captives, and nobody is given command. This is why journalists tend to be better at politics: In TV studios, as on the floor of parliament, they are already skilled at reaching and pandering to the widest possible audience. Few military recruits survive the sharp transition. They show up wearing an oversized jacket and sloppily tied tie instead of the dress uniform that they are used to wearing. They are easy to spot: They wander around the Knesset alone, mostly bearing a grimace combining a sense of offense, boredom, and mild disdain.

The legendary general Moshe Dayan was dispatched to the Agriculture Ministry, where he spent most of his time fighting a losing battle to get Israelis to switch from their beloved round tomatoes to a thinner, longer variety that was easier to export. Rabin was a disaster in his first term as prime minister; Sharon got fed up with the Knesset so quickly that he quit in his first term. All three became successful politicians only after years of exhausting boot camps.

When Ehud Barak retired as IDF chief of staff and segued straight into the role of minister in a Labor government, Sharon invited him for a meeting. "The most important lesson you've got to remember is this," he warned him. "When you kill someone in the army, he's dead. Here, you'll hear nonstop about so-and-so who was taken out, so-and-so who's finished. But the next morning, you'll bump into the people you've eliminated, alive and well and hungry for revenge, in the Knesset canteen."

One of Shaul Mofaz's aides once described for me what a typical Thursday looked like for the defense minister: At 9:00 a.m., the heads of the IDF regional commands sat down next to him in perfect order for the situation assessment. They left at 10:00 a.m., and in came the top brass of a special ops unit to discuss a secret mission in Syria. At 11:00 a.m., air force commanders entered to go over plans for the next war against Lebanon. And at 12:00 p.m., at the exact same table, sat a cacophony of party activists from Afula and Holon. For men used to hearing, "Sir, yes sir," the chaotic mess known as a "party" is intolerable.

In any case, the Knesset has never had any difficulties attracting military veterans. Fourteen of the IDF's twenty-one ex–chiefs of staff went into politics, including seven in a row, from Ehud Barak to Benny Gantz. Every soldier is an officer-in-waiting, and every chief of staff is a potential prime minister. Instead of bringing more security to politics, as originally intended, the generals ended up dragging politics into security issues.

Ehud Barak became the interior minister in Rabin's government just weeks after retiring as chief of staff. A whole battalion of political reporters accompanied his successor, Amnon Lipkin-Shahak, on his last day in the army in 1988. Shortly afterward, he gave a speech in civilian dress, announcing that he would join politics, because the prime minister he had just served under was "endangering Israel." Shaul Mofaz returned to the Kirya defense compound as defense minister just two months after leaving as the outgoing chief of staff. But the record goes to Dan Halutz, the first and last pilot to have commanded the IDF, who headed it during the Second Lebanon War: He saw the General Staff's boardroom table as a launchpad that would propel him into the government. He expressed support for the Gaza disengagement while still in uniform,[15] and was widely seen as the military branch of the Kadima party.

People often think that the "cooling-off law," which was passed in 2007 and forces generals to take time out before entering politics, was introduced to protect political old-timers from military-grade rising stars, but the truth is that it protects the army. The much-maligned initiative to keep senior officers away from the Knesset for three years was born between the Gaza disengagement and the Second Lebanon War, in the context of the corruptive relationship that had developed on Prime Minister Ariel Sharon's ranch between generals and politicians. It was called the "Halutz law" at the time, and no law is more just. If a reporter interviews a party leader and then jumps into his arms, that's inelegant. If a lieutenant general builds a political strategy while still sending soldiers into battle, and a brigadier general plays an active role in a discreet political forum—that's a catastrophe. Israeli mothers must feel confident that their sons have been sent into combat in order to fight the enemy, not to boost the commander's prospects in party primaries.

In the fictional job advert of the Israeli public's imagination, a leader must satisfy another prerequisite (besides extensive security experience): native-level English. Israelis' obsession with English goes back years. It is doubtful that any German ever devoted any thought to Angela Merkel's English before voting for her as chancellor. Nor have the British given any thought to the level of Boris Johnson's French. But Israelis have a particular soft spot for those who can seamlessly switch between the present perfect and present simple on foreign television, preferably without a hint of a local accent. And they have an even stronger aversion to those who stumble through the English language, like startled refugees on foreign soil, sinking under the weight of their accent.

Israelis who grew up in the 1980s can still remember the jokes about Foreign Minister David Levy—like the one about the man who asked him, "What's the matter?" and received the reply, "A meter, a meter and a half." These jokes, at the expense of a future Israel Prize laureate, obviously had a strong element of racism because the Moroccan-born minister spoke fluent French—an important language of twentieth-century diplomacy.

He was not alone. Amir Peretz's prospects as a viable alternative prime minister were famously squashed when he was photographed looking through the wrong end of a pair of binoculars during the Second Lebanon War. But they had been gravely damaged nearly a year earlier, when Peretz went to give a speech to an audience of American Jews. The font was too small, his confidence was too great, and the result was a massive embarrassment, which made that evening's nightly news. Kadima and the Likud sent the video out by email (that was how videos went viral in the first decade of the millennium), presenting Peretz as unfit for the role of prime minister, and from there, he only continued to sink.

For the whole of the 2009 election campaign, Peretz would try to maneuver between his desire to avoid speeches in English, which he could not speak particularly well, and his need to correct the impression of disaster. His aides carefully organized for him several meetings in English with foreign leaders. The media pounced on these events, which unfolded as follows: Peretz recited a few memorized sentences in

English, and Israeli journalists, cruel as they are, insisted on asking him questions in English in order to make him stutter again. In one event where I was present, we completely ignored his guest, a newly elected US senator, who was not even asked a single question. When the reporters finally left the room, the senator told Peretz, "Those reporters had a bad look in their eyes." Who was the senator? Barack Obama.

Israelis are, in many respects, just another frightened Jewish community in a two-thousand-year-long chain of frightened Jewish communities, even if they are larger and more independent than those that came before. The sense of existential insecurity makes Jews want to speak with their feudal lords in *their* language, and not in Yiddish or some other inelegant argot. This was true of Don Isaac Abarbanel in Spain, who pleaded with Spanish monarchs Ferdinand and Isabella to reverse the expulsion of the Jews; of Nachmanides, who publicly debated with priests under the watchful gaze of the king; and of legendary Israeli foreign minister Abba Eban, whom the satirist Ephraim Kishon once described in a sketch as someone who, whenever he spoke in the United Nations, had the envoys of Britain and the United States running to their dictionaries in order to work out what he had said.

This is also true of Israeli politicians in media appearances with hostile interviewers on American or British networks. When an Israeli prime minister can speak with world leaders as an equal, Israelis perceive him as more serious and better suited for his job. Israeli politicians' compulsive need to speak English has led to risible scenes over the years, such as peace ceremonies in which the Arab leader speaks in Arabic, the American leader speaks in English, and the Israeli leader gets his tongue tied around a vowelless Israeli English.

And then along came Benjamin Netanyahu. He was the first Israeli prime minister—if we don't count Golda, who grew up in the United States—who dreamed in English. It used to be said that Ariel Sharon evaluated people by their handshake: Calloused hands from farm work raised one's value in his eyes, and he had much less respect for lawyers with pale, manicured hands. Netanyahu evaluated people on the basis of their English. His conversations were interspersed with all sorts of elaborate words ending with "ism," and his office conversations with his aides—many of whom were English-speaking immigrants—were conducted in English. When he formed his government in 2009, a photographer in the Knesset press gallery snapped him swapping notes in English with his bureau chief, Ari Harow. When he called me one evening in October 2018, after I reported on a loophole that would allow him to ask the Knesset for immunity from prosecution, he was excited. Our whole conversation was in English: "It's shocking; it's amazing; it's a game-changer," he gushed.

Netanyahu's greatest moments in Israeli public opinion were in a foreign language, on foreign soil: calling the bluff of United Nations Secretary-General Kurt Waldheim, who turned out to be a Nazi war criminal; delivering speech after speech in front of the green marble wall of the United Nations General Assembly; lecturing an astonished US president on Israel's history and the dangers of withdrawing to the 1967 borders; and addressing Congress, repeatedly over three decades, to decry the Iranian nuclear deal. His English speeches are better than his Hebrew ones. "His Hebrew education was insufficient," once sniffed his father, Benzion Netanyahu, in a media interview. "There are things he still has to catch up on. His Hebrew is not as idiomatic as it could be."[16]

With or without English, the Israeli left, having lost power in 1977, tried to recapture the hearts of Israelis by calling up reserves from the General Staff. It still had in its service the richest reservoir of Israeli political hopes: the IDF. Even in Israel's eighth decade of independence, the overwhelming majority of the military top brass still leans left. Right-wing voters tend to complain about why, despite an abundance of national-religious junior officers, there has not been a single kippah-wearing major general in recent years, insinuating that there is a left-wing conspiracy to block them. The truth is more prosaic: the IDF General Staff of 2021 reflected the incoming class of 1985. The generals around Aviv Kochavi's table were conscripted before the national-religious premilitary academy in the settlement of Eli was established.

The Likud has lost power three and a half times since 1977. Each defeat can be explained separately, but if we connect the dots, they form the shape of a military beret and Uzi submachine gun. In 1992, after repeated electoral defeats, Labor's civilian leader Shimon Peres was replaced with former military chief Yitzhak Rabin, the liberator of Jerusalem in the Six-Day War. Labor trounced the Likud and became the ruling party for the first time in fifteen years. In 1996, Peres returned to the helm after Rabin's assassination—and was defeated by Netanyahu. In

1999, Labor learned its lessons and ran with retired general Ehud Barak, the most decorated soldier in IDF history. Election ads showed images of him taking part in the famous operation to free hostages on board a hijacked plane. He crushed Netanyahu, winning by the biggest electoral lead to date.

In 2006, the third ruling party since Israel's establishment was born. Ariel Sharon, the retired general who founded commando Unit 101 and crossed the Suez Canal in the Yom Kippur War, dismantled the Likud and founded Kadima. He lent heavyweight security credentials to this new political escapade. When Sharon fell into a coma, Ehud Olmert ran on Sharon's fumes to victory, albeit a smaller one than expected. One newspaper offered this very apt description the following morning: "Sharon won these elections with his eyes closed."[17]

The 2019–2020 elections set new records. After the Likud's back-to-back victories against lawyers Tzipi Livni and Isaac Herzog and journalists Yair Lapid and Shelly Yachimovich, the generals were called up once again. No fewer than three former chiefs of staff formed the Blue and White list together. Just to be safe, they also recruited another two retired major generals, two former police deputy commissioners, and a former deputy chief of Mossad. The party's leadership was dubbed "the cockpit," until Gantz and Gabi Ashkenazi activated their ejector seats and dismantled this alliance in order to form a government with Netanyahu. One election broadcast boasted of the party leaders' cumulative "117 years of security experience," which was really 120 years, if you count Yair Lapid's three years writing for the IDF's magazine. All this was enough to force Netanyahu to form a government and agree to rotate the role of prime minister—an agreement that was not honored. The only exception was the rotation that Peres forced Shamir's Likud to accept in 1984. The fact that he had founded the nuclear reactor in Dimona probably helped.

Having a general at the helm seems to be a necessary but insufficient condition for the left to reclaim power in Israel: Given the perception that the right is more credible on security matters, the Likud has only been defeated at the ballot box when the rival party presented, in addition to a shiny new military acquisition, a civil agenda. In 1992, Rabin rose to power in the context of growing public discontent with corruption in the Likud and Labor's promise to overhaul the national priorities. In 1999, Ehud Barak exploded with rage when his American advisers showed him that his former subordinate in the Sayeret Matkal commando unit, Benjamin Netanyahu, was polling better than him on security and counterterror issues. But when he calmed down, he followed their advice and focused on the high unemployment rate and the case of an old lady treated in the corridor of a hospital in Nahariya, which became a symbol of the ills of the healthcare system. In 2006, the Likud plummeted from forty seats to just twelve in the wake of Finance Minister Benjamin Netanyahu's tough economic policies, which slashed the wages and welfare payments of hundreds of thousands of angry right-wing voters. Likewise, Gantz, Ashkenazi, and Moshe Yaalon hardly said a word about security throughout the 2019–2020 elections, focusing instead on Netanyahu's corruption charges—allegations of illicit gifts of cigars and champagne and attempts to buy positive media coverage—and the question of whether a prime minister could serve under indictment.

It turns out that when it comes to economics, right-wing voters in Israel are not particularly right wing. On the socioeconomic axis, unlike the diplomatic-security axis, the average Israeli is slightly left of center. They are not a socialist but definitely not a capitalist. For Israelis, the leading value when it comes to the economy is, in two words, "mutual responsibility": the babies of Israel's rich and poor get vaccinated at the same health clinics, and as they grow up, they are taught by the same public education system, even if the former have access to private after-school tuition and robotics and debate clubs. In Israel, unlike the United States, there is close to zero tolerance for the idea of homeless people sleeping in the streets, even if it means that skyscrapers must scrape the skies from a greater distance. The right's dominant lead on security issues since Golda Meir picked up that telephone is almost completely offset when the cost of phone bills, housing, and public transport are on the agenda.

Since the Six-Day War, which launched the debate about peace, and the Yom Kippur War, which launched the debate about security, economics have not preoccupied Israeli public opinion. Of course, there have always been parties with clear capitalist policies or socialist agendas. But voters hardly ever devote any thought to this. Instead, they reward bold statements like "toppling the rule of Hamas" or "terror cannot be defeated by military means" more than coherent platforms about direct versus indirect taxation or the right way to structure health insurance. I still remember how one opposition lawmaker was totally dumbfounded when asked whether he supported raising or lowering taxes. One senior Likud minister could even allow herself to claim that there were only two problems in Israel: taxes that were too high and a budget that was too small. It was as if the nation's money grew on trees in Negev greenhouses.

The Israeli right is a big tent, and for many years, living inside as good neighbors are ultra-capitalist right-wing leaders such as Benjamin Netanyahu, Naftali Bennett, and Ayelet Shaked, and radical left-wing parties such as Shas and UTJ, which trumpet the cause of massive welfare payments and handouts. In contrast, it has been years since the "Labor" party won the support of a single laborer. In recent decades, the social-democratic camp has been led by a businessman residing in a tower (Ehud Barak), the head of a law firm serving Israel's 1 percent (Isaac Herzog), the CEO of a massive monopoly (Avi Gabbay), and, of course, a series of people on inflated public sector pensions.

Ze'ev Jabotinsky, the founding ideologue of the Israeli right, once wrote that if he were ever pickpocketed in the middle of singing "Hatikvah," he would not continue standing to attention. I thought about this every time I went up from the Knesset parking lot to the committee wing. I noticed that on days when the media obsessed about coalition crises, the parking lot was relatively empty. But it was completely jam-packed with new and shiny cars during deliberations in the finance and economy committees, which hardly anybody bothered covering: The truly dramatic decisions, those worth billions of shekels, were made there under the cover of the media's boredom.

In the summer of 2011, a single tent was erected on Tel Aviv's Rothschild Boulevard. One week later, there were forty thousand tents there. Within a month, these tents attracted half a million protesters. A wave of protests swept Israel, without a single word about security, Iran, or the settlements. The people, in their masses, demanded social justice. There had never been anything like it since the Yom Kippur War. But these were two distinct protests riding the same wave. The first, a neo-liberal protest, looked at Israelis as consumers and asked: Why is Israel so expensive? Why does an apartment in Tel Aviv cost the same as in

Manhattan? Why is Israeli-made chocolate mousse more expensive in Ashdod than in Berlin? The second, a social-democratic protest, looked at Israelis as workers: Why are they earning so little and working so many hours? Why are their pensions so low, and why is there no job security anymore?[18]

The immense enthusiasm on the streets disguised some glaring paradoxes: Most of the protesters belonged to the upper-middle class, but the cry for social justice meant helping the weaker sections of society (from higher taxes to be paid by the protesters). The social justice protests called both for taxes and tariffs to be lowered and for more public services; they demanded that citizens be allowed to earn more and the welfare state be rehabilitated. You know what this was like? It was as if the settlers' council and Peace Now held a joint rally calling for the immediate annexation of the settlements, to be followed by their immediate evacuation. Strange, right?

Except that this protest was a desperate attempt, the first after almost fifty years of futile arguments about security, to say that it was time to talk about something else as well. By an extraordinary coincidence, the masses of Israelis who thronged the Kikar HaMedina plaza in Tel Aviv in 2011 did so in the same year as the masses of Egyptians who thronged Tahrir Square in Cairo. These were very different protests, but they shared something in common.

The Arab Spring, to which naïve people around the world pinned their hopes, quickly turned into a bleak Islamic winter. Syria burned, Egypt seethed, and Lebanon was turned inside out. For the last Israelis who still believed in the prospects for peace, it became clear that, until further notice, there was nobody to talk to. The jungle, to borrow part of the famous analogy from Barak, was aflame with uncontrollable wildfires. And it was precisely then that Israelis—who for sixty years had been peering into the jungle in suspense through the windows of their proverbial villa to watch out for nasty predators on the prowl—shut their blinds in despair, realizing that they had no control over the events outside. For the first time, they turned their attention away from the jungle and instead to the villa itself.

To their astonishment, Israelis discovered damp walls, broken tiles, and outrageous electricity bills. *Forget the jungle*, cried the protesters without realizing it, *it's time to renovate the villa!* The next elections, in

2013, witnessed a massive, unprecedented, and as-yet unrivaled swing toward parties that focused on the economy and the cost of living: Yair Lapid's Yesh Atid, running on the slogan "Where's the Money?" was just one seat away from blocking Netanyahu and his talk about being "strong against Iran," which had already exhausted the electorate. All newly built homes in Israel must have their own rocket shelter, and like in many Israeli apartments, voters wanted to paint their national rocket shelter in pretty colors and convert it into a toy room.

But once in every few years, Israelis receive rude reminders of the purpose of their rocket shelters, coming from the skies of Gaza, the mountains of Lebanon, or the border with Syria. And once again, security returned to being the number one issue on which Israeli prime ministers rise and fall, and politicians went back to peddling fear. Because hope, as the philosopher Francis Bacon once said, is a good breakfast but a bad supper.

War and peace, fear and hope, were also intermingled on that rainy day in December 1978, when Golda Meir's coffin was led through the streets of Jerusalem. The previous year, she had managed to meet Egyptian President Anwar Sadat, shake his hand, and give his grandson a gift. When she died, Prime Minister Menachem Begin was woken up in Oslo. He was about to receive the Nobel Peace Prize that day for making peace with Israel's bitterest enemy, Egypt. When Golda's coffin was driven through Jerusalem, on its way to the burial plot for Israel's leaders, one mother in the crowd shook her fist. "Golda!" she screamed. "Send regards to Eli, who died in the war!"[19]

CHAPTER 3

The Good Jewish Kind

Menachem Begin's Decision— Building the National Camp

THE BEARDED MAN IN THE BLACK SUIT lifted his hand, signaling to the waitress to approach his table. "Coffee with milk," he told her, perhaps throwing in a "please." Time went by, and his coffee was nowhere to be seen. A few minutes later, the waitress came back. "I'm so sorry," she said, her eyes downcast, embarrassed to be imposing a kosher diet, "but you just ate goulash."

The date was June 1, 1949, and the setting was the oldest and best-known culinary establishment in Israel: a restaurant that is in no danger of closing, even though it gets dubious reviews, its customer base has not grown in seventy years, and there is no way of ordering takeout—the Knesset cafeteria.

The man at the table was Eri Jabotinsky, a member of the First Knesset representing Herut and the son of the founding ideologue of Israeli, Ze'ev Jabotinsky. His late father had been a literary genius, a wonderful statesman, and a proud secularist. "Prayers and religious customs did not touch my heart," Eri Jabotinsky wrote, dryly recalling his childhood experiences.[1]

The young Jabotinsky had been spared a religious upbringing. "The essence of Judaism cannot be boiled down to halakha, religious law, and the separation of kitchen utensils into meaty and milky tools," he wrote. His whole life, he was much stricter about separating religion and state than meat and milk. Lurking behind the lawmaker's request for coffee with milk, straight after eating meat, was probably something much more fundamental than a craving for caffeine.[2] The Knesset would have to address crises surrounding religion and state thousands of times, but the first one was a storm in a coffee cup.

Jabotinsky Jr. complained to the Knesset committee, demanding, as a matter of principle, two canteens: one kosher and the other "free." "He was livid," reported a *Haaretz* journalist, describing Jabotinsky's mood upon being refused coffee.[3] He was not alone. Lawmakers from the United Religious Front were astonished to hear that the Herut member was even demanding the sale of ham sandwiches in the Hebrew parliament. There was a clear logic to his thinking: If the Knesset represented the people, and if not all the people kept kosher, then everyone should be free to exercise their democratic right to the sandwich of their choice. The other members of Herut openly sided with this demand. The initiative to serve pork in the Knesset canteen was only thwarted in the end by Mapai's veto, at the request of the religious parties.[i]

Not only the State of Israel, but also the small Herut faction—fourteen members of the Knesset in total—found itself thrust into an identity crisis upon its establishment, torn between two competing values: nationalism and religion. The long-standing alliance between nationalist and religious parties in modern-day Israel, some of which are both nationalist *and* religious, has obscured the fact that modern nationalism and the Jewish religion have not always been the best of friends. Each value demands primacy over the other. Nationalism, for example, treats the state as a technical, secular entity. In contrast, the Prayer for the Welfare of the State of Israel, recited in synagogues, calls the state "the beginning of the emergence of our redemption"—which is laden with religious significance.

Ze'ev Jabotinsky, the founding father who imbibed Italian nationalism in his youth, left no room for doubt: "Until just a few months ago, we hoped that we would be able to live in peace with the Haredi element, and many of us were also willing to put aside our assumptions about their private behavior, lest the coming generation be offended. But now

---

i   In time, the Knesset canteen came to enforce the strictest kosher rules in the country, with kosher certificates from every possible denomination. Nevertheless, some Haredi members of the Knesset still avoid eating there.

we are forced to suspect that there is no avoiding a culture war here too."[4] At another opportunity, he shared with his readers "another, more regretful fact: that among us, in the lives of Jews who cling onto difference, many primitive customs have been preserved...for example, a woman to whom a man does not extend his hand for a handshake."

Jabotinsky Sr. had gone to his death nine years before the incident in the Knesset canteen, albeit closer to Judaism and spirituality than at the outset of his career as a public intellectual. But even from his grave in America, he remained the undisputed leader of the Herut party, much more so than its mustachioed thirty-five-year-old leader Menachem Begin, who could not even dream of one day becoming Israel's sixth prime minister. No wonder that religious and Haredi politicians—who for the first and last time in Israel's history managed to unite into a single list—preferred Ben-Gurion and his more pragmatic colleagues. The leaders of Israel's ruling party were, of course, complete heretics, but they understood their limits in Israel's governing system, and instead of getting bogged down in debates about theology and constitutional law, they preferred good old-fashioned compromises. Thus emerged the famous "status quo" on matters of religion and state, military draft exemptions for yeshiva students, and government funding for religious institutions. "I don't go to synagogue," Prime Minister Ben-Gurion was quoted as saying, "but the synagogue that I don't go to is Orthodox."

The early Herut party, in contrast, was bourgeois, extremely Ashkenazi, quite secular, and most importantly—ideologically purist. "For the unity of the homeland, the ingathering of exiles, social justice, and human liberty" read the principles on the first page of the party's founding charter, without mentioning any religious tenets whatsoever. The party appealed to property owners, who were appalled by Mapai's all-encompassing state interventionism, as well as to those who wanted to expand the young country's borders as far as the eastern bank of the Jordan River. Every single Herut representative in the First Knesset was born in Europe. This ideological rigidity did not pay off at the polls. Begin blamed Ben-Gurion for the division of Jerusalem and championed the cause of the capital city, but it repaid him with successive electoral setbacks. It is hard to believe nowadays, but for many years, the hedonistic, free-spirited Tel Aviv was considered the stronghold of the right-wing opposition. At one right-wing rally there in the 1960s, Begin addressed a crowd of forty thousand people.[5]

Most voters back then probably had no idea that Begin never smoked on Shabbat and only ate kosher food. Unlike most of his friends, Begin never turned his back on tradition, nor could he understand why Zionism and Judaism were somehow supposed to be in tension. Jabotinsky, a scholarly man, had treated religion and nationalism as competing values, but in Begin's mind, they simply coexisted peacefully, without need for academic arguments.[6] Behind his back, many in his movement thought that he was reconciling religion and nationalism through cheap, unintellectual populism. "Like the screeching of a door" was how Jabotinsky once unfavorably described one of Begin's speeches. When Begin, as the commander of the Irgun resistance, went on the run from the British and disguised himself as a rabbi called Israel Sassover, he seemed to slip into the role quite easily. But his party, torn between two approaches, was still far from capturing the hearts of Israel's more traditionalist voters.

Power was nowhere on the horizon, not even on the clearest of days. Ben-Gurion's movement, Mapai, positioned itself in the center of the political map as a key player without which it was impossible to form a government. It formed coalitions with whichever parties it pleased, sometimes with the Haredim and other times with Mapam, sometimes with religious Zionists and other times with liberals. Only two parties were beyond the pale: the communist Maki party and Herut, whose supporters, Ben-Gurion declared, were "Jewish Nazis" and whose leader, Menachem Begin, was a "clearly Hitlerian type." In a feat of parliamentary finesse, Begin retorted that the prime minister was "a great dictator and a little maniac."[7] He was so isolated, so thirsty for love. One day, he gleefully told a friend: "Ben-Gurion smiled at me today in the Knesset."[8] On less optimistic days, he was convinced that he could see a secret service agent following him from the visitors' gallery in the Knesset, obviously on Ben-Gurion's orders.[9]

But at least for now, he posed no threat to Mapai's rule, at least not a political one. Begin did not have a single supporter among Israel's elite. Even years later, in the 1977 elections, not a single professional broadcaster in the whole country agreed to feature in the Likud's election ads. When the actor Sefi Rivlin volunteered to appear in them, most of his performances were canceled overnight and his fellow actors asked for his name to be scratched off the posters of their productions, fearful of being tainted by association. "They say that we hired a man to shout, 'Begin for prime minister!' every morning," the Likud's leader once said in a moment of self-deprecation. "[When] asked why he wanted the role, he replied that it was a job for life."[10]

It took twenty-nine years in the end. And along the way, Begin would build, in a process of trial and error, what is now known as the "national camp." He had plenty of time for this trial and error: He lost eight elections, far more than Shimon Peres. But those were different days. He had almost no voters—just 49,782—when he began his journey to the top, but he had time in abundance.

Begin wanted to create a new center of political gravity, one that might somehow rival Mapai's power. He found his opportunity in the center: the General Zionists—"a party with no taste or smell," as my grandfather, an Irgun veteran, once dryly quipped. The General Zionists were a party for bourgeois property owners, who did not hold hawkish views on expanding Israel's borders but at least presented an ideological alternative to the Labor movement's centralized economy. The Maccabi health fund associated with it supported—to the ruling party's horror— the patients' right to choose their doctors.

Like the old joke about the man who was young at heart looking for a girl his age, this was a strange marriage of interests: a leader with right-wing views on the Arab-Israeli conflict but without an economic agenda was in search of an economically right-wing party without views on the Arab-Israeli conflict. Begin had no interest in economics, and the calamitous consequences of his ignorance would prove themselves in the runaway inflation that gripped the Israeli economy right under his nose when he was prime minister. He once shocked his colleagues when he announced at an elections rally: "We will allow the use of foreign currency only for the genuine needs of the collective and the individual, so that we may each serve as a personal model of modesty."[11] For his own part, he was indeed a modest man, whose favorite food was boiled chicken. His opposition to Israel's centralized socialist economy was more the instinctive response of one whose ideological bedfellows were excluded from key positions in the economy than the product of a deep understanding of supply and demand.

Begin's fifteen years of electoral courtship only paid off ahead of the elections for the Sixth Knesset, in 1965. When Ben-Gurion stormed out of Mapai for the last time and established Rafi, his own party, Herut and the Liberal Party spotted a window of opportunity to present an alternative and founded Gahal (an acronym standing for "Bloc of Herut and Liberals"). The Hebrew letter lamed emblazoned on the Likud's current logo is a throwback to the old Liberals.

Begin was forced to forgo in his party's manifesto his demand for the liberation of Judea and Samaria, which looked—just two years before the Six-Day War—completely delusional. His partners agreed to let him speak about his demand for the banks of the Jordan River, "but only to hint at it" in order not to scare away voters. Begin thought that this was still worthwhile: "God willing, we'll hit the thirties," he said, audaciously predicting a high number of seats. But the voters were less enamored with the union, making a point that would prove itself in nearly every Israeli election: In the case of party mergers, one plus one is almost always worth less than two. The joint faction dropped a seat, winning just twenty-six. Nevertheless, this was the first time that Begin came to head the second-largest faction in the Knesset, which could no longer be ignored. From now on, he was no longer "the gentleman sitting to the right of Mr. Bader." He was the head of a party that was center-right on security and right wing on economics. Now, all that he was missing was voters.

It took these voters time to make it to Israel, "on eagles' wings," as the young country poetically described Jewish immigration from Arab lands.

One day, in 1965, a Jew stepped off a boat that had just sailed in from Morocco. Perhaps he kissed the soil. There was no festive ceremony to welcome him. His name is a mystery, to this day, and nobody knows whether he is still alive. But he triggered a historic upheaval: When he sailed into the harbor, Ashkenazi Jews, those of European origin, were still a majority in Israel. But the moment he disembarked, the Ashkenazim became a minority. In its seventeenth year of independence, Israel was still trying to change the Jewish immigrants from Arab lands, to transform them in the great (Ashkenazi) melting pot. But these Jews, known as *Mizrahim*, would soon transform Israel itself.

The seeds of the electoral upheaval of 1977 had begun to germinate even earlier: Back when the votes were counted for the Constituent Assembly, which declared itself the First Knesset, Mapai was rocked by a minor scandal—it turned out that in ten Mizrahi neighborhoods in Tel Aviv, Herut had won 2,500 votes out of 3,300.[12] The Histadrut, the national labor federation, declared a day of mourning: "On this the state was founded, and on this it will fall," warned Mapai secretary-general Zalman Aran. "If the state succeeds over the next four years to rehabilitate life for Mizrahi Jews in Israel—we will have eliminated Herut. If not—a cancer will grow in the country that will imperil its existence."

To Mapai's credit, it did not play electoral politics and continued to actively facilitate the immigration of hundreds of thousands of Mizrahi Jews. To its discredit, it did nothing to curb ugly manifestations of racism. A *Haaretz* article declared: "This race [is] quite unlike anything we have known in Israel. These people are extremely primitive. Their level of education borders on complete ignorance, and they have no ability whatsoever to absorb anything spiritual. In general, they are only slightly better than the Arabs...and above there the matter of their chronic laziness and work-shyness."[13] Once, as a young reporter for Army Radio, I had asked President Moshe Katsav to share a personal story. To my astonishment, he told me about how officials once threw his family into a transit camp near Haifa in the pouring rain, promised to be back the next day to move them to permanent housing—and never came back. The president burst into tears and disappeared into his chambers.

The State of Israel was planned on a European drawing board and was therefore intended to be a German-speaking, opera-loving extension of Europe in the heart of the Levant. Jabotinsky shared this aversion to all things Eastern. He dedicated a whole article to explaining the inferiority of the East to the cultured and developed West. The "East," to which the Mizrahi ("Eastern") Jews belonged, was for him synonymous with the lowest possible form of human society.[14]

In the *ma'abarot*, the transit camps where many Jewish immigrants from Arab lands languished, there was no electricity and certainly no public libraries. Their residents were not familiar with Jabotinsky's writings. But they loved Begin. Contrary to the patronizing urban legend, they never thought that he was born in Meknes or Marrakesh, but they appreciated his affinity for Jewish tradition; they knew that he did not talk down to them, and they saw in the establishment's exclusion of him its discrimination against them too. They also liked that when he gave speeches, he wore a suit and tie, not khakis like Mapai's leaders did. "*Yaish Begin! Yaish Begin!*" they cheered during his first election campaign. "Don't they know my name's Menachem?" wondered Begin, until someone explained that *yaish* is Arabic for "long live."

Till today, most Mizrahim vote for the right, and most Ashkenazim—for the left. Since the 1955 elections, Mizrahi Jews have accounted for at least 55 percent of Herut and Likud voters, but in the Knesset, the number of "Sephardi" lawmakers, as they were known then, from the Likud was much lower than for the Alignment: only two out of twenty-six seats in the Sixth Knesset.[15] For anyone brought up believing the fashionable theory of identity politics—in which people are supposed to vote for people like them—this is surprising.

Most right-wing voters are from the Middle East, but most right-wing leaders are from the east of Europe: the ancestral surnames of Israel's four right-wing prime ministers, before most of them were Hebraicized, were Begin, Yezernitsky (Shamir), Mileikowsky (Netanyahu), and Scheinerman (Sharon). Surprisingly, the Likud's rise to power did nothing to increase the number of Mizrahi ministers in the government. Even more surprising was that this fact did not at all erode Mizrahi voters' support for the Likud. This is another quite strong hint that contrary to the claim of identity politics, women do not necessarily want to vote for women and national-religious voters care little for how many kippot are on their representatives' heads or, even for that matter, how many Arabs there are.

Israel's Mizrahi voters have never seen themselves as a "sector" of Israeli society. In their eyes, they *are* its society. "They don't want to be liberated from anything," explained the sociologist Prof. Nissim Mizrachi. "They did not arrive in a neutral country, where all they want is to be universalist citizens…. They came to Israel because they harbor deep feelings for the Jewish people."[16] Indeed, in the party institutions of Herut and the Likud, Mizrahim accounted for almost half of apparatchiks, but they did not necessarily elect candidates who came from the same countries as them—just the ones who struck them as the most suitable. When Yitzhak Shamir, born in Ruzhany, Russia, competed in 1983 against Rabat-born David Levy for the chairmanship of the Likud, orphaned by Begin's resignation, he swept much of the vote share of Mizrahi party officials.[17]

When the Labor Party lost the last crumbs of its support among Mizrahi voters, it tried to reclaim its former glory by diversifying its leadership. Over the years, it has crowned as its leader the kippah-wearing Avraham Burg, the Moroccan-born Amir Peretz, the veteran Iraqi immigrant Binyamin "Fouad" Ben-Eliezer, and Avi Gabbay, who grew up in the transit camp of Katamon without electricity. But as long as Labor put off changing its platform, its chairmen looked more like saccharine icing on a tasteless cake than leaders capable of reviving the historic relationship with the social groups that represent the majority of Israel's voters. Rabbanit Yemima Mizrachi once recalled on the radio that on the eve of the 2019 elections, she was shocked to hear her taxi driver, a religious Jerusalemite born to Moroccan immigrant parents, telling her that he planned to vote Labor. Only when she stepped out of the taxi, baffled, did the driver remember to chime, "Oh, by the way, Avi Gabbay's my brother."

The rest of the electorate was harder to persuade. In the same month that Amir Peretz was elected leader of Labor, it was abandoned by a quarter of a million voters—seven seats' worth of votes—in favor of Kadima, which Labor veteran Shimon Peres had just defected to. Labor set up an emergency campaign office, headed by party elder and member of the Knesset Aryeh Eliav, to attract them back. It was called the "Veterans' HQ," but Peretz's people privately gave it the more appropriate moniker of "Ashkenazi HQ." Labor's chairman promised to do everything to attract "social" voters (as Israelis call social democrats), but it was clear to everyone who the party was targeting. Ehud Barak called me to his office at the time. In the middle of our meeting, he pulled out a box of Abadi cookies, a Mizrahi treat, and asked sarcastically: "Would you like a few social cookies?"

A decade earlier, Barak did not hide behind political correctness. In 1997, as Labor's newly elected chairman, he outraged party veterans by apologizing to Jewish immigrants from Arab countries for Mapai's injustices: "We were unable to respect the richness of your culture. In people's memories, there remain deep scars connected to the Labor Party's actions. On behalf of myself, and on behalf of the leadership of the Labor Party, I ask for forgiveness."[18]

Barak was working to bring back the voters who had abandoned the party when he was still serving in the IDF's elite commando unit, undercover as a woman on the streets of Beirut. Hoping to rekindle the electorate's long-lost love for his party, he changed its name from "the Labor Party" to "One Israel." He also watered it down by running on a joint list with a national-religious party (Meimad) and former Likud minister David Levy's Gesher party, which had recently been formed with the aim—which it did not achieve—of attracting votes from Israel's social and geographic periphery.

This was practically the last attempt in Labor's history to rely on something other than the party's natural base of white Ashkenazi voters in the greater Tel Aviv area. Most of the left's attempts to return to power since then have been based on outsourcing: It hoped that Avigdor Liberman's loathing for Netanyahu would galvanize Russian Israeli voters, Moshe Kahlon would sweep voters in the social periphery, Naftali Bennett would mobilize the national-religious vote, and Aryeh Deri would bring in the Haredim.

But they were not fighting against Netanyahu the man but against the warm house built by Begin. Netanyahu understood this perfectly well when he reacted to Barak's apology by saying, "There are people and movements in Israel who think that we should be a melting pot that boils and blends every community until eventually a uniform Israeli pops out. The sort who will forget his community's unique heritage and disconnect from everything special and different built by his ancestors over the generations." Then he leaned into the microphone, as if to share a secret with the crowd: "In fact, you know what they wanted? They wanted us all to be Ashkenazi."[19] When the Likud faced the four-headed Blue and White party in 2019, Netanyahu mockingly called its leaders "three Ashkenazim—and Gabi Ashkenazi."

But let's not get ahead of ourselves. In the late 1960s, Begin could count on the support of veteran Irgun and Lehi resistance fighters, a large part of the Mizrahi electorate, and most of the Liberal's base. He was the leader of the second-largest party in the Knesset, and after the Six-Day War, when he joined an emergency national unity government, he also had a seat at the government table and a chauffeur. At his disposal was Ezer Weizman, his first general—an indispensable post in any political party serious about going far. But he had two tiny problems:

His party had no political partners in the Knesset, and it was still lagging behind Labor, which had a small lead of a mere thirty seats.

First, Begin turned his attention to closing the gap. Ahead of the 1973 elections, four years after Golda Meir formed the Alignment out of a cacophony of rival workers' parties, Begin chose to present a united list of his own. After protracted and exhausting negotiations, he formed an expanded bloc of Herut and Liberal parties together with the Movement for Greater Israel, a few refugees from Ben-Gurion's old spin-off party, and recently retired IDF commander Ariel Sharon. This was the revered general's first seemingly impossible operation in that unforgettable year, the second being the crossing of the Suez Canal soon after, during the Yom Kippur War. This united list was originally supposed to be called the "Counter-Alignment."[20] Fortunately for everyone, it ultimately decided on the catchier name "Likud," meaning "consolidation."

Menachem Begin had come a long way since his Herut days. The growing pains were acute: Accustomed to being the only leader in his movement, he suddenly found himself with roommates. In May 1975, most members of his faction voted against his economic plan and blocked his demand for the party to publicly call for Israelis to settle the Palestinian town of Nablus (the ancient city of Shechem). Nevertheless, when the votes were counted, this all paid off. On the last day of 1973, in the saddest winter in Israel's history, Israelis for the first time faced two major parties: One that had just failed with the Yom Kippur War and another that wanted to replace it at long last.

Nevertheless, when the clock struck midnight and ushered in 1974, the loudest celebrations were at the Alignment's HQ. The sense of relief was encapsulated in just six words in the following morning's headline: "It Could Have Been Much Worse." Golda Meir and Moshe Dayan had been dealt a blow but still controlled fifty-one seats. The Likud had received a big boost, but with thirty-nine seats, Begin was fated to deliver his eighth consecutive concession speech. The poet Haim Hefer mocked Begin the next day as a latter-day Moses, doomed to see the Promised Land from afar but never enter. But this hubristic verse would not age well. The Alignment had proven itself to be a cat with nine lives, but soon, very soon, would the tenth truck come to run it over.

But which partners were Begin expecting to form a government with? A browse through the newspaper archives reveals that the phrase "right-wing camp," to describe the political bloc that won power in 1977, first appeared only in the 1980s, long after Begin had gone home and severed contact with the outside world. If you had asked Begin at a rally whether he was right wing, it is doubtful that he would have known what you were talking about and even more doubtful that he would have wanted to define himself this way. His only association with the term "right" was from Betar's anthem: "May my treacherous right hand be forgotten if I forget the left bank of the Jordan."

What was the massive shift that Begin triggered? In order to understand it, we must remember that politics is far less rational than we tend to think. Few of us can remember the moment at which we formed our political opinions, because most of them were not formed in our heads but in our mothers' wombs. Most of us will spend our whole lives voting for the same side as our parents, and if we change our minds, it is usually as an act of rebellion against them or because we discover religion, lose faith, or suddenly come into money.

Often, as I am driving home after another argument on TV with my left-wing colleague Amnon Abramovich, I am warmed by the fuzzy narcissistic feeling that I had really showed it to him this time. But then I remember that if Amnon had been born to settler parents in Ofra like I was, and had I grown up on his kibbutz, he probably would have been the one calling for Israel to extend its sovereignty to Judea and Samaria while I would have been rooting for a minority government propped up by Arab votes. The most futile activity in nature, besides pressing an elevator button to make the doors open faster, is a political argument.

But if our identities remain fairly stable—assuming that we do not join a cult or decide to switch genders—why do such dramatic changes often happen between one election and the next? The answer is that each of us has multiple identities. A thirty-seven-year-old woman from south Tel Aviv might be someone who remembers the suicide bombings of the early 2000s and is afraid that they will come back, *and* a mother of three struggling to afford daycare, *and* a daughter appalled by the poor care given to her elderly parents, *and* a traditionalist Jew who lights Shabbat candles, *and* a citizen annoyed that her sister cannot visit on Saturday because there is no public transport. Which identity will she choose? That depends on who tells her the best story.

Politics is not a conference of accountants sitting down to compare percentage points and numbers. Politics is a storytellers' festival at a Galician marketplace. One person tells a scary story about nasty enemies who are secretly building big, evil bombs to drop on us. A second storyteller, eyes glistening, describes a Western country with open borders. A third reduces everyone to tears by talking about a poor old woman lying in the corridor of a hospital. Whoever can attract a bigger crowd by the end of the day wins.

The Begin of the early 1970s still lacked a political camp, but for the first time, he had a good and compelling story. He was no longer the head of a small party of disgruntled oppositionists, nor simply the center of a loose and unlikely alliance of capitalists, paramilitary veterans, and Jewish immigrants from Arab lands. He went from town to town, village to village, speaking about a new generation unashamed to be Jewish, united by national pride, tradition, and Jerusalem. He described the nation as a big family, which welcomed around the table its religious Zionist relatives, its Haredi relatives, and the biggest, most important, and silenced branch of the family: those who were simply traditional.

In 1973, after the Likud was founded, Begin gave this political family a name for the first time—one that not only described reality but shaped it. A name that would transform the country: "the national camp." It was as if, in one go, a grid of millions of people across Israel, who previously had no idea that they belonged to the same movement, was suddenly electrified. From then on, Begin would not stop using the phrase—all the way to the prime minister's office.

If the Haredim retained any lingering suspicions toward Begin—a throwback to Herut's secular beginnings—they had long since stashed them away. Begin suppressed his famous zeal for civil rights and supported a law that almost totally banned the rearing of pigs in Israel. "When I was a schoolboy, other boys tried to smear the fat of this animal on my lips," he recalled with horror at the Knesset podium. "I fought with all my might, and I succeeded." Eri Jabotinsky's ham sandwiches had become a distant memory.

After years of striking rock, water suddenly came out, and when it did, it came gushing out: The Labor-led government was no longer headed by a revered figure from Israel's founding generation, but by a young, rookie prime minister—Yitzhak Rabin. The German-born, aging, dovish leadership of the religious Zionist movement had been replaced with fresh blood, veterans of combat units and supporters of the settlement movement. Religious Zionists clashed on the hilltops of Samaria with police and soldiers, marking the end of their "historic alliance" with the Alignment and the start of their "natural partnership" with the Likud. Demographics also contributed their share. People joked that every ambulance in the street was carrying one young Likud voter on their way to being born and one old Alignment voter on their way to die.

Begin might have been plucking the same chords for years, but only now, in the mid-1970s, did the whole country start humming along. Israel—after the Yom Kippur War—felt more downhearted and less sure of itself, and it stashed away the secular melting pot in favor of religious traditions once left by the wayside. The massive groundswell of Jews rediscovering religion after the war was a vivid testament to this. The entertainer Uri Zohar, who became Haredi in 1977 practically on live radio, and Menachem Begin, who rose to power the same year, were different verses of the same song.

Begin enjoyed the natural adulation of religious voters. The day after the 1977 elections, he became the first Israeli premier to place a note in the Western Wall, in a gesture of gratitude for his victory. He was also the first to pepper his speech with "God willing." Groups of young religious Zionists danced around him in ecstasy. Rabbi Zvi Yehuda Kook, their leader, declared the Likud's victory to be a "divine revelation."[21] His support among the Haredim hit levels that would make any Hasidic rebbe jealous, because as much as one rebbe is revered by his disciples, he is also despised by his rivals' followers. Begin, in contrast, enjoyed total consensus in Bnei Brak. The zealous, Ashkenazi, secular, bourgeois Herut party had morphed into the traditionalist, Mizrahi, popular Likud. "The national camp" turned out to be the *Jewish* camp.

Begin's instinctive genius was proven a generation later in polling conducted by Jewish American pollster Arthur Finkelstein. His thesis began with a practical question: Let's say that you want to work out whether a close friend is right wing or left wing, and she refuses to tell you. How might you figure out the answer indirectly? If you ask her where she served in the army and she replies that she got out of military service, she might be a fan of an Arab party or a Haredi party. "Where do you live?" Well, even Tel Aviv gave one-third of its votes to the Likud, not to mention Haifa, which splits its vote equally. "What do you think about Netanyahu?" If you drew the line there, the whole of the Likud's Knesset faction, besides Netanyahu himself, would be considered far left. Finkelstein developed a devastatingly accurate metric, far more effective than Pfizer's COVID-19 vaccine. Just ask your friend, "How would you define yourself: Jewish or Israeli?" Fully 95 percent of those who answer "Jewish" are right wing, and 95 percent of those who say "Israeli" are on the left.

"Jewish" and "Israeli" are, in fact, two of the main tenets of Israel's identity as a Jewish and democratic state. Contrary to constant scaremongering, they are not in direct tension with each other. Most of Israel's citizens identify strongly with both the state's Jewish character and its democratic character. But sometimes they rub each other the wrong way. Like asking whether strawberry-banana yogurt is more strawberry or banana, Israelis often reflect on whether they are slightly more Jewish than democratic or vice versa.

Armed with this insight, you will find that most stories on the news in Israel, most push notifications on people's phones, and most of the quarrels that are a part of life in Israel are basically reiterations of the same tired argument—Jewish or democratic?—with a thin veneer of real news on top. In October 2020, Israel became the first country in the world to be plunged into its second coronavirus lockdown, in one of the most depressing periods of its history. Only to an untrained eye did Israel's news shows discuss public health and which activities the government should restrict in enclosed and open spaces in order to prevent transmission. On the surface, they debated a bill to ban left-wing protests in front of the prime minister's residence, the Haredi pilgrimage to Uman, restrictions on businesses, and ways to reduce mass prayer gatherings over the High Holy Days. But beneath the deafening noise in the news studios, one could hear echoes of a fierce debate about principles and about what was more important: the supreme democratic value of freedom of expression and protest or the supreme Jewish value of freedom of worship and prayer?

Before the COVID-19 pandemic, three consecutive Knessets had crashed in a political Bermuda Triangle. The debate about Haredi enlistment was really about which value was supreme: Torah study, in the name of which many yeshiva students were given draft exemptions, or equality, the name of which was proposed to force yeshiva students to enlist. The Nation-State Law, passed in 2018, also unleashed a firestorm: Did it really give the state's Jewishness legal precedence above its democratic character? Or was this just the right's late and ineffective entry into a constitutional pitch that is still controlled and unchecked by the left and the activist Supreme Court judges? Moreover, if you look at the names of right-wing parties, you will find the "Jewish Home" and "UTJ" and on the left, the Democratic Front for Peace and Equality (Hadash) and the Democratic Union. Could anything be clearer?

During the nonstop election cycle of 2019–2021, my fellow reporter Dr. Avishay Ben-Haim sent Israeli social media into a frenzy with an observation. He noticed an interesting phenomenon, which was not reflected in the close results at the national level: In towns such as Beit She'an, Netivot, Dimona, Yeruham, and Kiryat Shemona, the right-wing bloc won a crushing majority of 90 percent, with most people voting Likud. In contrast, in towns such as Ramat HaSharon, Hod HaSharon, Raanana, and the northern neighborhoods of Tel Aviv, the center-left enjoyed similarly fantastical levels of support, reaped mainly by Benny Gantz and Yair Lapid's Blue and White party.

Ben-Haim's conclusion was that Israel already has "two states for two peoples." There is "First Israel" in the greater Tel Aviv area—an Ashkenazi, economically established, secular, left-wing place, which loathes Netanyahu. And there is "Second Israel" in the country's periphery—a poor, Mizrahi, religious, right-wing place, which reveres Netanyahu.

The theory is disarmingly simple, but it raises a few questions. First, the Arabs: They are hardly Ashkenazi, and most of them live in Israel's social and cultural periphery, the bottom income brackets, and the towns where, as Ahmad Tibi says, "Everything is covered in tar, except the roads." What could be more Second Israel than that? At the same time, the religious Zionist community is mostly Ashkenazi, well-off, and lives in the center of the country. Yet since 1977, it has been a cornerstone of the right. And if distance from Tel Aviv is the key variable, then why is Sderot solidly right wing while the neighboring kibbutzim of Nir Am, Kfar Aza, and Negba are strongholds of the left?

Or maybe the strength of Israelis' attachment to Judaism is what correlates with their support for the right? Here is a fact and a hypothesis.

Fact: The more strongly that Jews in Israel identify as religious, the more likely they are to support the national camp. Haredi voters identify most strongly as right wing, followed by religious Zionists, then Likud and Yisrael Beiteinu voters, and at the far end of the scale—the left-wing Meretz party. Hypothesis: The more synagogues in a neighborhood, the more right-wing voters live there. In Bnei Brak, a Haredi city with a synagogue on every corner, almost 100 percent of voters side with the national camp. In the Arab town of Umm al-Fahm, which as far as I know has no synagogues, Chabad houses, or Carlebach services, the left won 99.63 percent of the vote in the 2020 elections.

Even when Benjamin Netanyahu first rose to power in 1996, he did so as the driver of a retrofitted car built over the frame of Begin's design. With all due respect to his manufactured slogan, "Making a Secure Peace," the slogan that really won him the election was less contrived and was never tested on any focus group: "Netanyahu: Good for the Jews." It began as an impromptu initiative by Chabad devotees in the last week of the election campaign. The morning after Netanyahu's stunning victory, with a razor-thin lead of just one percentage point, Shimon Peres showed up for work at the prime minister's office, as usual, at 7:00 a.m. He summarized the previous night's events with a single, pithy observation: "The Jews defeated the Israelis."

Peres astutely spotted that the Oslo Accords and suicide bombings, supposedly the hot-button issues of the elections, were only thinly disguising the true battle for hegemony in Israeli society. Indeed, the architect of the accords, Ron Pundak, admitted at the time: "I want peace, because I want there to be a sense of Israeliness. Peace is not an end in itself. It is a means for moving Israel from one era to another, to an era of what I consider a normal country. The Israelization of our society instead of its Judaization." One decade later, the journalist Yair Lapid would pen similarly honest thoughts about the Gaza disengagement: "It was not despite the settlers but because of them. It was never about the Palestinians.... There was a completely different motive: Over the past twenty years, the religious Zionists made extensive use of the secular nation to fulfill a series of political and mostly religious aims...but Israelis don't like being anyone's mules, no matter who's riding them."

The foundations of the camp that defeated Peres were laid in 1977. The day after Begin's victory, he did not stop at building a coalition; he also wanted to build a stable political bloc for generations, and the construction costs were high. For the first time since Israel's establishment, the education portfolio was given to a religious party: the National Religious Party (NRP), or Mafdal. The Haredim, kept out of Israel's coalitions since 1951, were tempted to enter through the front door, not just to peek through the window. In exchange for their consent, Begin scrapped the cap on draft exemptions for yeshiva students and grounded El Al flights on Shabbat. Overnight, the Haredim became the kingmakers of Israeli politics. The religious Zionist electorate was annexed by the right-wing bloc, and the Haredim were delighted to play the role in which they were cast.

Israeli elections became, in time, a question of who would get to form a government with the Haredim: They had a handsome cluster of seats, controlled by a handful of rabbis without any grassroots pressure against unpopular policies, because Haredi voters do not really express a choice as much as they follow orders from their supreme rabbinical councils. Most importantly, the Haredi parties have never had delusions of grandeur. They have never dreamed of controlling the defense, foreign, or finance ministries, and certainly not the prime minister's office. They have always swum against the political currents. Everyone keeps trying to climb the greasy pole, but the Haredim always keep their feet on the ground, even at the cost of giving up pricey real estate.

The Haredim were ideologically opposed to the Zionist state, but an old parable used by Rabbi Yisrael Meir (who was also known as the "Chofetz Chaim") eased their lawmakers' consciences in making budgetary demands from this state. It likened their situation to "a woman standing in the marketplace, selling apples. Some young rascals passed by her stall and started pinching her wares. The woman started crying and shouting. A wise man walked past and said, 'Don't cry. Everyone's grabbing—so stand there and start grabbing too.'"

As long as Begin was around, the Haredim kept him in their good books. Just before the handover from Rabin at the prime minister's office in 1977, he was asked by the young reporter Ya'akov Ahimeir what kind of prime minister he intended to be. "The good Jewish kind," was Begin's succinct reply.

The family known as the "national camp," established in the 1970s, was blessed in the 1990s to welcome a new, young, adopted son, who was not even around in Begin's days: Jewish immigrants from the former Soviet Union. These one million immigrants, startled masses flown in on packed flights following the collapse of the communist empire, would transform the Middle East. Israel's newspapers suddenly filled up with Cyrillic text; the streets, with unfamiliar sounds. Yitzhak Shamir managed to get Western countries to close their skies to divert this massive airlift of Soviet émigrés to Ben Gurion Airport, in what he saw till his dying day as his crowning achievement as prime minister.

In the first elections afterward, the vast majority of immigrants from the former Soviet Union gave their votes to the party opposing Shamir, led by Yitzhak Rabin. The great Russian immigration wiped out forty years of the steady growth of the Haredi and religious share of the population and, therefore, also threatened to erase the right-wing majority that had crystalized over the previous years. The Mizrahim, for example, reverted practically overnight to being a minority again. But in 1996, helped by Likud director general Avigdor Lieberman, himself an immigrant from the former Soviet Union, Netanyahu managed to galvanize the immigrant vote. Maybe it was the wave of terror attacks, or maybe it was the fact that a new Russian party, Yisrael Ba-Aliya, was led by two religious former prisoners of conscience: Natan Sharansky and Yuli Edelstein. Either way, the right-wing Israeli family had suddenly grown.

This political home was riven by tensions practically from the get-go. Israeli history teaches that immigrants from left-wing dictatorships tend to vote for the right (just as those who fled Argentina's right-wing dictatorship usually vote left). And indeed, the "Russians" mostly oppose territorial withdrawals, distrust the Arabs, and are intensely nationalistic. But still, what was this secular electorate doing in a partnership with the Haredi and religious parties? Israelis from the former Soviet Union supported civil marriage and the use of public transport on Shabbat and fueled a surge in supermarket sales of pork. In short, they were much more nationalistic than religious. Jabotinsky would have felt at home among them, but for his successors, things were more complicated.

It is no wonder, therefore, that a personal dispute with Netanyahu pushed Avigdor Lieberman, one generation later, to walk out of his home, taking 150,000 Russian-speaking voters with him. Once the debate over peace and territorial withdrawals had slowly subsided, his attachment to the right also frayed. Lieberman's voters feel much more comfortable with the secular Yair Lapid and Nitzan Horowitz than in the national camp, surrounded by kippah-wearing lawmakers. The immigrants from the former Soviet Union are the real weathervane of Israeli politics. For the past thirty years, whoever won the Russian vote won the elections.

Nevertheless, Menachem Begin's national camp long outlived him. It was able to survive long after the political alliance against which it was formed had shriveled up and disappeared. Leaders are judged by their legacies' resilience to the ravages of time and their successors' mistakes, and on this test, Begin still passes with flying colors. The house that he built is still standing, despite the cracks that formed in the walls around an issue that was supposed to be its centerpiece: opposition to territorial withdrawals and concessions. Begin pulled out of Sinai, Netanyahu signed the Wye River Memorandum, and the Likud divided Hebron, also uprooting settlements in the Gaza Strip and three in northern Samaria. But the argument over the territories, momentous as it was, was also derivative from the major debate of Jews vs. Israelis. The right's support for Judea and Samaria is rooted in a powerful sense of Jewish identity, not vice versa.

True, there is no shortage of contradictions in Begin's camp: The right-wing demand for the state to keep out of people's private affairs does not sit easily with government budgets for synagogues and the rabbinate's state-sanctioned monopoly on marriage. Nevertheless, by force of personality, Begin managed to dissolve the tension between the two constituent parts of his alliance and then fuse them together. He did so just like he managed to simultaneously outflank the Alignment on the right with his demand for a free market and on the left with his demand to boost welfare spending. Not for the last time, it became clear that internal contradictions do not always impede the creation of victorious political alliances; sometimes they are even a hallmark of them.

Fifteen years after entering the prime minister's office, Menachem Begin was laid to rest on a cold winter's day, accompanied by hundreds of thousands of admirers at a funeral unlike that of any Israeli prime minister: His body was carried on a simple stretcher, not in a polished wooden casket. He was buried in silence, without eulogies by world leaders, and not on Mount Herzl with Israel's other leaders, but on the Mount of Olives. There, overlooking the Old City of Jerusalem, stands a plain, unadorned headstone of the "good Jewish kind."

CHAPTER 4

Silence Is No Crime

Shamir and Eshkol's Decision—
Forming Unity Governments

FRAU KRUG CALLED THE POLICE in Munich in September 1962, a veneer of Bavarian politeness disguising her panic. Her husband, Heinz, had not come home from work at his company, Intra, the night before, and oddly, the guard downstairs had not seen him leaving. A few hours earlier, Herr Krug had returned from a visit to Egypt, where he had business that he did not discuss with his wife. His secretary told the police officer sent to the scene of his disappearance that a Middle Eastern–looking man had entered the building around the same time Herr Krug was last seen. No trace of him has ever been found.

We now know what happened. Krug was selling advanced weapons to the Egyptians, and the mysterious man in his office was a Mossad agent. After assassinating the German arms dealer, the agent had been instructed to dispose of the body in the most efficient way possible: dissolving it in a bathtub of acid.[i] The commander who proposed this nifty idea was known over the years as Michael, or Markovich, or some other alias, always changing his nickname. His real name was Yitzhak Yezernitsky, later using the last name of Shamir. He headed the Mossad spy agency's special operations department. For years, he hid behind newspaper pages in Parisian cafés, tracked down Nazi war criminals in Vienna, and

---

i   According to the journalist Ronen Bergman, Krug's body was disappeared this way he Krug was smuggled to Israel.

assassinated villains around the world. Many years later, accompanied by a member of the Knesset, he got lost walking around his hometown of Tel Aviv. "I know the streets of Damascus and Cairo much better," he apologized, embarrassed.[1]

It was a rare moment of indiscretion from Israel's seventh prime minister. "Two people can keep a secret, as long as one of them is dead," he once said, having sent quite a few to their graves himself. As the commander of the Lehi paramilitary during the British Mandate, he had ordered the execution of another paramilitary leader, Eliyahu Giladi, who had gone off the rails and risked jeopardizing the whole organization. After Israel declared independence, Shamir had authorized the assassination of the Swedish mediator Count Folke Bernadotte. He always acted with guile and discretion. People joked that until his dying day, he rarely spoke on the phone for fear that the British were still listening. Shamir was an outlier in Israeli politics: First he sat in jail and only then in the Knesset, not vice versa. He had an intense aversion to self-promotion, perhaps ever since his face had graced the British police's "most wanted" posters. During his leadership of the Likud, he was so absent from the party's election adverts that one could be mistaken for thinking that the actor who presented them was the party's candidate for prime minister.

Unlike the founder of his movement, Ze'ev Jabotinsky, Shamir did not believe that silence was a crime. He led the most sensational life of any Israeli politician, and yet, when he left Mossad and entered politics through the Likud, the public responded with an apathetic yawn. "Yitzhak Shamir is an odd sort in the human horizon of our party system," opined a journalist sent to interview him on the eve of the 1977 elections. "On the eve of elections, when everything is in a frenzy, everything is boiling over, and politicians are all panicking to spread their wares for journalists to see and add some color and glamour and grace and beauty and interest—often far beyond the basic qualities of what they have to sell, just as long as their image gets a boost—this man sits on the eleventh floor of Metzudat Ze'ev [Likud HQ] in Tel Aviv, and says nothing."[2]

Back then, just before the Likud's victory, the party was gripped by a drama hidden from public view: Menachem Begin had suffered a serious heart attack. The Likud's campaign managers did not know whether they could still film election broadcasts with its top candidate. One day they discussed possible substitutes. When Shamir's name came up, one official responded wearily: "Be my guest! Put him on TV and plaster the streets with his image. You couldn't give the Alignment a better gift than Yitzhak Shamir. Finally, they'll get their Knesset majority."[3] Every time Shamir appeared on television, the Likud's public relations manager, Ezer Weizman, cursed at the screen in Arabic. Whenever he wanted to speak with Shamir, he told his secretary: "Get me the small Smurf on the line."[4]

In the end, Begin recovered, the Likud pulled off its historic victory, and in the summer of 1977, Shamir became the Knesset Speaker. What followed should not have surprised anybody: One day, the members of the Knesset entering the plenary discovered that the microphones on their desks had been unplugged. The Speaker, fed up with their constant shouting, had decided to tone down the heckling and to put an end to the "deleterious parliamentary practices that have accumulated over thirty years."

The former Lehi commander who was slowly and silently scaling the political ladder was the complete opposite of the former Irgun commander who held the role of prime minister. There was no love lost between them, perhaps because of the glaring personality differences. "I was not a big fan of Begin's famous speeches," Shamir later confessed. "I often thought that his pathos and intonation were overdone. Like a stage actor, he drew his strength, even his inspiration, from the audience's cheers. I took a dim view of his responsiveness to flattery, and I hoped, in vain, that he might be weaned off his intense passion for popularity." In a rare glimpse of his mischievous spirit, he wondered "how Begin managed to survive in the resistance in all those months when he had to hide from view and abstain from such distractions."[5]

Like all great leaders, Menachem Begin never stopped changing, even after his death. Maybe there should be a law banning people from expressing nostalgia for politicians they did not vote for at the time. In modern-day Israel, Begin's leadership is universally revered, and even the Likud's rivals see him as a role model. They miss Begin, his emphasis on *hadar* (a value somewhere between "dignity" and "majesty") and his respect for the rule of law. But Begin the politician, not the artificial memory, was despised by his rivals. The placards reading "Begin

Is a Murderer," brandished during protests against the Lebanon War, offer just one snapshot. Even earlier, when Begin was celebrated as the architect of peace with Egypt, a left-wing party handed out electoral propaganda designed to look like a "most wanted" poster: "Wanted: this man, bald, 1.68 m, a danger to the state." In the same election campaign, in 1981, Peres announced that he would no longer address Begin as the prime minister. For his own part, Begin did not always act in a way befitting his office. He delivered one toxic, borderline incendiary speech against "millionaire *kibbutznikim* with their swimming pools," showing crowds in Kiryat Shemona a photograph of the swimming pool in the neighboring kibbutz of Manara.

Nothing was more ridiculous than the notion that the successor to the charismatic Begin might be this diminutive, camera-shy, mustachioed old man. "This speculation might sound delusional to people outside of Herut," reported Nahum Barnea in 1978, "but the candidate with the best prospects of succeeding Begin if he resigns…is not the sprightly Ezer Weizman or the flighty Ariel Sharon, nor even Dayan, Erlich, Yadin, or Shimon Peres. The most realistic candidate is a sixty-three-year-old Jewish dwarf, who bears no military ranks and launched his political career only six years ago. The public has not heard of him, even though his bushy eyebrows have brushed the corner of the screen in many TV reports. His name is Yitzhak Shamir."[6]

Five years later, in the last week of August 1983, the Israeli government convened for its weekly meeting. Everything proceeded like clockwork: Ariel Sharon attacked everyone else, one minister got a promotion over somebody else, and Yitzhak Shamir, now the foreign minister, sat in the corner in silence, as always. Just a routine day in Jerusalem. But then Menachem Begin asked for the floor. "My dear friends, I hereby inform the government that I intend to resign from my role as prime minister. I cannot continue to fulfill this role."

"We sat there around the government table," Shamir later recalled, "and at first, we couldn't talk to each other, or even look at each other. I remember how I felt: shock, an intense feeling that something momentous had happened that could not be reversed, that nothing would go back to being as it was."[7] When Shamir regained his senses, to his fellow ministers' surprise, his eyes welled up: "Nothing could justify this," he said, choking. "This will cause jubilation among Israel's enemies abroad and the Likud's enemies at home. The people sitting here would do anything in the world for you. We have followed you. Recant!"[8] But Begin stared into space and said nothing.

In a perfect role reversal, the moment that Begin fell silent was the moment that Shamir started talking. In the race for leadership of the Likud, he pulled off a shock victory over the younger and more charismatic David Levy. "Sha-mir! Sha-mir!" someone tried to call out from the crowd, but not even the rhythmic chanting of his name sounded like the "Be-gin! Be-gin!" of the good old days. "I see the role entrusted to me tonight as a temporary trust," he promised the crowd, as if consoling them with a promise that Begin would return sometime. But Begin never came back. That night, he went to sleep early, without even staying up to hear the news about who would replace him as prime minister.[9] When an aide woke him up with a telephone call to update him about who his successor would be, Begin mumbled something and hung up.

Begin's majestic style of leadership gave way to a government of anonymous soldiers. Israel's seventh prime minister entered his new office in Jerusalem like a conscript reporting for basic training. He was strict about not eating between meals or smoking, and he even stopped drinking the occasional glass of brandy. Shamir also added a new entry to the prime minister's daily schedule: Every day, he drove home in his official car to eat lunch with his wife and to take a nap.[10] Like Levi Eshkol, he too appreciated a good siesta. Shamir's afternoon naps said as much about his personality as did his speeches: Anyone capable of stopping everything and not drowning under the never-ending avalanche of events and crises in the prime minister's job clearly has a healthy sense of proportion. "I did not want to be thrust into a perpetual sense of emergency," said Shamir, explaining the rationale behind his naps.[11]

* * *

Two decades earlier, it was equally impossible to think of Levi Eshkol sitting behind the prime minister's desk. He had been a late bloomer in the workers' movement. While his contemporaries, such as Haim Arlosoroff, Eliezer Kaplan, and Pinhas Lavon, had been promoted to senior roles in their thirties, Eshkol was left behind.[12] He was put in charge of economic affairs, while all the glory, then as now, was reserved for those engaged in matters of national defense and foreign policy.

Eshkol's climb to the top took nearly forty years. Behind his thickset glasses and Yiddish accent lay an especially sharp mind. Not even David Ben-Gurion imagined that Eshkol would be the one to stand between him and power, proving that no man is greater than his kingdom. When Israel's first prime minister "went on vacation" in 1961, his ministers were alarmed and censored reports about it, in order not to spark panic. For weeks, the Israeli public had no idea that Levi Eshkol was in charge. Two years later, when Ben-Gurion resigned as prime minister for the seventh and final time, Eshkol took the reins reluctantly—or so it seemed. "This will be a continuity government," he said coyly, as Shamir would say decades later. Ben-Gurion praised his successor and gave him his stamp of approval, fully intending to decapitate him after a year or two, as he had done to Moshe Sharett a decade earlier. Sharett had been prime minister in name only, while Ben-Gurion ran the country behind the scenes. The IDF carried out operations without his approval, and bureaucrats and officers ran their own independent policies, steered by Israel's founding father. After a year and a half, Sharett resigned as prime minister, with no plans to return.

Eshkol had no intentions of ending up like Sharett. He cunningly and slyly entrenched himself in power and sidelined Ben-Gurion, who was doing his best to interfere. Israel's first prime minister cursed the third prime minister, whom he now saw as totally unfit. "This is a corrupt and imbecilic government," he publicly taunted in 1965, announcing that he would not rest until Eshkol was booted from office.[13] Ben-Gurion constantly spoke out against Eshkol at party conventions, called his leadership into question, and undermined him just as he had undermined Sharett. But Israel had moved on and had grown tired of its founding father's Spartanism. "You have this whole place to yourself?" Ben-Gurion harangued his daughter after inspecting her new apartment in Tel Aviv. "What do you need a carpet, curtains, and a lampshade for? All you need is a bed, a desk, and a bookcase."[14] Times had changed, and Israelis were buying carpets. They no longer stood to attention for every whim of the "old man," as he was known, and tragically for him, Eshkol proved to be a much sharper and more skilled adversary than Sharett.

Unlike Ben-Gurion, Begin never broke his silence as a former premier, even though some words of support would have helped Shamir against his hostile party and disappointed supporters. He did not bother to go to the Knesset to vote in favor of his successor's new government or even to honor him with a congratulatory phone call. In subsequent elections, he did not even vote.

The first hint that Eshkol was not planning on continuing his predecessor's legacy was a rare gesture toward someone Ben-Gurion had fiercely resisted, even though this person had been dead for nearly a quarter of a century: Ze'ev Jabotinsky. On a personal level, relations between Ben-Gurion and the founder of the Zionist right were surprisingly cordial. Despite the ideological chasm between them, the pair struck a peace deal between their movements in the 1930s. It was the fruit of several private, face-to-face meetings, in which Ben-Gurion cooked scrambled eggs for Jabotinsky when he was hungry. Jabotinsky died unexpectedly a few years later and was buried in the United States. In his will, he wrote: "If I am buried outside the Land of Israel, my bones must not be transferred there other than by the order of the Jewish government, when it is formed."

But this Jewish government had no intention of respecting the will of a man it regarded as a fascist. "The Land of Israel needs living Jews," decided Prime Minister Ben-Gurion, "not dead bones." When the pressure intensified, he explained: "Only a man's work survives his death. His bones are dust and ashes, and they have nothing to do with the man. And this country mustn't be turned into a graveyard." He had no desire to give Begin and his party the honor of a state funeral for their movement's founder: "I am completely sure that this vapid, demagogic, wily, and unscrupulous party cannot reach power in Israel, but its mere existence is a national disgrace," he said.

Levi Eshkol saw Begin as a legitimate opposition leader, not a fascist. At the first opportunity, he announced his consent for the repatriation of Jabotinsky's bones. Begin recalled the moment he updated his party colleagues, with characteristic brio: "A sacred silence gripped the hall, but it quickly gave way to rapturous applause. They all stood on their feet in unison, expressing their joy at this good news."[15] Jabotinsky received the happiest funeral in Israeli history. The event, attended by the country's entire leadership, was known as "Ze'ev Jabotinsky's return to the homeland." There was a limit to this generosity: The prime minister personally visited the designated burial site on Mount Herzl to ensure that it was sufficiently far away from the grave of Theodor Herzl. Nevertheless, the

Israeli right, excluded and persecuted under Ben-Gurion, was embraced by the state for the first time. Ben-Gurion responded with some especially venomous invectives in the press against the government.

Eshkol seemed unruffled. In his position as a one-man reconciliation commission, he set about bandaging another bleeding wound from the Ben-Gurion era. He abolished the regime of military rule over Israel's Arab citizens, which had endured since the War of Independence and was imperiling Israel's basic definition as a democratic state. Every time you hear someone warning about "dangerous trends" or a "slippery slope" toward dictatorship in modern Israel, remind them of the eighteen years in which Israeli Arabs in certain areas were barred from leaving their villages without permission from the military; the nightly curfews imposed across swathes of the "Triangle" and Galilee regions; and, of course, the terrible Kafr Qasim massacre, in which dozens of Arabs were massacred simply for being late to return home. Israel's military censor barred any reporting on this horrific event for a whole month and a half, and even later, it censored plays about it. Ben-Gurion stubbornly refused to abolish the nightly curfew, even once it was clear that Israeli Arabs posed no military threat to the state. Eshkol scrapped it in 1966, creating the first opening for the integration of the large Arab national majority in the small Jewish state.

But the final rift between Ben-Gurion and his successor was triggered by Eshkol's ambitious initiative to unite all of Israel's workers' parties. Ben-Gurion still harbored old animosities from the pre-state period, the legacy of ideological disputes about details so minor that nobody in the young state could understand them anymore. Eshkol, in contrast, had his sights fixed on the future. The official reason for the merger was a "capital outflow" that risked Israel's socialist values.[16] But in fact, Eshkol understood that Israel's demographics were changing. The Ashkenazi working class, formed by the waves of immigration in the 1920s and 1930s, could not afford the luxury of ideological quarrels over every dot and comma if it wished to remain in power. In 1963, a senior apparatchik penned an article titled, "The Courage for Change, Before Disaster." Eshkol's initiative delayed this disaster by over a decade.

The Alignment, as the new party was called, appealed to the center: The word "socialism" was expunged from the party platform and replaced with vaguer terms, such as "social equality" and "just allocation of income."[17] Ben-Gurion boiled over with rage again, but this time, nobody in the party could understand why. The Alignment's politburo convened, and it was a wheelchair-bound Moshe Sharett who drove the longest knife into Ben-Gurion's back. "A movement must draw inspiration from its leader," said Sharett, speaking in a weak yet scathing voice, "but the leader cannot subordinate the movement, silence its thoughts, and impose his personal opinions on it purely by virtue of his immense authority."[18] Confronted by two prime ministers, one past and one present, not even Ben-Gurion stood a chance. He quit the party, this time for good. His new party, Rafi, was thumped by the Alignment in the 1965 elections. The Alignment's secret weapon was a recording of Levi Eshkol's speeches, which was posted to every household in the country.

* * *

In December 1966, bookstores were suddenly filled with a bestseller from a mysterious publishing house called "Isser Publishing." Its title: *Eshkol Jokes*.[19] Its immense popularity was a sign of the prime minister's plummeting popularity. "It was the worst thing that could have happened," recalled Eshkol's then-press secretary, Yossi Sarid. "It is worse to be laughed at than hated." Every single Israeli heard the joke about the university that decided to award Prime Minister Eshkol an honorary doctorate in biochemistry because of his success in turning the Israeli lira into organic waste; in every living room in the country, Israelis heard the joke about the minister in Eshkol's government who broke his wrist trying to lift the nation's morale; and until today, everyone knows the quote on the last page of the book, even if its source has been forgotten: "A sign was put up at Lod Airport: 'Last one out, please turn off the lights.'"

The mass emigration from Israel that year was just one sign of the sense of national despair resulting from a severe economic recession. Eshkol broke the number one rule in politics: Don't argue with the voters' feelings. In a radio address to the nation, he tried to persuade Israelis that things were not so bad after all. "I know that when grocery prices go up, taxes rise, and households must replan their budgets, citizens tend not to compliment their government and the person heading it. I can understand this. Let's speak frankly about living standards: We are dressing much better and eating much better than before. Despite what some people claim—people are moving to bigger apartments, buying new furniture, and equipping their homes with refrigerators, better stoves, television sets, vacuum cleaners. He's bought a motorcycle; she's bought a motorcar."[20] Propagandists and media mouthpieces for Rafi, Ben-Gurion's party, generously heaped jokes on the coals of protest. They called for cuts to the national defense budget, claiming that it was exaggerated.

In the spring of 1967, the reason for massive defense spending became painfully clear. When Egyptian forces moved into Sinai and blockaded the Straits of Tiran against Israeli shipping, national anxiety peaked. But not even then did Eshkol enjoy any public credit: How could Israel go to war under the leadership of a prime minister (and defense minister) who last wore their uniform fifty years ago, during the First World War, in the Jewish Legion? "If we had security because Mr. Eshkol were capable of steering the ship of war in days like these," said an attack article in *Haaretz*, "we would gladly follow him. But this security does not exist, and it seems to be increasingly absent for increasing numbers of people.... We need Ben-Gurion to reclaim the premiership and Moshe Dayan to serve as defense minister." Shamir might have maintained his silence, but Eshkol chose to speak—and stuttered. His address on national radio on the eve of the war, in which he struggled to read handwritten changes to his speech, became a symbol of malaise. A poll found that before the speech, 51 percent of Israelis supported going to war, but four days later that rate had dropped to just 26 percent.[21]

Under pressure, facing picketing action and scenes of young Israelis digging mass graves in the heart of Tel Aviv, Eshkol was forced to climb down. He knew that the army was ready, but his public image and standing, which had already suffered from a long recession, could no longer reassure an anxious nation. Grudgingly, he was forced to appoint Dayan as defense minister. The extent of Eshkol's fear of totally losing control is clear from a secret telegram to his new defense minister: "I hereby put in writing the principles that we agreed on:.... The defense minister shall not act without the prime minister's permission in regard to launching general military activity or a war against any state whatsoever."[22] The fact that Dayan was Ben-Gurion's protégé and a member of his party contributed to Eshkol's fear of winding up like Sharett.

The prime minister who prepared the Israeli military for this stunning triumph was almost completely erased from the victory album of the Six-Day War, which ended with Israel tripling in size with the conquest of Judea, Samaria, the Gaza Strip, the Sinai Peninsula, and the Golan Heights. IDF generals became household names, and Moshe Dayan's face was plastered on the walls of student dorms around the world. Eshkol also toured Israel's new borders in military uniform, but who wanted a framed photograph of an old Yiddish grandpa wearing khaki pants pulled far above his belly button? Nobody was laughing at Eshkol now. It was worse: They ignored him.

It was Eshkol's stutter that helped him, against his better judgment, to make the most important political decision of his life: Ninety-six hours before the outbreak of the war, threatened on three fronts, he made peace at home. The Alignment prime minister invited Menachem Begin and his eternal opposition party Gahal to join the government. The man who had dodged IDF artillery that was fired off the shores of Tel Aviv less than twenty years earlier when he commanded a rival militia, now sat in the windowless room where ministers decided to liberate Jerusalem. Had Begin not been a member of the government during this historic period, it is doubtful whether Israeli voters would have trusted him enough to elect him prime minister a decade later. Eshkol opened the doors of Israeli officialdom to him, and he did so with an open heart.

The choice that Eshkol made under fire was also graciously made by Shamir in more peaceful times. When he received the mandate to form a government in 1983, he offered the Alignment to join a unity government on very generous terms.[23] One year later, with the inauguration of the rotation government of 1984, in which Shamir and Peres agreed to rotate the premiership, Shamir told the Knesset that he hoped that this coalition would send "a message of unity, reconciliation, love of Israel, and genuine cooperation."[24] Since he was forced to relinquish the role of prime minister that day for the next two years, he probably meant this sincerely. After the Likud's clear victory in 1988, Shamir still preferred a broad coalition to a narrow one, which he saw as trouble. He had little love for the groom, Shimon Peres, but he bitterly regretted being forced into a divorce two years later with the stinking maneuver of 1990, which we shall get to soon.

Shamir's support for unity with the left was not a product of ideological agility. His whole life, Shamir never budged a millimeter from his principles, and he refused to concede an inch of territory to the Arabs. "When you are asked why the Land of Israel belongs to the Jewish people," Shamir urged Herut lawmakers in December 1982, "answer them with one word: 'because.'" On another occasion, he warned that if terror attacks continued, Arab areas of Hebron would be "razed to the ground." But as a rule, in his political life, unlike his role in making Nazi scientists disappear, Shamir disapproved of a culture of assassinations and attacks of acidic nature. The archives reveal that neither Shamir nor Eshkol made a single harsh remark against their political foes.

An advertising executive once told me that since the launch of commercial television in Israel, the biggest advertising budgets have been invested in promoting not tourism, food, or vehicles—but mineral water. Why? Because probably not even the CEO of Evian could identify his own product in a blind taste test. The more money is spent accentuating differences, the smaller those differences become. Maybe this is what Eshkol and Shamir noticed about Israeli politics: From a historical perspective, the ideological differences between the movement that founded the State of Israel and the party that succeeded it in power are extremely minor. The two major parties wanted a Jewish state, supported *aliyah*, favored a free market with certain disagreements about the role of the government, and wanted peace despite certain reservations about Israel's borders and the preferred negotiating partner. In the end, these were two different brands of bottled water. The constant political squabbling in Israel serves to cover up these increasingly minor differences.

There was another reason for Shamir's support for national unity: He preferred to bargain on wholesale terms with one big party than to be forced into haggling at extortionate retail prices with many small parties. This phenomenon was still in its infancy but would soon swell to almost mafia-like proportions. After the 1988 elections, in which the right won a ten-seat lead over the left, Shamir was shocked by the demands made by Shas and the NRP—"fragments of parties" as he called them, but ones with a healthy appetite. Shamir preferred to shrink them back to their natural size, and for this he was willing to pay the Alignment a generous price: two out of the top three ministerial posts. Shamir was fortunate not to live long enough to see how, in 2019, the leader of a three-person faction received the defense portfolio, while a party with seven seats refused to settle for anything less than the premiership.

The problem is that while unity governments started off as a heart-warming idea in times of emergency, they soon morphed into a strategic threat to the credibility, stability, and values of Israeli politics. National unity in times of routine is a raised middle finger at the most fundamental idea of democracy: the permanent existence of an alternative to the government of the day. In Britain, the head of the second-biggest party is called the Leader of Her Majesty's Official Opposition; in Israel, sometimes it feels like sitting in the opposition is a grave breach of the Knesset's ethics rules. In Britain, it took the Second World War to force the creation of a temporary unity government. In the United States, not even that was enough. Maybe World War III will do the trick.

When opposition politicians constantly look for ways to join the government, they are expressing their lack of faith in their supreme democratic role: to make the government's life miserable, to criticize it without end, and to keep challenging it. In Britain, the Conservatives and the Liberal Democrats spent ages languishing in the opposition in the early millennium, and nobody died. What was so urgent that they had to join a coalition with Labour? War?

The damage inflicted by mistimed unity governments is startling: The opposition becomes insignificant, the government balloons in size, and decision-makers' capacity for serious policy reforms disappears. If everyone gets to sit around the table, then elections are just a cynical charade. Public disillusionment with politics and falling turnout are predictable consequences. There is a time for broad governments and a time for narrow ones, just as there is a time for bellicose leaders and a time for conciliatory ones.

* * *

Israel's third and seventh prime ministers now belong in the history books. Despite their successes, Eshkol and Shamir's careers died a sad death: Eshkol, in poor health, became increasingly absent from his work. His diary reveals the steady deterioration of his health: from "suffering a cold" in May–June 1968 to "rest and recuperation" in December 1968, a "runny nose" in January 1969, and "sick" in February 1969. "Many people," wrote one reporter, "are asking why thousands of people suffer nasty colds and yet only Eshkol takes dozens of days off work because of a runny nose." One morning, when Eshkol did not wake up, Israelis discovered that it was not a "runny nose" after all. Ben-Gurion refused to even publish a remembrance notice. "Even if I am sorry for a man's death," he said, "I cannot be sorry that he is gone as our country's leader." "I won't come to pay respects to a criminal, a fraudster," he sniped. "Do you want me to praise him just because he is dead?" In private, he went even further: "Just as I wouldn't have wanted him to visit my grave, I won't visit his, either."[25]

Shamir inherited the Likud from Begin with forty-eight seats and a decade later bequeathed it to Netanyahu exactly one-third smaller, with just thirty-two seats. The public had pivoted left, while Shamir remained stubbornly opposed to conceding even a grain of sand. The nation became younger, and Shamir grew older. On the day he vacated his seat in the Knesset for Prime Minister Yitzhak Rabin, sixty thousand young Israelis attended the Arad Festival to celebrate. Shamir consoled himself with a cup of tea brewed by the Likud faction manager.

Historians have been kinder to Eshkol and Shamir than the voters were. Nowadays Eshkol is nostalgically remembered for leading Israel to its most stunning victory, nursing its divisions, and healing the nation. Shamir succeeded in diverting one million Jews from the Soviet Union to Israel instead of letting them emigrate to the United States. He is widely considered a role model for Israel's leaders: Ehud Barak considers Shamir one of Israel's finest prime ministers, Ehud Olmert remembers him with longing, and even Benjamin Netanyahu said some uncharacteristically warm words about him.

In hindsight, Eshkol and Shamir's terms in office are remembered as catastrophe-free periods of great progress for national defense, the economy, and aliyah. Their success in holding onto power for a combined dozen years seems less surprising now than it did to their contemporaries. Those who grew up under Ben-Gurion or Begin, like those who grew up during Netanyahu's decade of power, tend to forget that there is more than one way to be prime minister. Some premiers are hot sensations; others are closer to room temperature. Some favor total victory; others prefer reconciliation.

When Yair Lapid was a talk show host, he used to ask politicians: "If you were an animal, which would you be?" With a slight twist, we might ask: "If prime ministers were vegetables, which would they be?" Ben-Gurion, Begin, and Netanyahu were, of course, cilantro: You either love it or you hate it. Nobody can be apathetic to herbs with such a distinct aroma, and there is no point in trying to persuade people to change their minds. Nobody who hates cilantro has ever been persuaded to give it a chance because of its nutritional value. Ben-Gurion was loved and despised; Begin was revered and loathed. Some people cannot bear Netanyahu; others cannot imagine life without him.

Politics is a pendulum. There is no "end of history," and no movement remains in power forever. There is also a constant swing between leaders' personalities. After the leaders who invoke strong emotions are viewed in black-and-white terms, there almost always comes a leader in some shade of gray. For thirteen years, Britain was governed by Margaret Thatcher, a leader whose policies and personality divided the country and provoked mass strikes and violent demonstrations. Thatcher was succeeded by John Major, who was portrayed as uniformly gray in every television satire show.

In France, the gaffe-prone and controversy-stricken Nicolas Sarkozy was followed by the pallid François Hollande. Fed up with scandals, the French warmly embraced him as "Monsieur Normale." Donald Trump made as much noise as an out-of-control jackhammer for four whole years, until he lost to Joe Biden, a professional politician with nearly fifty years' experience. Biden's presidential schedule included, instead of angry tweeting, tea with his wife in the morning and fireside cuddles with her in the Oval Office. An American journalist wisely identified the reason for Biden's victory: "I want to spend two weeks of my life without having to think about my president even once."

Franklin D. Roosevelt led the United States into the Second World War by force of charisma. When he died in office, he was succeeded by Harry Truman, a quasi-anonymous politician with little oratorical skill. And it was Truman, of all people, who dropped two atomic bombs on Japan, spearheaded the Marshall Plan for the reconstruction of Europe, and is now considered one of the finest presidents in American history. Truman earned much less respect from his contemporaries than from historians: Not daring to run for reelection, he quit politics. It is no coincidence that he was one of the American presidents whom Yitzhak

Shamir most admired. That's how it is: Sometimes politics is like *The Truman Show*, and sometimes it's just like Harry Truman.

The politics of shaking hands instead of twisting arms can produce considerable achievements. I personally witnessed this onboard a faulty plane grounded in Poland in subfreezing temperatures of 5 degrees Fahrenheit. The plane had flown around sixty members of the Knesset and dozens of Holocaust survivors, reporters, and political operatives to a short memorial visit to Auschwitz in 2014. After an exhausting day, it turned out that the plane's engine had broken down, and it was stuck on the frozen runway at Krakow's military airport. When the replacement plane landed, the Polish air hostess made the mistake of opening both doors, front and back. In an instant, a massive, two-way human bottleneck developed in the aisle: Those at the back tried to push toward their seats at the front, and those at the front tried to force their way to their seats at the back.

For forty-five minutes, Israel's biggest movers and shakers, ministers who prided themselves on being "bulldozers" and lawmakers who had built careers out of promising to "get things moving," stood completely stuck, unable to solve a very simple problem: to place two hundred people in two hundred seats after a sleepless night. In the end, the problem was solved by Isaac Herzog, who has since been elected president. With untiring gentleness and interpersonal skill, he coaxed one person to budge and someone else to scootch, and by tapping on shoulders and shaking hands, he unblocked the pile on. Years later, when pundits said that Herzog was unable to take off because he was too nice, I left some room for healthy doubt, because everyone had seen that it was only thanks to his niceness that this planeload of Israeli politicians had taken off.

Eshkol and Shamir proved that the same approach is possible in the Israeli prime minister's office: "I compromise and compromise," Eshkol once confided in someone, "until I achieve what I want."

CHAPTER 5

The Man Who Missed Twice

Peres's Decision—
Honoring the Rotation Agreement

A DISTINGUISHED DELEGATION STRODE anxiously toward the Knesset in the summer of 2004. The senior politicians from Mongolia had arrived with an unsolvable problem vexing the citizens of their expansive faraway country. Mongolia had recently held dramatic parliamentary elections around an issue that had divided the country for years: the tax rate on private horses that were not part of a herd. When the final votes were counted, the results were inconclusive. The elections ended with a perfect tie between the two sides. What were they to do?

For weeks, Mongolian politics was gridlocked. Lawmakers had to cancel flights to prevent the other side from exploiting their absence to swear in a new government. They would have been grounded forever had the political adviser of one of the party leaders not turned out to be Jewish. He vaguely remembered that in a faraway, tiny country called Israel, an election had already ended in a perfect draw once. He also knew an important Hebrew word—*rotatzia*: rotation.

The special exploratory mission that landed in the Middle East to study how to wriggle out of this bind was formed from two groups of representatives, each half from one of the two major parties. I learned about this fantastic story when the group's Knesset tour guide bumped into me in the corridor and asked me for directions to Shimon Peres's office.

Israel's eighth prime minister was still quite young, aged just eighty-one, and a rank-and-file member of the Knesset. The inveterate globe-trotter was used to passionately promoting Israeli inventions, such as advanced computer chips or multicolored cherry tomatoes, but this time, he was lecturing about another made-in-Israel world first: a two-headed government. One month later, at 2:00 a.m., I was sitting in the Army Radio newsroom, looking for stories for the next bulletin. Suddenly I saw on Reuters's website an article about a "large government" that had just been formed in Mongolia, comprising both parties.

My late grandfather used to say that historians in a thousand years will think that "Shimon Peres" was not the name of a person but an aristocratic title passed down by heredity. They will not believe that in the course of nearly seventy years after Israel's establishment, the same person served in every single role: director general of a ministry, member of the Knesset, deputy minister, minister in practically every ministry, prime minister *twice*, and president. In his old age, people said that Peres was the tragic hero of Israeli politics: the man who lost five national elections, three leadership primaries, and one presidential election.

But the truth is quite different. Peres may have been a hero, but he was far from a tragic one: Indeed, without winning a single clear victory at the ballot box, he was awarded the Nobel Peace Prize for a peace that never materialized and held nearly every possible office despite the many unflattering eulogies that he kept hearing about himself throughout his political career. The newspaper *This World* ran a big, red headline in 1960: "The End of Peres's Career?" But Peres's career survived another fifty-four years, much longer than the newspaper that printed this forecast.

In the State of Israel, there are eight positions that are considered symbols of the state: the president, prime minister, foreign minister, defense minister, finance minister, leader of the opposition, Speaker of the Knesset, and Supreme Court president. Peres served in seven of these eight offices, more than any other Israeli. If that makes him a loser, then what does a winner look like?

When Ehud Barak was elected prime minister in 1999, he decided to send Peres back home to his wife Sonia. In the government that he was about to present to the Knesset, there was no room for a seventy-seven-year-old former prime minister. But then a member of the Peres family asked for a few minutes of Barak's time for an urgent matter. "You should know," he told the prime minister–elect, choking up, "if you don't make him a minister, my father won't survive the week." Faced with these waterworks, even Barak's heart of marble softened up. He invented the Ministry of Regional Cooperation for Peres, whose life was miraculously saved. But we are getting ahead of ourselves.

* * *

The theatrical production known as a "rotation," which the Mongolians envied, first appeared on the national stage in 1984. Until then, it had been staged at fringe theaters, mostly in the Haredi and Arab communities. It was a modern adaptation of the Judgment of Solomon, but instead of dividing a baby between two women who both claimed to be its mother, it was about splitting the term of a religious judge or member of the Knesset between rival sheikhs or Hasidic dynasties.

The United Arab List, a party of pro-Zionist minorities that contested the 1977 elections, comprised Arabs from Nazareth, Druze from the Galilee, and Bedouins from the Negev. Unfortunately, it won only one seat. The solution was a rotation deal between Sheikh Hamad Abu Rabia and Druze activist Jabr Moade. Its wording was odd for a political agreement in the Jewish state: "We swear by Almighty Allah, by all the holy books and by history, that we shall be without conscience and honor if one of us violates any of these conditions. If Sheikh Abu Rabia does not resign, his presence in the Knesset will constitute theft and breach of trust, and he shall lack honor and a conscience."

One year later, when the date of the handover arrived in 1981, Abu Rabia forgot all about Almighty Allah and his oath. He explained that he had a duty to protect his Bedouin brethren from government schemes to build an airport in the Negev. A furious Moade appealed to the Knesset Ethics Committee and then to the courts but received an answer that would also dawn on Benny Gantz forty years later: In Israel, political agreements are legally unenforceable. No power in the world can compel members of the Knesset to resign against their will.

Abu Rabia received anonymous phone calls (he lived in the only house connected to a phone line in the unrecognized Bedouin villages) with death threats. Having already waited a year to enter the Knesset, Moade explicitly threatened him to his face: "May Allah take revenge on you and your children." Abu Rabia took no chances: He hired two bodyguards to escort him everywhere he went. Back then, not even the prime minister enjoyed such tight security.

Ten months after the deadline for the rotation, on January 12, 1981, the sheikh wrapped up another day at the office. He chatted in Arabic with a member of the Knesset from the Alignment in the Knesset canteen. Then he sat down with Shimon Peres for a friendly cup of coffee. At 8:00 p.m., he left the Knesset in a green Peugeot 500, license plate number 800-805, and drove to the Holy Land Hotel in Jerusalem. He had fired his bodyguards just a few months earlier, after paying Moade 60,000 shekels to call off their agreement. He had no doubt that the danger had passed. It was a mistake that cost him his life. When he parked his car in front of the hotel, two masked young men walked up to him. They shot him in the head through the windshield and escaped in a Jeep. For the first time in Israeli history—a member of the Knesset was murdered.

Two days later, the assassins' identity came to light: They were Moade's sons, and one of them was an IDF officer. Just as the boys were being arrested, their father took his oath of allegiance in the Knesset—and the seat of the murder victim. A collective shiver went down the lawmakers' spines when the freshman parliamentarian stood with them for a minute's silence in memory of their slain colleague. They were watching a modern reenactment of an old biblical rebuke: "Have you not murdered a man and seized his property?" Just nine years later, Abu Rabia's killers were released from prison. One hundred thirty sheep were slaughtered at the celebrations in their honor.

It is understandable, therefore, why a rotation was not an especially popular format in Israel in the 1980s. But three years after Abu Rabia's burial in a state funeral, the idea of a rotation was resurrected from the dead. Begin resigned and shut himself away at home. The new government of his unpopular successor, Yitzhak Shamir, trundled along for seven months before collapsing.

It was a dark period in Israeli history, which has arguably been repressed in popular memory. Israel was embroiled in war in Lebanon, and hyperinflation was out of control. The stock exchange went into meltdown with the bank stock crisis. The shekel rapidly lost its value. No wonder that the elections were set for the middle of the summer vacations, on July 23, 1984: Few Israelis had enough dollars to fly abroad on vacation anyway. "Dear readers," announced the *Yediot Aharonot* newspaper to subscribers the week of the elections, "owing to rising costs, the price of the newspaper will be eighty shekels." When the new government was sworn in forty days later, that price had already risen to 180 shekels.

Every poll suggested that the Alignment's seven years in the wilderness, since the upheaval of 1977, were about to come to an end. The last polls predicted fifty-three seats for Shimon Peres's Alignment and a landslide over the Likud. "Why were the pollsters wrong?" wondered a newspaper headline two days after the elections and not for the last time in Peres's career. Israel is the only country in the world, Peres later complained, where people say the truth in polls and lie at the ballot box. When the last votes were counted, it turned out that while the Alignment had pulled ahead of the Likud by three seats, there was a perfect tie between the blocs: It was sixty-sixty. For several days, Shamir and Peres tried to pinch seats from each other's bloc. They both courted Rabbi Ovadia Yosef, who had just catapulted his sensational new party Shas into the Knesset, and they argued about whether it was legitimate to form a government with the votes of the non-Zionist Arab parties. But eventually they understood: The public had strong-armed them into working together to try to dislodge the ship of state, which was mired deep in the mud.

But who would head the government? Shamir loathed Peres, and Peres despised Shamir. A quarter of a century later, while flying with President Peres on a state visit to Europe, I read a book by the late Shamir. Moseying past the journalists, Peres asked to have a peek at my book, and when he saw Shamir's picture on the front cover, he pulled a face. "You won't learn anything from that man," he rebuked me loudly. Later, over the skies of Warsaw, he called over the press corps to lecture us about the late prime minister's myopia, as if he and Shamir were still fighting another election and decades had not passed since the 1980s, with one of them in his grave and the other in the president's residence.

For weeks, in plain sight of President Chaim Herzog, the Likud and Labor claimed the premiership and refused to let go, recalling a wonderful Talmudic story about the split of the kingdoms of Israel and Judah between King Rehoboam and King Jeroboam. In the fable, God personally advises Jeroboam to reverse his secession and offers to join him for a stroll with King David in the Garden of Eden. "Who will walk at the front?" asks Jeroboam. "Rehoboam," God answers. "Not interested then," the king replies.[1]

The solution was born in Switzerland, of all places. Zevulun Hammer, an NRP minister, was on vacation there after the exhausting election campaign when a eureka moment suddenly sent him running to the payphone to make an expensive international call to the president's office: Maybe *both* Peres and Shamir could be prime minister, for two years each? If it worked for NRP hacks in local elections, why not at a national level?

As with all successful compromises, everyone was equally appalled. One journalist wrote that by the same token, "We might as well have a penalty shoot-out, like in soccer when nobody wins the national championship: Shamir could take five shots at Peres's goal, Peres could take five shots at Shamir's, and whoever wins, wins." Others wondered why Shamir and Peres should not just rotate the job one week on, one week off, like army cooks.

Shamir was especially suspicious: He had never trusted Peres, and he was convinced that he would never be able to cash in his guarantee. In general, the Alignment's chairman had never enjoyed much public trust. His own actions contributed to this, of course, but so did Likud propaganda: The most recent elections were the third in a row in which the actor Sefi Rivlin roasted Shimon Peres for public entertainment. Everyone in Israel was mimicking his impersonations of Peres, answering every question with "Yes and no."

After a few more weeks of intense fighting for the number one spot, Israel received the first rotation government in its history. It was propped up by an unprecedented coalition of ninety-seven members of the Knesset, but astonishingly, not by a single legally binding document committing Peres to resign on the appointed date. The pair were photographed with the president, one to his left, the other to his right, in front of a record number of twenty-three ministers, all men (when it came to gender, they were not such fans of equality). The document listing the government's core principles was a masterwork of creative wording to bridge an ideological chasm. Settlements? "Between five and six" would be built a year, "by agreement." The country's borders? "No annexation and no withdrawal." Peace negotiations? "By agreement of the two major parties."

Shamir did not believe for an instant that Peres would step down. He had flashbacks to Abba Eban, Israel's legendary diplomat, who was once asked why Peres did not honor his promise to appoint him foreign minister and replied sarcastically: "He didn't want to set a precedent."[2] Nor had the Likud chairman forgotten what Ben-Gurion used to say about Peres: "Shimon isn't always accurate with facts."[3]

But as much as Shamir could not stand Peres, and Peres could not stand Shamir, the public loved this new government. It was one of the most successful governments in Israel's history. In just two years, it pulled the IDF back from Beirut into the new "security belt," close to the Israeli border. It stamped out inflation before inflation could stamp out the Israeli economy. French President François Mitterrand invited Peres to the Élysée Palace in Paris, curious to hear about his relations with Shamir. "It's not exactly the Garden of Eden every time Adam and Eve are together," replied the Israeli premier in French.

Mitterrand later warned Peres to honor the rotation agreement, but most of Peres's associates urged him to do the opposite. The date of the switchover, October 17, 1986, was approaching. The eighth prime minister's popularity rose as he neared the end of his term. The last poll gave him a whopping thirteen-seat lead over Shamir. The Likud, mired in infighting, was horrified by the prospect of early elections and inevitable defeat. On the night of the big decision, Peres's family and advisers gathered at his Tel Aviv home. "How would I look my grandchildren in the eyes if I didn't keep my word?" wondered Peres.[4] Then Sonia spoke. Peres's quiet, reclusive, camera-shy wife, the ultimate proof that opposites attract, uttered just four words: "Promises must be kept."

To everyone's shock, that was exactly what happened. Shimon Peres kept his word. On October 20, albeit with a three-day delay because of last-minute squabbling about issues that have long since faded into insignificance (Would Yossi Beilin be Israel's ambassador in Washington? Would Benjamin Netanyahu continue as the ambassador to the United Nations?), Peres stepped down. From the prime minister's office, he drove to the Knesset, and for the first time in Israel's history, the party that founded the state voted for a Likud prime minister. Then they raised a toast, with juice, and switched seats. The ceremony was short and low-key, partly because of the breaking news passed to the incoming and outgoing premiers on a piece of paper: An air force navigator called Ron Arad had been taken captive after his plane crashed in Lebanon. Shamir summarized the moment thus: "Two years of teeth-grinding had come to an end."

What happened there? It is possible that the trauma of the 1981 and 1984 elections deterred Peres from placing his faith in flattering polls. But it seems that it was his public reputation for untrustworthiness, which had plagued him for most of his political career, that pushed him into making the ultimate display of trustworthiness: He became the first person in Israeli history who voluntarily, not because of a decline in physical or mental health or alleged criminality, resigned from an office that he very much wanted to keep. There had never been anything like it, and there has never been anything like it since.

The totally extraordinary nature of Peres's decision is evident from the second prime ministerial rotation agreement, signed thirty-five years later. After three inconclusive elections, Blue and White party chairman Benny Gantz decided to "pull a Peres." After a campaign in which Netanyahu insinuated that Gantz was literally insane and being black-mailed by the Iranians, and Gantz accused Netanyahu of treason and receiving bribes to harm national security, the pair decided to break the exhausting political deadlock—and all their promises—and form a rotation government. The coronavirus pandemic spared them from having to shake each other's hand. Gantz had fewer seats than Peres did and also much less political experience. Netanyahu promised him "no tricks or schticks," in what would quickly turn out to be another of his schticks.

But Gantz did not trust Netanyahu—it is hard to believe how deep his distrust was at this point—and he therefore introduced a new, special Basic Law in the Knesset that was supposed to cuff Netanyahu to the switchover date and throw the keys into the sea. The solution was for the Knesset to swear in a two-headed government, with the handover anchored in law. It was no use. Netanyahu managed to wriggle out of the deal with a political maneuver as cynical and malicious as it was sophisticated. And Gantz? He became the answer to a trivia question: Who took an oath as prime minister but never served in the role? Peres, who started playing the political game when Netanyahu was not even a twinkle in his father's eye, simply honored the agreement.

Some people believe that politics and ethics are two parallel universes that are never supposed to intersect; that on the road to the top, one must run people over without mercy, throw friends under speeding buses, and lie and cheat. Indeed, politics often works like this, although one does not have to climb the greasy pole like a jungle animal. Nevertheless, in hindsight, it seems that Peres made a grave mistake by deciding not to break his promise.

Would Peres definitely have won the hypothetical 1986 elections? Absolutely not. But he did lose the real elections of 1988 by a painfully familiar margin—a single seat. Would his credibility have been ruined for good? Maybe, but honoring his promise to Shamir did nothing to repair it anyway. Even in the race against Netanyahu a decade later, the Likud hammered him for zigzagging and being untrustworthy. So, after so many losses, what did Peres have to lose by breaking his promise? It would have been immoral, cruel, and unfair—but all would have been forgotten once he took his seat. Peres, however, did not do this. "This is my last day as prime minister," he said at the short handover ceremony with Shamir, adding with his signature optimism: "for this term."

* * *

Peres was right. Nine years later, in the early hours of the morning, Peres opened the door to the prime minister's office, walked in, and sat down again on the padded blue chair. He had left the office that he so coveted in the most organized way imaginable, with a leaving date penciled in two years in advance, and he returned in the most terrible and spontaneous way of all. The drawers of his wooden desk still held the possessions of Yitzhak Rabin, murdered by an assassin the night before in Tel Aviv: half a box of antibiotics to treat his toothache, half a tube of toothpaste, and half a pack of cigarettes. The slain premier's toothbrush was still in the private bathroom. Rabin's staff never forgave Peres for not waiting even a short while, at least until the funeral.

Rabin's murder transformed Israel: In November 1995, Israel registered the sharpest-ever drop in the number of road fatalities, at least until the coronavirus lockdowns of 2020. The widespread shock after the murder made Israelis more considerate on the roads, and it made them curse and protest less. The right-wing demonstrations against the Oslo Accords, the biggest and most sustained protests in Israeli history, disappeared without a trace. The IDF pulled out of Nablus, Ramallah, and other Palestinian towns in Judea and Samaria with almost no public protest. *Yediot Aharonot*'s first poll after Rabin's murder showed that Israel was no longer divided: Peres won 54 percent, whereas Netanyahu had crashed and burned to just 23 percent. The Likud chairman was convinced that his short political career had come to a juddering end.

Everyone—Peres's associates, Labor Party leaders, and even the Rabin family—urged Peres to dissolve the Knesset immediately and hold snap elections. "Two terror attacks will take us back to playing catch-up," warned Defense Minister Binyamin Ben-Eliezer.[5] Israel's old-new prime minister could have asked the nation for a mandate, claiming that he was holding Rabin's in temporary trust. Nobody would have raised a peep, and nobody would have dared to target him with the sort of toxic yet effective attack ads that the Likud used so effectively against Peres since the 1970s. Seared by the murder, Israelis still recoiled from even the tepid temperatures of standard election propaganda.

But Peres waited. Officially, he explained that it was not the time to divide Israeli society with another election after the trauma of the prime minister's murder. In reality, he had his own reasons: He was hoping to negotiate a peace treaty with Syria in exchange for a full Israeli withdrawal from the Golan Heights and then to take this to the nation for a vote. But there was also another, less-spoken-of factor: Having suffered so many personal defeats, Peres did not want to go down in history for having won an election just because his predecessor was assassinated. He wanted to bolster his position as prime minister in his own right, not just by virtue of an assassin's bullets.

Like always in politics, personal impulses also played a role. Contrary to rewritten versions of history, the animosity between Rabin and Peres never truly subsided. For decades, they had run against each other, loathed each other, and slandered each other in public and in private. When the author who helped Rabin write his memoirs suggested calling Peres an "indefatigable schemer," Rabin beamed with joy. "This is the first time a chief of staff salutes a sergeant," he gushed.[6] The two Labor leaders relied on the mediation of the only person they both trusted, a wise and discreet political operative by the name of Giora Eini. On the stage at the left-wing rally in Tel Aviv, just minutes before the murder,

Eini was still scuttling between the two of them, trying to get Rabin to honor a secret promise to Peres that he was pushing off. "Shimon will haunt me till my last day," Rabin snapped, on the stage, in front of Minister Binyamin Ben-Eliezer.[7] Then he walked to his car, but he never made it there.

Peres was determined to escape Rabin's long shadow. In his new government, he made himself defense minister, just like the man he called his "older brother." Although the public did not view him as "Mr. Security" like Rabin, Peres resisted calls to appoint former military chief and freshman member of the Knesset Ehud Barak to the role. For one hundred days, Peres avoided calling snap elections, giving the Likud an opportunity to pick itself up off the floor, rewrite its platform, and present Netanyahu as a leader who could make a "secure peace."

Only in February 1996 did Peres finally dissolve the Knesset. His excuse was entertainingly absurd. The government needed a fresh mandate for a plan to develop the Negev, he told reporters in snowy Davos. Benjamin Netanyahu, shocked by the prime minister's crude political error, told his wife Sara that Peres had just lost the elections.[8]

Two weeks later, at 6:45 a.m., a suicide bomber blew himself up on the number 18 bus driving down Jaffa Street in Jerusalem. Volunteers from the ZAKA emergency response team had to collect scattered body parts from trees and balconies. This was the first act of revenge for the assassination of terrorist mastermind Yahya Ayyash in Gaza using a telephone boobytrapped by the Shin Bet. One week later, there was another suicide bombing—at the same time, on the same bus, on the same road. I still remember the presenter of the breakfast radio show telling listeners, "For those joining us now, this is not a repeat broadcast." Peres visited the scene of the massacre, and just like in the days before Rabin's murder, he was confronted by crowds of angry citizens. He understood the meaning at once. "I'm cursed," he told his bureau chief.

The next day, the eve of the Jewish holiday of Purim, at the most iconic crosswalk in the country, outside Dizengoff Center in Tel Aviv, another suicide bomber blew himself up. Sixty Israelis were killed in just two days. Overnight, stickers handed out by a right-wing activist appeared on cars across the country: "Shalom Chaverim" ("That's peace, friends"), a play on Bill Clinton's famous eulogy for Rabin at his funeral: "Shalom chaver" ("Goodbye, friend"). It was a signal that the right was back in the game. The next day, Peres's lead in the polls was completely wiped out. In the bloody electoral arithmetic of that awful winter, the suicide bombings offset Rabin's murder. In the direct election for prime minister, Benjamin Netanyahu beat Shimon Peres by just thirty thousand votes.

In Israel's history, some people were touching distance from being prime minister: Netanyahu foolishly gave up on the chance in 2001 and then languished for nearly a decade before returning to the Balfour Street residence. Benny Gantz received the mandate to form a government and returned it to the president untouched. But nobody besides Peres dropped the ball on two occasions. Twice in a decade, in 1986 and 1996, Shimon Peres could have guaranteed himself many more years in office. The first time, all he had to do was to serve the rest of his term, but he resigned; the second time, he only had to relinquish the rest of his term, but he stayed put. These two defeats proved the truth of a cliché often printed on fridge magnets: Timing is everything in life.

Thirteen years went by, and Peres forgot the bitter taste of defeat. He was now the beloved and revered president of Israel: not the one seeking a mandate to form a government, but the one awarding it. And then, when he was in the president's residence, it was someone else's turn to perform a spectacular volley kick right into a bucket full of milk: Kadima chairwoman Tzipi Livni.

When Ehud Olmert resigned, President Peres gave Livni an opportunity to be the first woman after Golda Meir to serve as prime minister. But to everyone's astonishment, after several weeks of fruitless negotiations, she failed. She claimed that she had refused to give Shas 1 billion shekels of kickbacks. "The public is fed up with political games," she announced next to Peres, who only thanks to fifty years of experience in diplomacy could conceal his incredulity. Nearing his ninetieth birthday, Peres was still secretly checking the possibility of resigning as president and running against Netanyahu for prime minister. But to give up on a dream for a measly billion shekels? Had Peres been in Livni's place, he would have gladly offered 2 billion shekels, just to get Shas to sign already. Livni, a self-proclaimed purist, still claims that she does not regret losing the premiership in order to save the public purse. Who knows what is secretly going through politicians' heads? Maybe this is what she truly believes, living now as a pensioner in affluent north Tel Aviv?

But as with Peres, it is also possible that the process of trying to form a government is the last public audition for the job, a fateful test of suitability. On the campaign trail, candidates can win seats from a successful interview with a hard-nosed interviewer or lose them because of an unfortunate gaffe. On the face of it, this is exceedingly stupid: What does body language or the ability to answer random questions on the spot have to do with handling a hostile US president or stabilizing a jittery economy? But elections are one long job interview, in which a recruitment committee of nine million citizens inspects how candidates behave under pressure. This system rewards a healthy bonus to those determined to reach the top at any price. If you don't want the role badly enough, you are clearly unworthy. Few people get a second chance in front of this committee. When it comes to being prime minister, Ariel Sharon was right: If you don't jump at it now, two hours will fly by, and you'll be left far behind.

CHAPTER 6

Shtreimels for Peace

Rabin's Decision—
Forging an Alliance with Shas

E VERY FRIDAY WHEN I CAME HOME from school, the weekend newspapers were all spread out on the coffee table. In Israel, and especially
in a place like Ofra, where I lived—an opinionated settlement surrounded
by hostile neighbors—there are two ways to catch up on the news: open
a newspaper or open a window. Growing up, current affairs and real life
were not two parallel tracks but constantly intersected: Muffled gunfire
at night became a news report about a terror attack in the morning; a
headline about a prospective peace deal became a bus with reinforced
windows heading to another mass protest in the evening.

From time to time, I noticed that certain pages in the newspapers had
been ripped out, leaving me to wonder what was so outrageous that they
were thrown in the trash: Was it an overly revealing interview with a TV
star, an explicit sexual reference, or images that left little room for the
imagination? When I entered fourth grade in 1992, the number of these
missing pages rose rapidly. The retro version of Israel, with its generic
"white cheese" and black-and-white newspapers, had quickly given way
to a brasher and more audacious Western country in glorious Technicolor.
A famous photo from the Gulf War shows the trail of an interceptor missile against the skyline of Tel Aviv, a tired and tattered old city without any
skyscrapers. The next year, its skyscrapers started soaring.

The Soviet Union collapsed, the Berlin Wall came down, and borders and armies started to be seen as an irritating nuisance from the eighties. The first commercial advertisements on television did sell products but the main "commodity" was a brazen Tel Aviv attitude. Michael Jackson entertained tens of thousands of young Israelis, who paid astronomical sums for a ticket, in Yarkon Park. At school, our mid-morning sandwiches gave way to "hot meals": instant noodles, which you just had to add hot water to and wait for five minutes before downing the monosodium glutamate. Achinoam Nini launched her first album, whose cover showed her with nothing but her hands covering her breasts. Israel's second TV channel was launched in November 1993 with a documentary about a young gigolo in Eilat.

But the ground really shook when nineteen-year-old Aviv Geffen walked into Israelis' lives, singing words that nobody had ever imagined airing on the radio: "We're a f**king generation!" the radio blared every few hours. The young Geffen boasted about dodging military service. When he appeared on the cover of *Yediot Aharonot*, covered in nothing but a big red slogan—"It is good to die for ourselves" (a rhyming spin on "it's good to die for one's country")—there was an uproar. The adults in Ofra hated Aviv Geffen, his makeup, and his nasal voice, but we could not take our eyes off this offensive sensation. He probably had no idea that children wearing big kippahs and sweatpants knew all the words to his songs by heart, including the punch: "Let's march toward our dream / without races or nationalities."

The odd thing is that Yitzhak Rabin, who returned to the prime minister's office in the summer of 1992 after a period of political exile, hated Aviv Geffen no less than my parents did. There was a fifty-year age gap between the quick-tempered general who forced open the road to Jerusalem with armored vehicles and the singer who rebelled against all authority and performed songs that seemed to have been written with the sole purpose of making people angry: "Because the dove has already choked on the olive in its throat / look who that drunkard is, it's the prime minister." Yet in hindsight, both men appear to have been songbirds heralding the same Israeli spring. It was probably a coincidence that Israel's cultural revolution overlapped with the political upheaval of 1992, which gave the left its first Knesset majority in fifteen years. But it gave this moment a modern soundtrack. It was definitely a cool time to be left wing.

These sensational developments all overlapped with the emergence of a new political list—a merger and neon-green rebranding of three left-wing parties, two of which were politically quite red: the socialist Mapam, the liberal Shinui, and the progressive Ratz. Mapam hated the rich; Shinui, the Haredim; and Ratz, the settlers. But the united list had the catchiest jingle and a female leader, and although most of its candidates were old white men, this political union was *the* hot trend of the 1992 elections. The right-wing Tehiya party ran adverts with old men speaking in lofty Hebrew about the Jewish people's rights to the land, while Meretz showed a cute dancing baby shaking its butt. Months after the 1992 upheaval, shoppers at Ofra's grocery store would stand in line and feverishly try to guess the identity of the three unknown neighbors in the settlement who fell for Meretz's audacious charm and gave it their votes.

When the last votes were counted, on June 23, 1992, it became clear that Labor had crushed the Likud with a twelve-seat lead, the biggest in twenty years. But the left-wing bloc's lead over the right was much thinner—about as thin as could be: Together with the five Arab lawmakers in the Knesset, Labor and Meretz hit sixty-one seats. This time too, right-wing parties had won more votes than the left, but they fell victim to their own fatal schisms, incessant infighting, and an electoral threshold that had just been hiked up to 1.5 percent. Tehiya, a boutique right-wing party, had voted in favor of raising the electoral threshold, only to find itself crashing underneath it, together with a slew of right-wing parties with names as pompous as their voters were scarce: the Redemption of Israel party, the Torah and the Land of Israel party, and the New Liberal Party. "The right is like an AC unit: a split system that produces a lot of air," suggested the journalist Uri Orbach in a moment of gallows humor.

The fact that it won on a technicality did not dampen the victorious side's joy. It only intensified its leaders' urgent desire to yank the national steering wheel 180 degrees to the left. "I shall lead the way," blustered the incoming prime minister in a somewhat angry victory speech. But his natural partner, the Meretz party, had other plans. Yossi Sarid, the most eloquent politician in Israeli history, vowed that Rabin would be "Meretzified"—he might be the pilot, but Meretz would choose the flight path. But after spending a whole generation in the opposition, the Rabin-Meretz government first had to choose a national destination. And this decision would largely fall to a politician unlike anyone Israel had seen before: Meretz's leader, Shulamit Aloni.

Aloni was probably the first broadcaster ever elected to the Knesset, but not the kind who played gentle music on the radio. She invented the journalistic genre of helping the little guy caught in the wheels of Israel's bureaucracy. At the strikingly young age of thirty-six, she was elected to the Knesset for Mapai and soon caused a stir by showing up at the inauguration of the Knesset building in a tight-fitting, sleeveless white dress.[1] The reporters were scandalized and the Haredim were outraged: a combination that would become a recurring theme in attitudes toward her over the years. Aloni quickly became the most prominent woman in the Labor Party after Golda Meir. There was no love lost between them. The elderly, thoroughly establishment prime minister despised the young lawmaker, who obeyed coalition discipline only when it suited her principles and who had the cheek—God forbid!—to demand party primaries, instead of having a party committee select the Knesset list. Golda urged Israeli citizens to fulfill their duties to the state, while Aloni championed civil rights. "I don't know what *we* think," she once interrupted the prime minister, "I know what *I* think." This young politician was kicked off the party list at the first opportunity—kicked by Golda's own foot, of course.

Aloni signed a petition against settlement construction, but her new party's name showed where her heart truly lay: Ratz—the Movement for Civil Rights. The words "and Peace" were only added a few elections later. This erudite and sharp-tongued woman from the secular suburb of Kfar Shmaryahu railed against religious coercion. She denounced the unholy alliance between the major parties and the Haredim, which she warned would "take Israel back to the Middle Ages." From the opposition, she secured the decriminalization of homosexuality, and her crusade for LGBT rights—long before anyone knew what these initials stood for—led Prime Minister Begin to accuse her of "defending beasts." She demanded the cancellation of the annual Bible Quiz, even though her knowledge of scripture often put her religious colleagues to shame. She attended her local synagogue only once a year, on Yom Kippur, which was still a marked improvement compared to another member of the Knesset in Rabin's coalition, Yael Dayan, who was once photographed in the middle of this holy day on the beach, in a swimsuit.

Now, with a dozen seats and determined to be the ideological jet engine of the incoming government, Aloni set her sights on realizing all her dreams. But there was a problem: Even at the peak of its power, which would never return, the Zionist left commanded fifty-six seats. For a coalition with the power to transform the country, it needed another five for a Knesset majority.

The two Arab parties, Hadash and Mada, won five seats between them, but never, until Ra'am in 2021, had representatives of the Arab national minority sat in the government of the Jewish state. The establishment was not particularly interested in them, and in fairness, the feeling was mutual. In Israel, the government is the supreme commander of the IDF, which since 1948 had fought only Arab states and organizations. The Arab parties were to Israeli governments what Israel was to the moderate Arab states for most of its history: a mistress for the occasional liaison, not a legitimate partner for marriage.

The defeated Likud was not a potential coalition partner, both because the new government was bracing to hit Ctrl+Z and erase the previous government's policies, and because the movement, battered and bruised, had no leader with whom to do business: Its top figures were already busy with primaries to elect Yitzhak Shamir's successor. UTJ, an ultra-Orthodox party, won only four seats, and in any case, its rabbis were hardly eager to collaborate with the secular kibbutzim. The NRP commanded six precious seats, but a coalition with it would make secular reforms and negotiations with the Palestine Liberation Organization (PLO) impossible. Its election slogans—"The NRP to Your Right," and "Choose the Path of Faith"—left little room for doubt. Moledet, which called for an expulsion of Arabs, was never a serious candidate. This left Rabin with two choices: two relatively new right-wing parties, which had just performed impressively in the elections—Tzomet and Shas. They were both extremely colorful additions to the fairly monotonous landscape of the national camp.

Tzomet had just quadrupled to eight seats on the back of an intensely right-wing but also very secular manifesto. Its leader, former IDF Chief of Staff Rafael "Raful" Eitan, despised the religious establishment almost as much as he hated the Palestinians. He loved working at his rural olive press and hated the rabbinate with a passion. "Parasites" was just about the least inflammatory thing that he called the Haredim. He once called the Palestinians "drugged cockroaches in a bottle." Raful was a womanizer, who treated his guests to horsemeat sausage ends: sausage ends to save money and horsemeat because of his indifference to the laws of kashrut. He seemed to take a perverse pleasure in nurturing false rumors that non-Jewish blood ran through his veins.

On matters of war and peace, Tzomet and Meretz were polar opposites: on the right, the chief of staff who waged the Lebanon War; on the left, supporters of Peace Now who organized a four hundred thousand–person protest against that war. But on matters of religion and state, they were ideological twins. This was the first hint that the old division, between left and right, had gradually ceased to account for the new generation of voters' increasingly diverse tastes.

Shas was a completely different story. In fact, it was Meretz's mirror image, in black and white. It had already successfully contested three elections but still remained an enigma, wrapped in a mystery, inside a conundrum. The party was founded as a popular movement to contest local elections in Jerusalem and Bnei Brak, and all its Knesset representatives were ultra-Orthodox Mizrahi men, almost all with a beard and the title "rabbi." But its rapidly expanding voter base, which confounded the pollsters, mainly comprised traditionalist Mizrahi Jews from deprived neighborhoods, fed up with being taken for granted by the three hegemonic Ashkenazi parties: the ultra-Orthodox Agudat Yisrael, the NRP, and, above all, the secular labor movement.

Shas, whose name is an acronym for "Torah-observant Sephardim," appealed not only to observant Jews but also to traditionalists: the children of immigrants who were thrown off ships into Ben-Gurion's melting pot and those who were reserved a few token spots in the Ashkenazi-dominated yeshivas and were forced to relinquish their ancestors' liturgical melodies. For all of them, Shas offered a father figure: former Sephardi Chief Rabbi Ovadia Yosef. It also offered the most effective electoral slogan in the country: "Restoring the Former Glory." There was no doubt about who was being accused of depriving them of their glory: the Ashkenazim who had founded the State of Israel, cut off their sidelocks, and sprayed them with insecticide in transit camps. Israel's political elite, a cramped hot tub where the country's (largely secular, Tel

Aviv-based, left-wing) politicians, pollsters, and journalists sit in far too intimate proximity, was at a loss to understand this movement and grasp its true proportions.

In the United States, pundits tend to speak of "shy voters," those who are unwilling to tell pollsters that they plan to vote Republican. Long before this phenomenon was known, Israel had its own phenomenon of "Shas voters." For years, Shas was Israeli pollsters' Bermuda Triangle: They kept predicting its implosion, but they were the ones who imploded when it defied expectations. Even today, the Midgam polling institute massages Shas's poll numbers upward, because forty years after its establishment, its voters are still reluctant to admit their choice to pollsters for fear that it will cause them trouble.[2]

One Shas election advert in 1988 opened with the blowing of a shofar and then showed the eccentric sight of seven rabbis, led by Rabbi Ovadia Yosef, performing the Jewish ritual of the "annulment of vows" for voters who had sworn to vote for other parties. Indeed, for the first few years, Shas was a closed black box: It did not hire a spokesperson, and its members had little interest in the mainstream media. The big shift came when a new young leader leapt from being the interior minister's director general to the minister himself by ritually slaughtering Shas's previous leader, Yitzhak Peretz. In the first newspaper report about him, he was incorrectly called "Eliyahu," but soon enough, the whole country would know his name: Aryeh Deri—the youngest and most ambitious minister in any Israeli government. He was only twenty-nine.

Sociologically, Raful Eitan was a much better match for Rabin and his government than Deri and co.: He was a product of the Labor movement, an avowed secularist, and Rabin's former military subordinate. Rabin took personal charge of the mission to bring Tzomet into the coalition. But the meeting between the two retired generals went badly and was full of awkward silences. They both hated politics and chitchat (Raful's inaugural speech as chief of staff, a decade and a half earlier, was just thirty-four words long).

Labor grudgingly turned to Shas. The initial prospects were dire: What did this secular government have in common with the six Haredi men from Shas? Moreover, Shas voters have always been the most right-wing element of the Israeli electorate, much more so than Israelis who vote for religious Zionist parties or the Likud. Shas voters are more

nationalistic than the National Union, more hostile to the law enforcement system than the Likud, more resistant to territorial concessions
than the NRP, and to top it all—more supportive of the Likud's leader
than Likud voters themselves.

In a country where politics increasingly revolved around the question of "Are you more Jewish or more Israeli?" nobody was more Israeli
than Meretz and Labor voters, and nobody was more Jewish than Shas
voters. An old recording of Rabbi Ovadia Yosef talking about his future
coalition partners, mysteriously leaked to the media with devastating
timing, certainly did not help the negotiations: "The day Shulamit Aloni
dies, it's time for a celebration and a feast at home," he had said. "She and
the rest of these villains and Torah-haters and religion-haters."[3] Shas's
spiritual guru and Meretz's chairwoman had just one thing in common:
Neither of them selected their words with much care.

The loathing was mutual. One Meretz-affiliated columnist called
Shas a "despicable Mizrahi movement." Meretz was the antithesis of Shas,
which Meretz's supporters saw as systematically propagating ignorance
and poverty in order to protect its power. Its culture of amulets, bless-
ings, and promises of heaven was alien to the party that was demanding
the teaching of evolution in schools. Aloni had resigned from Rabin's
first government (in the 1970s) because of corruption allegations against
an NRP minister. Now, she was being asked to sit in Rabin's second government with Deri, who was already a bribery suspect. The road to peace
was paved with painful concessions.

In the summer of 1992, Yitzhak Rabin made what was perhaps the
most important decision in Israeli political history. There were early
clues in his victory speech: "We want to unite all positive forces in the
nation that identify with our cause: the promotion of peace, while safe-
guarding our security." Those listening closely would have noticed that
the incoming prime minister did not say a word about civil reforms or
protecting the rule of law.[4] Labor's election campaign had promised a
new national agenda and a war on corruption, but the party's leader had
no doubts about the purpose of his mandate: negotiations with Israel's
Arab neighbors, under the rubric of "land for peace."

As Israel's defense minister during the First Intifada (the Palestinian Arab uprising of 1987) Rabin had ordered soldiers to "break arms
and legs," but he was quickly convinced that the only way to end the

violence was to negotiate with the Palestinians, or as Israelis called them back then: the Arabs of Judea and Samaria. On the campaign trail, he promised not to talk to PLO chief Yasser Arafat, and he was probably sincere, but he did not give enough thought to how he could honor both promises together: to negotiate with the Palestinians while boycotting the chief of the PLO. The intended solution was broad Palestinian autonomy, with a strong Palestinian police force. As Shulamit Aloni put it, in her own delicate way, "Anyone who wants to live near Rachel's Tomb or the tomb of Rahab the Whore can do so at his own responsibility and his own expense."[5]

Rabin and Meretz chose the path of peace, which passed through the gates of religion. On the way to fulfilling their mission, they found Shas to be a more natural partner than it initially seemed. A few years earlier, Rabbi Ovadia Yosef had published a religious ruling that stated that "it is permissible to return territories that we have conquered in exchange for a long-awaited peace."[6] Aryeh Deri himself has always held a center-left worldview. Deep into the 2000s, he was still promising that if he were given the opportunity, he could persuade his voters and his rabbis to agree to a large-scale territorial withdrawal, even from East Jerusalem.[7] Israel's most hawkish voters placed their trust in a nest of two pure-white doves. As in the case of Tzomet, it turned out for much of the Israeli electorate that politics was not all about the right-left divide.

The sensitive task of brokering a coalition deal was given to Haim Ramon, perhaps the last Labor official who had not yet burned his bridges with Haredi society after the so-called stinking maneuver: Labor was still shell-shocked after the disgraceful fiasco of its attempt to form a government with Shas and Agudat Yisrael just two years earlier. Labor's basic distaste for the Haredi way of life was exacerbated by the sour taste of treachery. Party officials had assumed that there was no point continuing to invest in the Haredim when there was hope of seeing any returns. Whenever Shimon Peres, for example, was asked to make a gesture to the Haredim, as a way of "casting his bread upon the waters," he would reply sarcastically: "Cast my bread? I've already sent them whole bakeries!" But Ramon and Deri had gradually cultivated a warm friendship. They bridged the cultural gap between them, a product of their different ethnic backgrounds and life stories, with shared interests: their love of political intrigue, soccer, and smoking cigars with tycoons. Thus was born the most ambitious maneuver in Israeli political history: the use of Israel's most right-wing votes to sign the Oslo Accords with the PLO.

The road to Oslo passed through Hebron. Not the city, but the elitist Ashkenazi yeshiva where Shas's chairman had studied. Aryeh Deri is a product of this institution. He dresses like Haredi Jews from eastern Europe, picked up Yiddish at the yeshiva, and most importantly, back in the early 1990s, drew his political power and support from the patronage of Rabbi Eliezer Menachem Shach, the most important leader of the Litvak Haredi world. Rabbi Shach gave his personal backing to this young party, gave it legitimacy, and became its principal spiritual leader, even more so than Rabbi Ovadia Yosef himself.

But two years earlier, it was Rabbi Shach who, with a single devastating speech, foiled the previous attempted alliance between Rabin and Deri. After the Shamir government was toppled with the support of Shas and Agudat Yisrael, everyone waited to hear what Rabbi Shach had to say, which would determine whether Shimon Peres would be able to stroll into the prime minister's residence. Of all possible venues, the nonagenarian rabbi decided to gather his disciples at the home stadium of the Maccabi Tel Aviv basketball team. It was not the first broadcast from this sports venue that kept the entire nation glued to their radio sets, but it was definitely the first that required simultaneous translators for Yiddish.

Journalists waiting for the night's big headline—Would the Haredim side with Labor or the Likud?—almost missed it when it landed. "If there are kibbutzim that don't know what Yom Kippur is," Rabbi Shach said, hardly audible through the loudspeakers, which had known better days, "who don't know what Shabbat is and don't know what a mikveh [ritual bath] is, who breed rabbits and pigs, have they any connection with their father? Is the Alignment sacred? They have severed themselves from our entire past and want a new Torah. If they don't keep Shabbat, or Yom Kippur, what makes them Jewish?"

Wait, what's he saying? thought the baffled reporters, exchanging glances. They did not understand that Rabbi Shach had just closed the door on a unity government. The Haredim would no longer ally with the kibbutzim and the Labor Party.

Just two years had gone by, the earth had kept spinning, and Rabbi Shach was not one to change his opinions. He spent a whole night speaking to Deri in Bnei Brak, demanding that he not join a government in which Shulamit Aloni, as education minister, would "convert hundreds of thousands of Jewish children."[8] Deri was eager to enter the government: Shas's own school system, El Hama'ayan, was already, unsurprisingly, under serious financial strain. He was also personally entangled in a police investigation that would soon mature into bribery charges and a criminal conviction. Perhaps he believed that his participation in a left-wing government would make it easier for law enforcement authorities to declare his case closed. Rabbi Ovadia Yosef enthusiastically supported Shas's entry into the government. But Deri, as Haim Ramon wisely discerned, was more of a Shachnik than a Shasnik.[9]

After three grueling weeks, to Ramon's astonishment, Deri agreed to the formation of a Labor-Shas-Meretz government. It was another of the impossible alliances that makes politics such an impossibly captivating game: the old, secular, Ashkenazi elite was about to return to power with the help of the party founded as a revolt against it. "First Israel" and "Second Israel," to use journalist Avishay Ben-Haim's distinctions, were about to get married. The dowry was generous: the Interior Ministry and Religious Services Ministry, and an invaluable bonus—the role of director of Haredi education, manned by a Shas appointee. For the first time in the history of Haredi society, the Ashkenazim would have to beg for crumbs from the Sephardim, not vice versa.

Or would they? On the day of the signing of the coalition deal, Deri suddenly disappeared. Ramon left dozens of messages on his answering machine, but to no avail. The Labor lawmaker went pale: In his mind's eye, he saw the nightmare scenario of stinking maneuver version 2.0. After two hours, which felt like an eternity, Deri called him, his voice tense, and asked for two more hours. In the end, he turned up at the ceremony and signed the papers.

Deri later revealed to Ramon what had happened in those tense hours: He had freaked out because Rabbi Shach had flipped out at him, and he had decided to remain in the opposition. But when Rabbi Ovadia found out, he made his own way to the Knesset, for the second and last time in his life.[10] "Where's Rabbi Aryeh?" he asked. "Sleeping," Deri's secretary told him, as instructed. Rabbi Ovadia burst into Deri's office like a firestorm and found Deri on his sofa, wide awake and smoking. He yanked Deri off the sofa with both hands, pulled him down the stairs, threw him in his car, and said: "I'm ordering you to sign. No monkey business."[11] The tone of the 1990s was about to be set by two men wearing long black frocks: rockstar Aviv Geffen and Rabbi Ovadia Yosef.

What made Rabbi Ovadia and Yitzhak Rabin, two men whose life paths had never intersected before, place their faith in each other?

Rabin was the general who had won the Six-Day War, the liberator of Jerusalem, Judea, and Samaria, but as a young prime minister seven years later, he did everything in his power to prevent religious Zionists from settling the Arab-populated areas of the newly liberated territories. Unlike his Labor colleagues, Rabin was never a fan of the settlements or the settlers. When his defense minister, Shimon Peres, planted a tree in the settlement of Ofra—probably just to annoy him—Rabin was livid. He described the settlement movement as "one of the gravest dangers" facing Israel. "What is 'settlement' anyway? What kind of struggle is this?" he asked. "What kind of method? The settlement of Kadum is a bloated fart." He described Gush Emunim, the pro-settlement activist movement, as nothing less than "a cancer in the democratic social fabric of the State of Israel, a body that is taking the law into its own hands."[12]

Two years later, it was the religious Zionist movement that terminated Rabin's short-lived premiership and, as would become clear soon, his party's eternal rule. The Israeli Air Force's first F-15 jets, delivered from the United States, landed at Tel Nof Airbase on a Friday in December 1976. The weather was fair, and the planes were not targeted by enemy antiaircraft fire, but in their first mission, they failed: They arrived twenty minutes late, and the welcoming ceremony dragged into Shabbat. The dying gasps of the Labor movement's rule could be heard in the dying gasps of the historic alliance between the religious Zionists and the secular socialists of Mapai. Till his last day, Rabin felt compelled to explain to religious members of the Knesset that although he was still at the airbase at 4:00 p.m., just seventeen minutes later, when Shabbat came in, in Tel Aviv, he was already home. But it was no use: the NRP abstained on a vote of no confidence, Rabin got the message, and he resigned. The caricature in the following day's papers showed a fighter jet with the NRP's logo performing a nosedive in order to blow up a horrified Rabin.

The ground offensive in Samaria and the airstrike at Tel Nof were expressions of a broader struggle over hegemony in Israeli society, which boiled over on Rabin's watch. The prime minister was certainly aware of the religious Zionists' ambitions to supplant the kibbutz movement as the vanguard of Israeli society. Religious Zionists typically believed that secular Zionism had grown tired after the Six-Day War and that it was time to seize the reins—but the chief of staff from that war had no intentions of voluntarily signing over his estate.

Rabin, a ruddy-faced and short-tempered man, did not spare anyone's blushes. When party colleagues were late for a vote, he shouted, "Idiots!" at them in front of the whole Knesset. He called Peres an "indefatigable schemer" and Yossi Belin a "poodle." But he took special pleasure in coining derogatory nicknames for the settlers, the tip of the spear of religious Zionist society. He called their isolated settlements "political settlements" and mocked them as "Beit El, Emmanuel, and Schlemiel." His first step after returning to office in 1992 was to freeze and stifle the settlements' funding. The settlers feared Rabin and loathed his government. One day, when I was in sixth grade, I found the prime minister's home number in my family's phonebook (my father was a journalist). I called him with a few friends, and when we heard him say "Hello?" in his smoky, baritone voice, we shouted "Go home, Rabin!" without realizing that since he had just answered the phone, he was already home.

Shas fit perfectly into Rabin's diplomatic plans. Rabin saw it as the perfect partner: It was ultra-Orthodox but not messianic, right wing but open to territorial compromises with the Arabs. Rabin wanted Shas to hold the political balance of power instead of the old NRP. There were early signs of this during the 1992 election campaign: Labor's candidate for prime minister surprised his party colleagues by traveling to Netivot, with a black kippah on his head, to receive a blessing from a Moroccan mystic.[13] In this sense, Rabbi Ovadia was the ideal partner. Not only was he open to territorial compromise as part of a peace deal with the Palestinians but he also felt ill at ease in the right-wing camp for personal reasons. As the Sephardi chief rabbi, he had clashed with his Ashkenazi counterpart, Rabbi Shlomo Goren, who was revered by the NRP. In 1983, his tenure was cut short, and he was humiliatingly ousted in favor of Rabbi Mordechai Eliyahu, the doyen of the religious Zionist movement. Had he not been pushed out, Shas might never have come into the world. Joseph Cedar's movie *Campfire* keenly depicted the frustration and bitterness of young Mizrahim in the religious Zionist movement's elitist Ashkenazi schools.

Rabbi Ovadia's dismissal was stitched up by a Likud-NRP coalition. No wonder that these parties' "natural partner" did not see their partnership as such. The rabbi slammed Shamir for "eating bugs and impure fish" and called his wife a "shrew"; and when Sharon booted him out of his government, he joyously announced that God would "give this wicked man a smack, and he won't wake up." He never spoke about Rabin or Peres this way.

When Deri became the subject of a criminal investigation a few weeks after the implosion of the stinking maneuver, Rabbi Ovadia was convinced that the Likud was stitching up his protégé as cold revenge for his dalliance with Peres. "I told you we mustn't go with the Likud," he berated Deri. "They're wicked."[14] And now, suddenly, heaven gave him an opportunity to repay the wicked in kind.

The new coalition was quite broad, with sixty-seven members of the Knesset, but from its inception, it had to be flexible, because its ideological spectrum ranged from Friday sermons in mosques in Umm al-Fahm to Saturday night Torah classes in Sephardi strongholds of Jerusalem. One guest invited to Rabin's office in the first weeks of his premiership found Deri sitting there, as if he owned the place, with his feet up on the prime minister's desk. But three factors threatened to undermine this new partnership: Shulamit Aloni's big mouth, Deri's trouble with the law, and above all—the Oslo Accords.[15]

A parliamentary opposition tries to find cracks in the coalition and then widens them by proposing bills that divide and embarrass the government. In this case, the Likud did not have to look too hard: From the get-go, it faced not a crack but a gaping rift.

The new education minister, Shulamit Aloni, was eager to prove to her voters—and maybe also to herself—that sitting with Shas in a coalition had not dented her secular credentials. During Passover, when Jews traditionally avoid eating bread, she sat down with her whole team in a restaurant in Nazareth to eat freshly baked pita—as if only to wind people up. She later demanded the removal of the book of Joshua from the school curriculum on the grounds that it constituted incitement to militarism and racism. She called the chief rabbis "popes" and Joseph's tomb in Nablus "the tomb of Sheikh Yusuf." When Rabin eulogized the

Lubavitcher Rebbe, Aloni opined that the prime minister had "gone a bit overboard with his statement."[16] Shas was livid, but Rabin was apoplectic. The truth came out: He preferred Shas to Meretz.

When Aloni explained that humans came from apes and that the world was not really created in six days, news reached the prime minister during a tour of Carmiel. Since there was no cellphone at hand (and cellphones were huge black bricks back then anyway), he stormed into the office of a local supermarket, picked up the phone, and called the education minister himself. Everyone in the supermarket could hear him yelling.[17] Aloni organized a supportive rally for herself, in which one of the speakers said, "Haredi schools are schools for criminals." This was an attempt to put out a fire with gasoline. To make up for it, Aloni was forced to commit to speaking nicely and quietly from then on and, in a gesture of goodwill, to supporting a law banning imports of pork.

The coalition was rocked by seven Aloni-induced crises, and its first year was still far from over. When the education minister berated the prime minister for daring to end his speech at a memorial event in Warsaw by reciting the Shema prayer, it was game over for their partnership. The Council of Torah Sages, Shas's supreme rabbinical authority, was convened for an emergency meeting. Ultimatums were delivered, threats were made, and Rabin demanded Aloni's resignation in favor of a much more junior role in the Ministry of Culture, Science, and Communications. "It is hard to believe that people who breathe slogans about peace could bring about this government's collapse," he fumed. When Aloni cleared her belongings from the Education Ministry, Knesset colleagues consoled her with an old saying by Ezer Weizman that would later be attributed to her, causing her much anguish: "For peace, I'd be prepared to wear a shtreimel"—referring to the traditional fur hats worn by Hasidic Jews.

Rabin would probably have bitten his tongue had he not known something that the minister and the rabbi would soon discover: Far away in chilly Oslo, under a cloud of snow and secrecy, an unprecedented agreement between Israel and the PLO was in the works. Long before the IDF's withdrawal from Gaza and Jericho, the Oslo Accords began with quite a different retreat from the Education Ministry.

Half of the country was dumbfounded and the other half elated when the details of this secret agreement came out at the end of the summer of 1993: Israel would recognize the PLO as the legitimate representative of the Arabs of Judea, Samaria, and the Gaza Strip. It would allow Arafat and other PLO leaders to enter Gaza and Ramallah, and it would let them form a military-sized police force, armed with assault rifles and armored personnel carriers. Israeli troops would pull out of Gaza and Jericho first, but this would by no means be the end. The songwriter Haim Hefer penned a song about "white doves" fluttering over military cemeteries and proclaiming a song of peace, but the same week, another four headstones were erected in Israel's military cemeteries: the first victims of the terrorism that would soon erupt with extraordinary force.

The Knesset majority for the accords was guaranteed because of the Arab parties' support. But three hundred thousand right-wing protesters flooded the street outside the Knesset in a last-ditch effort to get Shas to oppose the deal and tarnish its legitimacy.

Aryeh Deri resigned the following morning.

The thirty-four-year-old minister's resignation had nothing to do with the Oslo Accords, but it threatened to doom them just four days before the official signing ceremony. One month earlier, Deri had been indicted on serious charges of receiving large bribes. Rabin desperately needed Shas's support and therefore refused to fire him in order not to weaken his coalition, which needed everyone on board for the historic test on its doorstep. And just then, after the accords were made public, the Supreme Court decided that as soon as Deri had been charged with bribery, the prime minister was obligated to sack him, along with Deputy Minister Rafael Pinhasi, who had also gotten into trouble with the law. In an incredible twist of historical irony, perhaps driven by something deep in his subconscious, Rabin had promised an anxious Israeli public the morning before the ruling that "the Palestinians will clean up Gaza without Supreme Court rulings."[18] And exactly then, the Supreme Court in Jerusalem triggered an otherworldly commotion.

Rabin was dumbstruck. He warned that Deri's resignation imperiled the peace process. Shulamit Aloni, who had already quit a Rabin-led government because of the entry of a religious minister suspected of corruption, now found herself calling on Shas to stay in the coalition. The prime minister frantically rushed to Rabbi Ovadia's house before taking off for the signing ceremony in Washington, to make sure that Shas's impending resignation would not imperil the Jewish majority in the Knesset for the accords. "Go in peace, and return in peace," the rabbi replied, hinting that everything would work out, and adding a friendly slap to make his meaning clear. Shas quit the coalition but abstained during the vote, allowing for a solid majority of eleven members of the Knesset. Deri has always maintained that Rabbi Ovadia forced him not to oppose the accords. But a recording of the rabbi that emerged after his death told a different story: "It was him, him, it was all him," snarled the rabbi, wagging a finger at his protégé.

One month later, the Supreme Court would drop another bombshell: It accepted the petition of a private company and overruled the ban on importing non-kosher meat. Giving a kosher stamp to both the Oslo Accords and pork was too much to swallow, even for Rabbi Ovadia. Rabin was beside himself with rage. He had an open account with one of the judges: Justice Aharon Barak. As the government's legal adviser, Barak had not left Rabin any choice in 1977 but to resign as prime minister because of the Dollar Account affair (the revelation that Rabin, a former ambassador in Washington, held an illegal US dollar account). One generation later, Rabin suspected that Barak was trying to torpedo his second term as prime minister as well. "Nobody but the government will run this country," he rebuked the judges. In order to make it clear that he was serious, he rammed a new law through the Knesset, overturning the court's ruling and stopping shipments of frozen pork on their way to Israel. For years, the right has been demanding that judges not have the final say, but the only government that has ever stopped them was a Labor-Meretz government. Shas was placated and continued to support the government from the outside.

Supporters of the Israeli Supreme Court's judicial revolution often cite the "Deri-Pinhasi ruling," just four days before the Oslo Accords, as roundabout proof that the court is not left wing. Look, they say, the judges followed their conscience and ignored their ruling's potentially calamitous consequences for the peace process. Indeed, the Supreme Court and the Israeli left have had different objectives in recent decades: While the left focused on promoting the two-state solution at the expense of Greater Israel, the Supreme Court's rulings have focused mainly on emphasizing Israel's democratic character at the expense of its Jewishness. Back then, the executive branch's ideological rival was the settlement enterprise, backed by the NRP and Moledet, while the judicial branch locked horns with the religious laws passed by Shas and UTJ. The Supreme Court has outraged right-wing Israelis in recent years with a string of rulings against settlement outposts, including overturning a law to legalize them, but to date, a quarter of all that it has overturned were initiated by the Haredi parties:[19] Haredi drafted exemptions and expanded welfare payments and scholarships for yeshiva students. It is no coincidence that the biggest protest in Israeli history was by half a million Haredi citizens in front of the Supreme Court in 1998.

In the two critical years of the Oslo Accords, Rabin's paradigm would be put to the test: Would Shas's right-wing voters give the pro-Oslo government a long lease of life? This would shape up to be an unbearably difficult test. Within days, settlers erected a protest tent outside the home of Shas's spiritual leader. They knocked on his door and ran away, honked all day, and shouted through megaphones all night. When Rabbi Ovadia's wife, Margalit, came home with the groceries, they chanted protest slogans at her. "This is no way to live," complained the rabbi after months of around-the-clock protests. "The settlers are interfering with my studies and won't let me rest." A few months later, Rabbi Ovadia's wife passed away. The protesters blamed him for the death of settlers in terror attacks, and he blamed them for the death of his wife.[i]

Rabbi Ovadia's hint was understood: As soon as he finished his sermon, hundreds of his acolytes marched to his house, set fire to the protest tent, and torched the car of one of the protesters. By the time the Border Police swooped in to separate the warring parties, three of the settlers had been evacuated to the hospital in a light-to-moderate condition. Rabin was hardly sorry. "The rabbi's followers were from the lunatic branch of the right," said an associate of Rabbi Ovadia, the attorney David Glass, "and they rushed ahead without thinking for a second. That's proof that their devotion to him transcended any other ideas."

* * *

One Saturday night, in September 1993, while Rabbi Ovadia Yosef was delivering another of his weekly sermons at the Yazdim Synagogue, a personal aide came up and whispered something in his ear.[20] The rabbi's

---

[i] A few months after the protests started, the daughter of one of the protest leaders, Rabbi Menachem Felix, was murdered in a terror attack in Ofra. On the eve of Deri's imprisonment in 2002, Rabbi Ovadia asked for and received Felix's forgiveness.

eyes watered up. "What did Yitzhak do to deserve this?" he asked out loud when the audience was also informed about the three fatal gunshots in Tel Aviv that killed Yitzhak Rabin.

The rabbi soon discovered, to his horror, that the shooter was a kippah-wearing Mizrahi Jew. Before Rabin was murdered, he still visited the rabbi and, over tea and a plate of nuts and seeds, strengthened the political safety net that was saving his government from collapse. By now, Shas was officially in the opposition; a month earlier, it had voted against the Oslo II Accords, which would see the IDF withdraw from Nablus, Ramallah, and all other Palestinian cities. The agreement was passed by a single vote, thanks to two shameless defectors from the right. Even so, a majority of Jewish members of the Knesset opposed the agreement, a fact that electrified the streets and filled them with pent-up violence. Thousands of right-wing protesters marched on the Knesset carrying torches.

In the subsequent elections, between Peres and Netanyahu, Rabbi Ovadia would also prefer the Labor candidate over the Likud's. But the masses were too powerful even for him. In 1996, under pressure from the increasingly right-wing Haredi street, Shas's spiritual leader gave his followers a free vote, which everyone interpreted as a call to support Netanyahu in the direct elections for prime minister. Rabbi Ovadia also allowed himself a free vote and cast it for Peres, giving the outgoing premier probably his only Haredi vote that year.

Less than three years later, the 1999 elections witnessed the very last opportunity to revive Rabin's political alliance, this time with his self-declared heir: Ehud Barak, who defeated Benjamin Netanyahu with a colossal twelve-point lead. His festive apology to the Mizrahim for the Labor Party's historical injustices certainly did him no harm, nor did Rabbi Ovadia's blistering epithet for Netanyahu, calling him "a blind goat." Now, borne on the wings of an unprecedented protest vote against Aryeh Deri's conviction, and buoyed by an electoral system that allowed voters to cast one ballot for prime minister and another for the Knesset, Shas scored a historic record of seventeen seats, almost on par with the Likud.

Once again, a Labor prime minister faced a dilemma: a secular state or a Palestinian state? Or more precisely: Shas or Shinui and the Likud? The huge crowds that filled Rabin Square for the victory celebrations were in no doubt: "Anyone but Shas! Anyone but Shas!" they roared on beat. It is doubtful whether anyone there realized the historic irony of chanting this in a square named for the man who forged the original alliance with Shas.

Barak heard the crowds—and ignored them. "I could have formed a government that would have addressed domestic affairs, a unity government with the Likud," he explained twenty years later. "But we were three years past the deadline for a permanent settlement [with the Palestinians], and Clinton had a year and a half to go. There was an opportunity to get into the peace issue, so was this the time to start dealing with domestic problems?"[21] Once again, into the trash went a pile of election promises: Barak's pledge to favor "waiters, not draft-dodgers" or Meretz leader Yossi Sarid's vow: "Read my lips: We won't sit in a government with Shas." Within a few weeks, Barak coerced Deri to resign the leadership of Shas and then signed a generous coalition deal with his successor, Eli Yishai. Barak, I discovered while writing this book, was willing to work with Deri; he only booted him after receiving covert requests from enemies of the convicted politician from within Shas itself.

Like Aloni, her nemesis, Yossi Sarid, lasted less than a year in the Education Ministry. History repeated itself all over again with arguments over Haredi education and weekly quarrels. Once again, Rabbi Ovadia Yosef deployed his sharp tongue, this time awarding Meretz's chairman the epithet of "evil Haman, Satan, who must be uprooted from this world."[22] Barak tried to terminate a century of enmity and hostility with the Arabs but could not even put an end to the Jewish civil war raging inside his own coalition.

Just a few days before the historic peace summit at Camp David, Sarid resigned in tears from his beloved Education Ministry so that Shas could remain in Barak's government. "I could not take responsibility for the collapse of the peace process," he said, promising to return. This would be Meretz's last day in government for more than twenty years. But it did not bring peace: Shas waited another three weeks before it, too, quit the coalition.

When Barak returned from Camp David, without peace and without a coalition, he suddenly remembered to remove his shtreimel. One Saturday night, he called over his party colleagues and declared a secular revolution: civil marriage, public transportation on Shabbat, and the dissolution of the rabbinic establishment. "For the sake of secular unity with the Likud," he announced, "I would even be willing to backtrack from agreements reached at Camp David." The Likud scoffed at the offer. After many years, Shas had finally come home from its wanderings on the left's turf. Now that Shas was knocking at its door, at long last, the Likud was not about to reply, "Sorry, we're not home."

In recent years, Israelis on social media have pined for an "enlightened liberal government," of the sort that would end Israel's rule of the territories and the religious establishment's rule inside Israel itself. But the truth is that this is impossible. The demographic shift since the 1970s has made it impossible to form a stable coalition without the participation of one of two religious movements: the religious Zionists or the Haredim. After the Gaza disengagement, the late journalist Uri Elitzur wrote that either religious Zionist synagogues could be evacuated with the support of the Haredim, or Haredi yeshivas could be shut with the support of religious Zionists. The left, therefore, had to choose: peace with the PLO or war with the rabbinate? Separation of religion and state or separation from the Palestinians?

What would Israel have looked like if Rabin had formed a government in 1992 with the secular nationalist Tzomet instead of Shas? Instead of suicide bombers on buses, would Israel have had buses on Shabbat? And what would have happened if Barak had heeded the call of the masses in Rabin Square and formed a coalition with Shinui and the Likud instead of the Haredim? Would he have managed to restructure the relationship between secular and religious citizens instead of the one between Israelis and Palestinians? These will remain hypothetical questions because of the special dilemma of the Israeli left—or at least, what used to be the Israeli left, until it shriveled up and evaporated.

"All over the world, the left is judged by its distance from Che Guevara," complained member of the Knesset Amnon Rubinstein at Meretz's inaugural conference in 1992. "Only in Israel is it judged by its distance from Yasser Arafat." If Rubinstein had been a Spanish or Belgian politician, his Shinui party's capitalist manifesto would have earned him a respectable place on the right. But in Israel, he found himself joining forces with a left-wing socialist party like Mapam. In politics, voters only get one ballot—and they can only use it to advance one goal. And the Israeli left chose, time and again, the supreme goal of ending the occupation, not creating a secular state. It called itself the peace camp, not the liberal camp.

It is traditionally said that the left can make war, but only the right can make peace. When the left wants to promote territorial compromise, the right floods the streets; and when the right last called up the reserves on a major scale, it ended with a four hundred thousand–person rally in Tel Aviv. It is doubtful whether these two old axioms are still valid (the Likud has since launched Operation Defensive Shield to retake Palestinian cities during the suicide bombings of the Second Intifada, and the Labor produced the Oslo Accords). But one deeply repressed truth still holds: Only the right can promote a secular agenda.

Israel has had only three governments in recent generations without the Haredim, and all three were headed by right-wing prime ministers. Ariel Sharon's 2003 government, with Tommy Lapid and Benjamin Netanyahu, slashed child benefits and sent labor participation rates soaring. Netanyahu's 2013 government, with Yair Lapid and Naftali Bennett, passed a Haredi enlistment law and a mandatory core curriculum for Haredi schools.

But even these two governments were quickly dismantled. Shinui's ministers supported Israel's economic recovery, until one evening Sharon booted them from his coalition in favor of UTJ as a way to advance the Gaza disengagement. He knew that even Shinui's leader Tommy Lapid, who vowed in 2005 to vote "by hook or by crook" against a budget that included 200 Million USD for UTJ, would have to support his bill even from the opposition, but he needed the UTJ onside. "The voters wouldn't forgive me if the withdrawal from Gaza were canceled on my account," said Lapid, rationalizing his vote. When the LGBT community wanted to march in Jerusalem shortly before the disengagement, the police were worried that they would have to divert massive forces away from the evacuation of the settlements in the Gaza Strip in order to secure the parade. Shimon Peres, the eternal Labor chairman, was furious: "The gays have crossed a line," he fumed.

The most absurd thing is that the right's partnership with the Haredim has been its Achilles' heel. The Haredim are a political asset, but the public price is high. Every study shows that a large majority of Israelis, including right-wing voters, supports civil marriage, equal rights for same-sex couples, and public transportation on Shabbat. The alliance with the Haredim traps right-wing politicians in an inevitable clash with their voters. During the nightmarish cycle of non-stop elections in 2019–2020, Netanyahu lost his ability to form a government after Avigdor Lieberman defected from his bloc, waving the banner of secularism instead of that of the right-wing camp. If the left were strategically sensible, it would have advanced a civil agenda, but Labor, Meretz, and Kadima's sense of historical urgency pushed them into the arms of the Haredim—and perhaps also toward their political demise.

Can the alliance between Shas and the left be revived? That would be a tough task, because the left does not exist anymore and neither really does Shas. The Labor Party imploded together with dreams of a "New Middle East" because it failed to offer an updated vision for a country that was gradually shaking off its belief in the Palestinians' willingness to make peace. From its ruins rose center-left parties that learned their lessons and sold voters a shopping list of anti-religious policies instead of talking about "the occupation": Tommy Lapid appeared on TV with kosher-certified soap bars in order to prime public opinion for a secular government with Sharon. His son, Yair Lapid, did something similar to Shas ten years later. Deri was in the opposition at the time with Labor chairman Isaac Herzog, the grandson of Israel's first chief rabbi. "God willing, one day we'll get to crown you prime minister," said Deri, but it is doubtful whether anyone in the room, maybe besides Herzog, truly believed him. Only Rabbi Ovadia could have led hundreds of thousands of right-wing voters in an orderly procession into a left-wing government.

In the past decade, news networks have tried to use hologram graphics to build a coalition between Shas and the left's candidate of the day, be it Herzog or Gantz. But Aryeh Deri, back from prison, could never really have pulled it off. In 2002, just before the heavy door of Maasiyahu Prison was slammed shut behind him, Deri—surrounded by crowds of supporters—stood in front of a microphone and asked for forgiveness from his old mentor, Rabbi Shach, for entering Rabin's government against his orders. That was the crime, Deri is convinced to this day, for which he served two years behind bars. Not the envelopes stuffed with dollar bills.

Shas has long stopped being the revolutionary movement that it once was. Rabbi Ovadia passed away in the fall of 2013, and eight hundred thousand people followed his funeral procession in the largest gathering in Israeli history, but far fewer followed his political party. There has never been and probably never will be another leader like him, capable of rallying by the force of his unique personality and intellectual acumen both the Sephardi yeshiva world and the Mizrahi traditionalists who make kiddush on Friday night and then watch the news.

Israel Bachar, a political consultant, explained that the Shas brand encompasses two movements: The original Shas was a traditionalist and social-democratic movement, but it was swallowed by a right-wing Haredi movement, until nothing of the first movement survived. In the 2020 election, in an effort to lock in its electorate, which had halved in size since its glory days, Shas plastered Jerusalem with posters hailing the Likud's leader: "Bibi," they said, "needs a strong Aryeh Deri."

CHAPTER 7

No Partner

Barak's Decision—
Liquidating the Left

THEY SNACKED ON NUTS and seeds from a small bowl in a large wooden cabin in Maryland and spoke about "the situation." Suddenly, someone spotted out of the corner of his eye that the prime minister was clutching his throat and gasping for breath. To everyone's horror, he started turning blue, slowly choking. A young aide instinctively grabbed the prime minister by the back and performed the famous Heimlich maneuver. A small peanut went flying to the floor, and everyone, including the prime minister, breathed a deep sigh of relief.

In July 2000, in the middle of the historic Camp David Summit, Ehud Barak nearly became another victim of peace.

Fourteen months earlier, a large group of young men in black suits was seen running late one evening along Hayarkon Street in Tel Aviv, heading south. The moment that Israel's only two television channels forecasted an unprecedented double-digit landslide, the Shin Bet bodyguards had heard a voice in their earpieces. In an instant, the defeated prime minister's large and despondent suite at the Hilton emptied out, and the prime minister–elect's large and festive suite at the nearby Dan Hotel filled up instead. The Shin Bet's personal protection unit did not wait for the final votes to be counted to switch allegiances. It was enough to hear Benjamin Netanyahu's announcement that he was taking a "time out," from which, everyone assumed, he would never return.

Ehud Barak's 1999 election campaign was a masterpiece of electioneering. His election ads reminded voters of his young days as the fearless commander of the Sayeret Matkal commando unit. They were shown, over and over, the famous photo of him standing on the wing of a hijacked airplane, next to the body of a terrorist who had just been eliminated with a single bullet to his head. Only in Israel does the leader of the peace camp try to gain popularity with such warlike images. Only in Israel can a candidate chase the Arab vote and in the same breath boast about how many Arabs he has killed in his many years in uniform. No less absurdly, Barak tried to get Azmi Bishara, a future traitor and fugitive, to withdraw his own candidacy by sending emissaries to promise him that in exchange for dropping out of the race, his government would improve the prison conditions of convicted terrorists.[i] But for the sake of peace, Arab voters gave the candidate of One Israel—as Labor was rebranded for the 1999 election—nearly 100 percent support.

The name "peace camp" was not always synonymous with "the left." Until the early 1990s, the brand referred to a small group on the fringes of the left: the Communist Party, Ratz, and *This World*, a popular weekly that promoted territorial withdrawals with the same passion as it promoted scantily clad girls on its front page. Labor was vociferously opposed to the creation of a Palestinian state. Golda Meir said that there was no such thing as a "Palestinian people" and said of the Arabs: "I cannot forgive them for forcing us to kill their children." Peres explained that "it is inconceivable for Jews not to be able to settle everywhere in the Land of Israel." Labor prime ministers were willing to pay a heavy price in blood for hostage rescue missions, from the Munich Olympics to Entebbe, because they refused to negotiate with the PLO about exchanging terrorists for hostages—much less about "land for peace."[1]

At the turn of the 1980s, everyone in Labor supported a Knesset resolution calling Yasser Arafat an arch-murderer. "Clearly wolves do not change just because you stroke them," said a Labor lawmaker. Eighty-eight members of the Knesset supported this resolution, and only five opposed it.[2] Twenty-two years later, having caught his breath after the peanut incident, the left's last prime minister stood poised to shake the hand of this wolf, in the hope that he would sign a permanent accord

---

[i] As told to me by member of the Knesset Jamal Zahalka in February 2019.

to end the conflict with the sheep. For Ehud Barak, this was a form of personal closure: As the commander of the Sayeret Matkal commandos in the late 1970s, he had once proposed ambushing Arafat's motorcade in Lebanon with a truck filled with half a ton of explosives.

This was the end of a slow, long, and agonizing process. Since the Yom Kippur War, Israel's control of Judea, Samaria, and Gaza had been the main issue in every election. Nobody believed anymore, as Moshe Dayan said, that it was "better to have Sharm el-Sheikh [a city in Egypt] without peace than peace without Sharm el-Sheikh." The argument over the formula of "land for peace" had begun.

The battle lines between the two sides, left and right, were drawn with the help of two very important civil society organizations founded after the war: Gush Emunim and Peace Now. The religious Zionist youth understood that in order to resist international pressure for a withdrawal, they would have to determine facts on the ground, and the secular left-wing youth understood that without peace now, it would be much harder to uproot these new settlements later. Between the winter of 1974 and the Arab Spring, for nearly forty years, the two sides clashed almost exclusively about this issue. The hawks did not notice that both sides in this protracted confrontation were absentmindedly drifting leftward with each passing election. The Likud and Labor kept arguing with the same fervor while inching closer and closer to territorial withdrawals.

As early as 1974, the Alignment accused Begin of stubbornly opposing any form of compromise. But even the Alignment's own positions back then would have been considered far right in Barak's time: From 1974 till 1988, its platform declared that "a Palestinian state would be a source of hostility, which would imperil the peace of Israel and the whole region." Deep into the 1980s, it still supported building new settlements in the major blocs. In 1992, Labor still opposed the idea of evacuating any settlements. Even Ehud Barak, on the eve of the 1999 elections, avoided using the words "Palestinian state" and let it be understood that even if such a state were formed, it would encompass at most "40, maybe 50 percent" of Judea and Samaria. Time and again, he promised that "Ofra and Beit El will remain forever under Israeli sovereignty." He even recruited for his campaign the mayor of Jerusalem, Ehud Olmert, who repeatedly promised that Barak would never divide the capital city—a statement that would be put to the test very soon and would fail.

* * *

Labor's transformation did not happen overnight. It happened because of two objects with similar ballistics but different ranges: a rock and a rocket.

In late 1987, practically without warning, Judea, Samaria, and the Gaza Strip were set aflame. Twenty years of relative quiet in the territories had given way to mass disturbances, as IDF soldiers were pelted with rocks and Molotov cocktails. Settlers beyond the Green Line replaced the glass windshields of their cars with dirty, rock-resistant plastic sheets. The first generation of Palestinians remembered the raw power of the IDF as it conquered the Gaza Strip between sunrise and sunset, and Judea and Samaria in sixty hours flat. The third generation would experience a similar trauma when the IDF retook Palestinian cities in 2002, in an attempt to suppress a wave of suicide bombings. But the generation in between encountered quite a different IDF: an army on the back foot, serving as a bewildered police force against a popular uprising, wielding relatively unsophisticated weapons. Instead of tanks, the IDF used rubber bullets; instead of fighter jets, it jet-sprayed tear gas.

The Labor defense minister, Yitzhak Rabin, ordered troops to "break arms and legs." A few years later, he explained that he had been misunderstood: He was not calling for disproportionate force, but the opposite—he was ordering soldiers to cause injuries, not deaths.[3] The heavy price tag of Israel's control of the territories gradually dawned on Israelis, including the leaders of the left.

Three years later, a conflict over petroleum in the Persian Gulf morphed into the most bizarre war in Israeli history: the Gulf War. The United States swooped in to defend Kuwait when it was invaded by Iraq, and the tyrant Saddam Hussein chose to mobilize the Arab street in the easiest way possible: by shooting at Israel. He fired old Soviet missiles at Tel Aviv and Haifa. Israel was gripped by hysteria, fearing that Saddam would fire missiles with chemical warheads, but it was a false alarm: Saddam's missiles were all conventional, except for the last one, which, for some reason, was filled with concrete.

Nobody can forget the nights, which were scary at first, strange later, and silly by the end, huddled in sealed rooms at home (as if wet rags and masking tape could seal anything). Like during COVID-19, everyone wore masks and school was canceled. From our mountaintop window, through nylon sheets, we could see the long trails of the rockets whizzing toward their targets on the coastal plain. Our Palestinian neighbors saw them too and danced on their roofs with joy: "Ya Saddam, ya habib, udrub udrub Tel Abib!" they chanted (roughly: "Yo Saddam, dude, bomb bomb Tel Aviv!"). They were thrilled to outsource to Iraq something that they had failed to do: to force Israelis into bomb shelters.

On the face of it, this was an extremely stupid move on the part of the Palestinians on their road to independence. "This week you proved to me how stupid I was for so many years," fumed Yaron London, one of Israel's leading left-wing journalists. "Next time you ask me to support your 'legitimate rights,' you'll find that your cheerleading for Saddam made me deaf to them."[4] Yossi Sarid, a veteran supporter of the two-state vision, could not hold back and wrote two columns for *Haaretz* against the Palestinians and Arafat in equal parts pungent, bitter, and sour: the first under a headline that translates liberally as "Get Lost," and the second, a few months later, "Don't Even Bother Getting Lost." Israelis had to wear gas masks, he wrote, to try to overcome the foul and toxic stench of the PLO's support for Saddam Hussein. "After the war," he wrote, "when Allah is less great, don't call me."[5]

In the end, Sarid was the one who made the call. The left's brief flare-up of anger against the Palestinians subsided. Instead, most Israelis settled on a new understanding: The new era of rocket warfare had greatly reduced, or so it seemed, the importance of controlling territory. Four million Israelis had sat in their sealed rooms, wearing US military surplus gas masks, with their children in strange gas-sealed bassinets, because of a deranged despot over five hundred miles away. They emerged from these rooms with a realization: If rockets could fly hundreds of miles, then why was it such a big deal to control the twenty to thirty miles from the Jordan River to the outskirts of Tel Aviv? *Let's sever the Palestinians off the evil regimes around us*, they thought, *even if the price is to surrender parts of Judea and Samaria.* Peace is more important than the territories.

On June 9, 1992, a warm late-spring night, three Mossad agents walked up to a man who had just stepped out of a taxi at the entrance of the Meridian Hotel in Paris and fired three bullets into his head point-blank. The man was Atef Bseiso, a top PLO officer and one of the men responsible for the massacre of Israeli athletes at the 1972 Munich Olympics. He was the last PLO official dispatched by Mossad to heaven with a bang. One and a half years later, on a lawn in Washington, Israeli Prime Minister Yitzhak Rabin would shake the hand of the PLO's leader, Yasser Arafat. The Rabin-Peres government had promised to negotiate with any Palestinian who agreed to recognize Israel and abandon terrorism, no matter how much Israeli blood he had on his hands.

The Israeli public supported this by a wide margin.[6] For decades, in an effort to decipher public opinion, pollsters have asked Israelis to place themselves on a scale of 1–7 about the Israeli-Palestinian conflict, from far left to far right. The nationwide average score tells us where the average Israeli stands—let's call her Vardit from Rishon LeZion. In 1993, when the Rabin-Meretz government was in power, Vardit gave herself a score of 3.8, slightly left of center. In other words, she was cautiously optimistic about peace.[7]

This was the first time since the Yom Kippur War that the Israeli public leaned to the left. It would soon prove to be the last. But in the meanwhile, the Likud seemed extremist and old-fashioned. Three Likud lawmakers defied the party whip ordering them to vote against the Oslo Accords. It looked like the peace camp had comprehensively trounced the national camp. In late 1993, a young officer by the name of Naftali Bennett hitched a ride to his base. The driver took one look at his uniform and said, "You look like a great guy. Aren't you wasting your time in the army? There's peace. War is yesterday's news."

The Oslo Accords, the most important diplomatic development of the past generation, were built as a temporary structure. They were hastily erected as an interim arrangement, in the hope that the passage of time and good neighborly relations would dissolve the biggest bones of contention: Jerusalem, the return of Palestinian refugees, the settlements, and final borders. Israel withdrew from Gaza City and Jericho first, and later from Ramallah, Hebron, and the other major Palestinian towns. Rabin, Peres, and Netanyahu shook Arafat's hand, giving him territory and arms. But six years later, there was no sign that any ground had been broken for a permanent structure. Israel kept ceding more and more parts of the territories, but there was no end to the conflict on the horizon. Israel's tenth prime minister, Ehud Barak, was determined to change this. Two months after his stunning election victory, in meetings that he liked holding at his favorite time—3:00 a.m. and later—Barak waved a pencil at his interlocutors. "You see this?" he asked, "It won't stand up unless I hold it. If I drop it, it'll fall. That's exactly the situation with the Palestinians. Either we reach an agreement—or we're on a collision course."[8]

One peace treaty was small fry for Barak. He wanted, in just one year, to usher in comprehensive peace in the Middle East, signing treaties with both Syria and the Palestinians. And then, he hoped, he could dedicate the rest of his premiership to domestic affairs. He secretly began scheming to bypass the law that limited Israeli prime ministers to eight years in office at the time. He was planning on staying in power for twelve years.[9]

Barak's attempts to court Syria's leader Hafez al-Assad were clumsy. He gave him his heart, but as George Michael sang, the next day Assad gave it away. Barak called the aging Assad "a brave leader, who shaped modern Syria," ignoring the fact that he shaped it by massacring tens of thousands of opponents with nerve gas. "As soon as I see a camera, I start heaping praise on Assad," he joked with reporters.[10] He was willing to pull out of the Golan Heights and even let the Syrians swim and fish in the Sea of Galilee. One morning, a newspaper headline announced, "Talks for a visit by Barak in Syria soon—maybe even next week." The first days of the new millennium were marked by heady optimism.

In the end, no Israeli flags were raised at the presidential palace in Damascus. The Syrian foreign minister's peace summit ended without any agreements. US President Bill Clinton flew to Switzerland especially to meet Assad, only to discover, within just six minutes, that he had nobody to talk to and nothing to talk about. As Benny Begin said at the time, Israel trying to make peace with Assad and Arafat was like a woman trying to seduce a gay man: whatever she might do, he just would not be interested.

Barak's ambitions for comprehensive regional peace were the mirror image of the all-out war in his government. Of the eighty members of the Knesset in his original coalition, fewer than thirty remained less than a year later. While trying to resolve the conflict with the Arab world, Barak struggled to resolve an especially daft crisis about the fateful question of when the national electricity corporation could transport a turbine through Israel's streets. Fearing a backlash from secular drivers if this caused major congestion on a weekday, he decided to have it transported on Shabbat. UTJ quit his government. This augured poorly for his ability to find creative solutions to slightly more dramatic issues, such as the return of Palestinian refugees or the fate of Jerusalem.

As his government crumbled at breakneck speed, Barak resolved to check once and for all whether his figurative pencil would stand or fall. He set himself a target: a clear-cut, historic resolution of the Israeli-Palestinian conflict with a comprehensive peace treaty, here and now. When he took off for the Camp David Summit, he no longer had a coalition. His ministers had dropped out one by one, leaving him carrying no fewer than ten portfolios. He knew that without a historic achievement, his days as prime minister were numbered.

Standing at the entrance to the US president's country retreat, in early July 2000, Barak did not downplay the magnitude of the moment: "One hundred years of enmity and struggle meet at this point in time." In a heavy hint, the Americans accommodated him in the cabin where Egyptian President Anwar Sadat had slept twenty-two years earlier. They were expecting him to make concessions of Begin-like proportions: if possible, down to the last inch.

Desperate for an achievement, Barak agreed to surrender nearly everything: He had long forgotten his election promise that a Palestinian state could be formed on less than half of the land in Judea, Samaria, and Gaza. He whispered his true, secret offer into Clinton's ear: 92 percent of the land, the evacuation of tens of thousands of settlers, and the pièce de résistance—dividing Jerusalem by giving Arafat the Muslim and Christian quarters of the Old City and splitting sovereignty over the Temple Mount. He smashed taboo after taboo, offering concessions that nobody had ever contemplated making.

It was an offer that could not be refused, and Arafat did not refuse it. The Palestinian Authority chairman never bothered responding to Barak's offer, which US President Bill Clinton conveyed to him. It was later claimed that part of the reason for the summit's collapse was that Barak was not nice enough to Arafat, but those blaming Barak's poor people skills still fail to understand what Arafat's adviser Ahmad Tibi said: The minimum that the Palestinians are willing to accept has never matched the maximum that the Israelis are willing to give. The summit lasted fourteen days, which felt like an eternity. In the end, Barak returned home without a peace treaty and without a government.

The pencil had fallen over and snapped.

On the red carpet at Ben Gurion Airport, Barak made his decision. It sealed not only his own fate but also that of the whole peace camp. "Today I return from Camp David," he said, in the formative speech of his premiership, "looking into the eyes of the millions of people who sent me, and I say with a tortured heart: We have not succeeded. For now." The prime minister glanced at the original text of his speech, written on the flight by his advisers. It read: "We have not succeeded, because there is no partner." He adlibbed a minor correction, in order to keep the door closed but not locked: "We have not succeeded because we have found no partner for a deal."

Collective memory can be misleading. Shimon Peres is popularly quoted as asking, "Am I a loser?" but in fact his words to Labor's central committee were: "They say that Peres is a loser. I'm the one who lost?!" In the 2015 election, Benjamin Netanyahu never referred to "Arab droves" but rather used the more moderate expression: "Arab voters are moving in large numbers to the polls." But in Israeli popular memory, Peres was a loser, and the Arabs voted in droves, and memory is flexible enough to adapt itself to preconceptions. The millions of eyes that Barak mentioned seemed to peek at his written speech and ignore what he actually said. The only thing that has survived from Barak's speech, and indeed his premiership, is the phrase "no partner." That was what the speaker was thinking and, as if by telepathy, that was what his audience heard.

With these two words, which he never even said, Ehud Barak liquidated the political camp that had governed Israel for most of its history, leaving it naked with only a torn flag around its midriff. He still shook hands with his ministers on the red carpet; an armored motorcade stood by to take him home; he slept at the residence on Balfour Street; and people still called him "Mr. Prime Minister." The Labor Party would continue to wander in and out of coalitions. It even notched up certain electoral achievements here and there. But at that moment, the left was finished. Political camps coalesce around ideas, and the left's big idea had just gone up in flames. This would probably have happened eventually anyway, but Ehud Barak dramatically hastened its demise.

* * *

After the epic failure at Camp David, the negotiations with the Palestinians never got back on track. Israeli prime ministers would meet Palestinian leaders again in Annapolis, Paris, Taba, New York, Washington, and Jerusalem. Near the end of his term, Ehud Olmert received from Bashar al-Assad a delivery of hummus prepared that morning in a restaurant in Damascus. It was creamy and delicious. It was also the only fruit of peace that anyone in Jerusalem would enjoy until the Abraham Accords with the Gulf States in 2020.

The unmasking of Arafat, as Ehud Barak called it, was a formative moment in Israeli political history. Until then, Israeli politics had a left and a right and maybe some crumbs of the center. But at that moment, the ship of state capsized. The camp that had comprised half of the nation, and sometimes more, started sinking until it was completely submerged.

In summary: Between the Six-Day War in 1967 and the First Intifada in 1987, most Israelis opposed negotiations with the Palestinians. Between 1987 and Barak's spectacular failure in 2000, most Israelis supported negotiations. It is no coincidence that this period saw three Labor prime ministers: Peres, Rabin, and Barak. The "New Middle East," as they saw it, meant a happy Israeli-Palestinian wedding.

After Barak, from 2000 till the Arab Spring in 2011, Israelis no longer believed in peace, but neither did they have any particular interest in continuing to govern areas densely populated with Palestinians. They wanted not to marry the Palestinians but to divorce them. The surprise result was widespread support for a unilateral withdrawal. The Kadima party, of blessed memory, won power promising exactly this, with a plan to evacuate nearly one hundred thousand settlers and to demarcate Israel's final borders. But the Israeli public gradually stopped believing in this solution. When Hezbollah grew more powerful after the unilateral withdrawal from Lebanon in 2000, and when Hamas grew more powerful in Gaza after the unilateral withdrawal in 2005, Israelis lost interest in further withdrawals, until further notice. In 2011, the Arab Spring destroyed the belief that additional withdrawals might do any good for Israel. Ever since, the Israeli public has been drifting to the right, or rather—away from the left.

This shift has been reflected most vividly in the public image of Yasser Arafat. In the 1970s and 1980s, he was considered a "two-legged creature," as Begin described him: "the man with all that hair on his face." In the euphoric Oslo era, a satirical show on TV presented him as a smooth and jovial character. A poll conducted in 1997 showed that Arafat was twice as popular as Netanyahu and Peres.[11] Just a few years later, the PLO chairman went back to being a bloodthirsty arch-terrorist: When he was placed under siege at the Muqata compound, dying of a mysterious disease, Israelis received, with schadenfreude, daily reports about the pita rations that the IDF allowed in.

The quarter century in which Israel experienced a bloody intifada, the Lebanon War, and another four exasperating operations in Gaza prodded the average Israeli—Vardit from Rishon LeZion—slowly but surely to the right. In 1993, still young and optimistic, she placed herself slightly left of center, with a score of 3.8 on a scale of 1–7. Eight years later, with the failure of Camp David and the outbreak of a wave of terrorism, Vardit had already moved right of center, to around 4.7. In 2020, now more skeptical and disillusioned, she moved much further to the right, at around 6.2. She needed a telescope to see the left. Until something dramatic changes her mind, the electoral math will remain brutal for Ehud Barak's camp: In Israel, a prime minister can only come from the right or the center-right, or at least head a government based on the right.

In later years, Barak summed up his failure with a pithy insight: "The right could not forgive me for offering Arafat everything, and the left could not forgive me when it became clear that not even that was enough for him." This was, of course, an elegant way to dodge several other defects that emerged during his tenure, such as his condescending attitude toward his partners or the fact that he managed to quarrel with every politician who gave him their trust. Barak offered a succinct summary of his experience: "Politicians are only human," he once said, adding: "and sometimes, not even that." He was not helped by his important and historic decision to pull the IDF out of Lebanon after nearly twenty years of pointless bloodletting in the "security belt." Hardly anyone in the defense establishment saw any point in holding onto the military outposts in Lebanon, but Barak was the only one with the gumption to follow through. Everyone in Israel was moved to see the last armored personnel carrier leaving Lebanon, carrying a soldier with a broad grin waving at the cameras.

That soldier's name was Sharon Shitoubi. Six months later, he was killed in a terrorist shooting in the Gaza Strip.

The Second Intifada, which erupted in September 2000 on the explicit instructions of Israel's onetime partner for peace Yasser Arafat, drowned what remained of Barak's government and his achievements in blood and fire. Israeli soldiers were massacred in Ramallah and defenestrated, and bloody riots broke out within Israel between Arabs throwing stones and police officers with live ammunition. Even before the snap elections, a million bullets had been fired, and sixty-eight fresh graves had been dug in Israel's cemeteries. By the time the IDF extinguished the flames through superhuman efforts, over a thousand more Israelis would pay with their lives for this catastrophic experiment.

In the elections of the winter of 2001, Barak set two dubious records: He became both the prime minister defeated by the widest margin in Israeli history—a staggering 26 percent—and the shortest-serving prime minister, relieving Moshe Sharett of this amusing title. I was there with Barak on the night that his turn came to announce that he was taking time out. Most of his bodyguards were quick to abandon him and dart to the new prime minister, Ariel Sharon. The Shin Bet's personal protection unit is not a sentimental place.

* * *

For six years, Ehud Barak waited on the outside, constantly searching for a way to get back into politics. In the end, an opportunity opened up in the north. The Second Lebanon War, a dunderheaded escapade by Israel's new defense troika—Prime Minister Ehud Olmert, Defense Minister Amir Peretz, and Chief of Staff Dan Halutz—triggered a small spike in public nostalgia for Barak. It is certainly ironic that he staged his comeback because of a war with Hezbollah, the organization that grew dramatically stronger in the wake of the unilateral withdrawal that he himself spearheaded as prime minister six years earlier.

But the Labor Party to which Barak returned was a pale shadow of the ruling party that he abandoned. He conquered the summit after it had already been flattened. Most of his voters, it turned out, had indeed been convinced that Israel had no partner for peace, at least until further notice. It would be hard to convince them to vote Labor for the sake of resuming negotiations with the Palestinians, having offered them practically everything at the start of the decade.

Barak emerged from the 2013 elections with a humiliating crop of thirteen seats. The peak, or rather, the nadir, was still ahead of him: For two whole months, he begged to join the government headed by his former military subordinate Benjamin Netanyahu. But the party that founded the State of Israel had to wait for the approval of Netanyahu's senior partner, Avigdor Lieberman, to give his approval. In a rare gesture of generosity, the new prime minister called the coalition between the large Likud and small Labor a "unity government," like the proverbial elephant marching through the desert next to a mouse and praising it for "all the dust we're kicking up together." The Likud has never been part of a government that it did not head. Labor has done this five times, with senior portfolios and chauffeured cars compensating for its loss of ideology. Barak's party colleagues begged him to end his partnership with Netanyahu and try to rebuild the party in the opposition, but he refused to listen.

* * *

In January 2011, a decade after sapping Labor's will to live, Ehud Barak tried to perform a mercy killing. Early one morning, he took another four party members with him, and in exchange for a scandalous share of government ministries from Netanyahu, he dismantled the party that had propelled him to the premiership. "We are fed up with the disturbing leftward drift," declared the first Israeli leader to have offered to divide Jerusalem and relinquish control of the Temple Mount. He accused Labor lawmakers of getting swept into "post-Zionism and post-modernism." The duo who served together during the Sabena airplane hostage crisis resumed their partnership forty years later.

Contrary to occasional appearances, Labor has never recovered from what Barak did to it during his two stints as its leader, in 2000 and 2011. Despite a brief comeback under Isaac Herzog, Labor has been dying an agonizing death for a whole generation. The party has switched leaders ten times in twenty years in a desperate attempt to find someone to run with. The Likud, for comparison's sake, has had only two leaders in the same period. In the Middle East, only ISIS has performed more beheadings than the party that founded the State of Israel. Labor members crowned, one after the other, a union leader from Sderot, a radio and television presenter, a high-end attorney from Tel Aviv, a businessman born in a transit camp, and a general. This was not a rejuvenation but a full-on panic attack. Self-confident parties do not feel the need to perform constant blood transfusions or to don camouflage (like Labor, rebranding itself as the Zionist Union and One Israel). With these constant upheavals, Labor looked more like a man drowning and hysterically waving his arms in the air than a trained swimmer peacefully bobbing through the water.

Labor kept changing not only its leadership but also its agenda: Amir Peretz and later Shelly Yachimovich tried to take the party back to its days as a militantly social-democratic workers' movement. After Barak split off, Yachimovich tried to change course on the Palestinian issue as well: The settlers, she said, were not the root of all evil after all.[12] But Labor's voters had long stopped working in factories and fields. They now belonged to the wealthy bourgeoisie, which was horrified by the red flag planted on the party's turf and its plans for dramatic tax hikes. It says a lot about Labor that in the past generation, Israel's workers' party had been headed by four millionaires with luxurious houses in Tel Aviv: Ben-Eliezer, Barak, Gabbay, and Herzog.

Ehud Barak popped up one last time, in the September 2019 elections, for the most pathetic attempted comeback in the history of Israeli prime ministers: He ended up with an unrealistic spot on an expanded Meretz list. At the age of seventy-eight, the penny had not yet dropped that it had all ended for him on that hot summer's day at Ben Gurion Airport.

In summary: Golda Meir deprived the left of the mantle of security; Ehud Barak deprived it of the mantle of peace.

CHAPTER 8

Neither Left nor Right

Sharon's Decision—
Pivoting to the Center

D AY BROKE OVER GANEI TAL, a village dotted with villas, greenhouses, and mortar shell impact craters, on August 17, 2005. It was to be the last day in the life of this small Jewish settlement in the Gaza Strip. At exactly 8:00 a.m., IDF soldiers were supposed to breach the settlement's gates, pack the belongings of those who agreed to be evacuated, and drag out those who did not. There were four soldiers for each adult resident— one for each limb—and armored buses.

Or would they? A rumor spread like the plague, hopping from the synagogue to the protest tent of teenagers wearing orange (the color of the anti-evacuation protest movement), and from there to the media: *Prime Minister Ariel Sharon had suffered a heart attack. He was in the hospital in Jerusalem. The Gaza disengagement would be called off.* The fact that the withdrawal had been approved by the Knesset and the government and that half of the IDF was already parked on the only road leading to the settlement did not dampen the outpouring of euphoria.

Four months and one day later, when Sharon suffered a stroke, the evacuees heard the news at hotels across the country and in their new caravan parks, their belongings stored in large army shipping containers. The rumors of Sharon's incapacitation were not exaggerated, just premature. They were right about one thing: If not for Sharon, the bloc of Jewish settlements in the Gaza Strip known as Gush Katif would still be standing. The State of Israel has demolished forty-nine settlements in its history, including in the Sinai Peninsula in 1982. Ariel Sharon's signature was on the evacuation order of all of them.

The interesting thing is that the same signature, by the same Ariel Sharon, also appears on the fading documents establishing over one hundred settlements across the land of Israel. For some of them, Sharon signed off on both their construction and their demolition.

During the Jewish festival of Sukkot in 1990, Sharon participated in the rededication ceremony for the settlement of Kfar Darom, which had been deserted during the War of Independence and was now being brought back to life. "Just as it is clear that if Israel pulls its forces out of Lebanon, towns in northern Israel will be shelled," he said in his speech, "it is also clear that if we vacate the Gaza Strip, the whole south of Israel will be hit." The following year, he urged American Jewish millionaires to donate money to strengthen Gush Katif. "Because nowadays, anyone can fire a Katyusha rocket, a small over-the-shoulder metal tube, and strike Ashkelon or Kiryat Gat or Netivot," he said. "What should we do then? Bomb the place? Retaliate? There is no answer to these problems other than a Jewish presence in the Gaza Strip."

If you have read this far, you should not be fazed by Sharon's flip-flop. We have already seen that big leaders come with big paradoxes. The thing is that even compared to all his predecessors, Israel's eleventh prime minister was a walking paradox. Most of his most important actions involved undoing his own decisions. He wrote and erased the same words, built and dismantled the same settlements, opposed and supported the same policies, and never once looked back. Only forward. "Never apologize for or regret anything," Moshe Dayan once advised him, and Sharon took this advice to heart.

Four years earlier, the lights were switched on at the Likud's campaign headquarters. On a bulky television set, the kind that existed in 2000, the Likud candidate for prime minister and his aides had just watched his latest election ad: Against a backdrop of gentle music, Ariel Sharon was shown hugging his grandchildren, driving a tractor around his ranch, and carrying a sheep over his shoulders. ("We don't eat friends," he promised the cameras, next to a terrified lamb.) The candidate blinked. Everyone waited to hear what he had to say. "I've got to thank you all for making me look like such a nice guy," he said. "But I'm warning you that with a single sentence, I might ruin all your hard work."[1]

No one in Israel thought that Sharon—now aged seventy-two—was *nice*, of course. He had been a man of war and strife his whole life. He once bloviated to Alignment ministers, "Abba Eban, your foreign minister, is an American spy. Check how many pairs of binoculars he has at home and why he needs them all."[2] He once threatened Yigael Yadin in front of a stunned Menachem Begin and fellow ministers: "I'll strip you stark naked on the cabinet table." He treated orders as recommendations and hierarchies as an irritating nuisance.

But now, there was a bloody intifada raging outside, and Prime Minister Ehud Barak had lost his last crumbs of public support and was dragged into certain defeat. Sharon was convinced that Netanyahu would return to politics and easily claim the leadership of the Likud. He even started planning for his retirement, which included writing his memoirs ("a five-volume encyclopedia"). Reality had different plans: Netanyahu surprised everyone by deciding not to run, and Sharon was suddenly catapulted from being the much maligned, hot-tempered defense minister of the First Lebanon War to a peace-loving, grandpa-like candidate for prime minister. With a fifty-year delay, Moshe Dayan's prophecy about him came true: "You'll be called in only when there's a catastrophe."[3]

When the votes were counted, it turned out Sharon had swept not only the settlements, Jerusalem, and other right-wing strongholds, but also the greater Tel Aviv area—not exactly a bastion of the right. The geographic center of Israel gave him not only its trust but also its political center. Amazingly, Sharon did not even win such resounding support in his party primaries. His colleagues were always quite critical of him and never quite took him seriously.

On the night when Sharon entered office as prime minister, he summoned his then-friend Reuven Rivlin to the Kirya defense compound in Tel Aviv. *Why does he want to meet me there, of all places?* wondered Rivlin. When he stepped into the prime minister's Tel Aviv office, a spartan old room, Sharon told him excitedly: "I wanted you to see me finally sitting on the chair I've been dreaming about since 1954, the first time I was in this room." Then he lay down on the couch. The whole way back to Jerusalem, Rivlin, a stalwart of the right, could not shake off a nagging thought: *Why did the Likud's new prime minister refer to the seat as "Ben-Gurion's chair"? Why not "Begin's chair"?* He would remember this incident when the pair parted ways in the wake of the Ben-Gurion-style partition that his party's leader was about to promote: the Gaza disengagement.

Strange as it sounds, the Likud's founder was never a true Likudnik. As a young adolescent, Ariel Sharon had joined the left-wing Haganah, not the Irgun or Lehi like the Begin, Shamir, and Netanyahu families. He was not a Jabotinskyite "prince," like many of his party colleagues, whose parents had been Jabotinsky loyalists, because he had never been a Jabotinskyite or a prince. He grew up in a strict, spartan home, the first in Kfar Malal to be surrounded by a high fence and keep a guard dog at the entrance. His parents, Mr. and Mrs. Scheinerman, were proud individualists who refused to grow what the village committee ordered them to grow in their allotment. This rebellious streak propelled Sharon to the greatest successes achieved by any IDF officer and also his fair share of trouble as a politician.

In 1958, when he was still in uniform, Sharon joined Mapai. He would later explain that it was the only way to get a senior command in the army. What stood between him and the ruling party was not a matter of ideology, but a generational gap from the older generals and clear differences of character. They hated the fact that he regularly took journalists for rides in his armored personnel carrier, and they envied his operational successes. His path to the position that he so keenly coveted—IDF chief of staff—was blocked. In 1973, he was discharged at the rank of major general and set about taking revenge on those who denied him command of the military: the party whose membership card he still held.

Thanks to two breathtaking maneuvers in 1973, Sharon eventually reached the position of prime minister: In the fall, he blocked the Egyptians in Sinai and crossed the Suez Canal, and earlier, in the summer, he had founded Israel's first large right-wing party. After excruciating negotiations, plagued with difficulties and ego, he merged five separate movements into a single list to be known as "the Likud." If not for him, Begin would never have become prime minister. Sharon was placed only sixth on the Likud's Knesset list, behind three doctors who have long since been forgotten. But at the end of the war in which he saved the country from Egyptian invasion, Sharon was the new party's number one public relations asset. His image, with a bandage around his forehead, helped the party achieve relative success: nearly forty seats.

The left's revenge was swift: Mapai passed a law preventing him from serving both as a member of the Knesset and as a corps commander in the reserves, suddenly remembering the dangerous link between generals and politics. Sharon was quick to resign from the Knesset. He was already bored of wandering around aimlessly in the hallways, and his affair with the right did not last long. He locked horns with everything that moved in the party that he had built. Ahead of the 1977 elections, he founded a new party—Shlomtzion—after an awkward political shopping trip that proved that ideology was not his chief concern: He started with the Likud, continued to the Alignment, took a detour through the NRP, and sauntered between almost all the Zionist parties.

The new party's manifesto was vague and focused on the "national" need for Sharon to serve as defense minister. The party's ideological malleability was clear from the fact that its founder offered a spot to the prominent left-wing lawmaker Yossi Sarid. "I want what's best for the country, and you want what's best for it," he said, "so what's the difference between us? We can and must run together." Sarid, a true verbal artist, was left speechless. Even the party's name, Shlomtzion, was telling: It was the name of the daughter of Amos Kenan, the man who once chucked a bomb at the home of a religious minister. Kenan also received an invitation to join the party, and he too politely refused. On the night when Likud celebrated its historic victory, Sharon was left alone with his sorrows and just two seats.

Begin spared Sharon's blushes, brought him back into the Likud, and appointed him agriculture minister. It was during this term that Sharon became the great builder of settlements, planting Israel's flag all over Judea, Samaria, and the Gaza Strip. But as soon as he was promoted to defense minister, inspecting honor guards in a white safari suit, he changed his tune again: He evacuated all of Israel's settlements in Sinai, including Yamit. Settlers who had danced with him all the way to Sebastia were hit with water cannons by soldiers sent to evict them on the defense minister's orders. When he was booted from office a year later, after the official inquiry into the Sabra and Shatila massacre, the left celebrated and the right was not particularly upset.

In 2001, therefore, right-wing Israelis treated Sharon with respect and suspicion, while left-wing Israelis focused only on the suspicion part. Sharon was not especially worried about either side. He correctly identified a very large and very silent part of Israeli society, which had coalesced in the decade that witnessed the murder of one prime minister and two thousand citizens and the maiming of two great dreams: the right-wing dream of Greater Israel and the left-wing dream of a "New Middle East." Amid the constant sirens and bombings, most Israelis just wanted a quiet, middle-class life. This shift reached peak absurdity one night when news channels ran a split screen: on one-half, footage of terror victims covered in blood after a suicide bombing in Jerusalem, and on the other half—a live soccer game.

Sharon gave Israelis the quiet that they desperately craved. He almost completely stopped giving interviews, unlike his predecessors, Netanyahu and Barak, who appeared in the media nonstop. But more importantly, he decided to base his leadership not on his party's operatives but on the growing majority in the center of the political map that was searching for a new home. Since the demise of the Democratic Movement for Change (Dash) in the 1970s, few new centrist parties had been founded in Israel. When Israelis went to the polls, they had to choose whether they were right wing or left wing, fascists or Arab lovers, eager to hug Arafat or desperate to expel him. Sharon offered them a third way. His associate Reuven Adler put it bluntly: What Israelis wanted was to thump the Arabs and pull out of the territories.

Sharon's premiership generously satisfied both demands. After the dark month of March 2002, when over 150 civilians were murdered in terror attacks, he sent the IDF into Palestinian cities for its most muscular operation since the Six-Day War. Once more, Israeli tanks were seen on the streets of Ramallah, Nablus, and Jenin. Israeli bulldozers razed whole wings of the Muqata compound, besieging Arafat ("that dog," as Sharon called him, as opposed to Netanyahu's preferred term: "that thing"). In one meeting with President Bill Clinton, wedged in a chair far too narrow for his body, Sharon surprised his host with a conciliatory message. "The Palestinians are good and noble people, besides two small shortcomings," he said, before leaning over to his bureau chief and asking: "How do you say, 'murderous traitors' in English?"[4]

But at the same time, and at first quite unintentionally, Sharon became the first Likud prime minister to openly support the idea of a Palestinian state. Israel, he announced one evening in a speech, wanted to give the Palestinians something that nobody had ever given them: the right to establish a state. He built a huge, unphotogenic concrete wall, ostensibly in order to stop terror attacks but in practice to sketch the first-draft border between the State of Israel and a future State of Palestine.

The Likud was apoplectic. On one occasion, Sharon's speech to his party committee was disrupted with the shrill sound of hundreds of whistles. Another time, at Netanyahu's initiative, the Likud passed a resolution opposing the two-state solution. Sharon, who had once famously heckled Prime Minister Shamir, now attacked those who dared to interrupt him. And having once outflanked the prime minister on the right, he now complained that his own ministers were outflanking him. Sharon mourned his rival's achievement, but to everyone's surprise, this defeat only strengthened the public opinion of him. The lesser his party's faith in him, the greater the public's. In the 2003 elections, Israelis who had never supported the Likud before now cast their votes for it—not because of the party, but despite it. They did not vote for the Likud: They voted for Sharon.

The Likud was now home to two rival, mutually antagonistic movements: One was ideologically right wing and opposed withdrawals; the other was centrist and pragmatic and favored compromise. Sharon was already fed up with the party that he had founded. Soon after doubling the Likud's strength to forty seats, he came under vocal attack from his right-wing opponents in the party. Most of them were virtually unknown freshman lawmakers. At one Likud faction meeting in 2003, Sharon used a word that no Israeli prime minister had ever dared to utter: "occupation." "To hold 3.5 million Palestinians under occupation—you don't have to love that word—but to hold them under occupation, in my opinion, that's a bad thing." Speechlessness gripped the room for a second, like the brief moment of stunned silence between a suicide bombing and the wailing of ambulance sirens. Then the whole room seemed to be propelled into the air. In his armored car, on his way home from the Knesset, Sharon confided in an aide: "I don't plan on staying on much longer with that gang of scoundrels."[5] Their opinion of him was not much better.

Sharon spearheaded two grandiose demolition projects in his second and final term as prime minister: the Jewish settlements in the Gaza Strip and the Likud. During the election campaign, he warned that "withdrawing under fire means pulling out without getting anything back... this would be a great danger to Israel's future." The electorate followed him. When he changed his tune soon afterward—whether because of the criminal investigations into him or because he had a sudden and unexplained change of mind—the withdrawal from Gaza enjoyed widespread public support. Sharon concluded that he no longer had any use for the party that he had founded. It had gone from being an asset to a heavy liability.

On his way to evacuating Gush Katif, Sharon elegantly ignored his past promises, as well as a poll of Likud members forbidding him from dismantling settlements. When rumors started spreading about the withdrawal plan, settler leaders who had once "grabbed the hilltops" on his orders phoned the prime minister's office, but his secretary refused to put them through. They learned an important lesson: When you treat someone as the ass carrying the messiah, he may well see himself as the messiah, and you will end up playing the ass.

* * *

The settlers were not the only ones to learn this lesson. So did the Haredim. One of the hallmarks of the Israeli political center is its opposition to Haredi political dominance. The Council of Torah Sages is the most extreme force in Israeli society on matters of religion and state, while centrist voters are quite happy to mix and match: They like to make kiddush on Friday night and then watch the news. They want their weddings officiated by a rabbi but with mixed dancing.

Politically, the center is a bitter foe of the Haredim: After all, Shas and UTJ's political stock had always risen with polarization in Israeli society around the never-ending argument about Israel's control of the territories. And these parties, which had no strong affiliations or opinions on this subject, remained a hot commodity at the disposal of the highest bidder. The smaller the political center, the greater the demand for the Haredi parties, and vice versa.

The first hint of Sharon's pivot to the center on matters of religion and state as well could be seen in his refusal as prime minister to visit the home of Shas's leader, Rabbi Ovadia Yosef, even when he greatly needed the party's support for key votes in the Knesset. As a minister and rank-and-file member of the Knesset, he had visited the courts of rabbis and Hasidic rebbes more than any other politician, wearing a big black kippah on his white hair. But the moment that he was elected to the highest office in the land, he dropped this old habit. "The prime minister doesn't go to anyone," he said. "They come to him."[6]

The Haredim were late to realize that they were no longer in charge. In May 2002, they torpedoed a scheme for government cuts to save the collapsing economy. Sharon wasted no time. That same night, he fired Shas and UTJ's ministers. With this, he became the first and last prime minister to date to have voluntarily booted the Haredim out of a coalition instead of begging them to enter it. He derived immense, almost sadistic, pleasure from this act. "Nu, have the letters arrived yet?" he kept asking his cabinet secretary every other minute, in case the courier with the dismissal letters had gotten stuck in traffic.

Only after the Haredim begged him did Sharon agree to let them back into his government, but not for long. After the 2003 elections, Sharon decided to bring into the government Tommy Lapid's secular Shinui party, which had just won fifteen seats, at the expense of the Haredi politicians, who were used to thinking of their ministerial seats as their private property. Shinui's new ministers walked around their new ministries like kids who were let loose in a (non-kosher) candy store. Their first act was to erase the letters "BS"D" (short for "with the help of Heaven" in Aramaic) from the Interior Ministry's letterheads.

For a year and a half, Ariel Sharon's government unleashed even more dramatic reforms: It mercilessly cut child benefits and increased Haredi participation in the work force. But then Shinui discovered that all sheep in Sharon's flock meet the same end: slaughter. When the NRP quit the coalition in protest at the disengagement and Sharon needed religious representatives around the table, he had no qualms about firing Shinui's ministers and bringing the Haredim back instead. "They're against everything that's Jewish," Sharon said in horror about Tommy Lapid and his colleagues with considerable delay, as if his retinue had just landed back from a state visit to Mars.

When the last Israeli soldier pulled out of the Gaza Strip in the fall of 2005, the typhoon that had ravaged Israeli politics for two years seemed to subside: Sharon had achieved his mission, the pockets of resistance in the Likud had been suppressed, and the party stabilized in the polls at around forty seats again. Benjamin Netanyahu, who had quit as finance minister a week before the disengagement in protest, was now a defeated, powerless, and utterly uninfluential backbencher. Had Sharon wanted to, he could have remained at the helm of the Likud for as long as he wanted to.

But he didn't want to. He leveraged his immense power for one final mission: the remaking of Israeli politics. After months of hesitation, polling, and late-night consultations at his ranch, Sharon decided to engineer an upheaval that would make 1977 pale in comparison: He planned to seize power with a movement unaffiliated with either camp, left or right, and independent of either bloc. He decided to consign the Likud and Labor to the junkyard of politics.

Kadima (meaning "forward") was not the first political party tailored to the proportions of a single person. Sharon's ambitious undertaking was almost a one-to-one replay of Ben-Gurion's formation of Rafi ahead of the 1965 elections. Both ventures had their roots in a long-running dispute within the ruling party: Mapai was torn apart by the Lavon affair, an elaborate scandal about failed Israeli espionage in Egypt, while the Likud was split over the disengagement. Both parties were created in an attempt to eliminate their mother parties, by the founding fathers of those mother parties: Sharon, who had founded the Likud, sought to terminate its rule just as Ben-Gurion had sought to liquidate Mapai, which he had led since before Israel's independence. Both men did so by jettisoning long-held ideological principles and lurching to the center. "Neither left nor right—marching forward (*kadima*)!" declared Rafi's election slogan, in an almost perfect preview of Sharon's "Neither left nor right—forward (*kadima*)!" in 2006. Oh, and both parties fielded Shimon Peres third on their lists: once as a promising young politician and the second time as the responsible adult in the room.

Rafi crashed and burned in its attempt to lead an upheaval, winning just ten seats and quickly disappearing. Sharon hoped to succeed thanks to one particular advantage over Ben-Gurion: He was still the prime minister. "The movement that we have founded today will serve the People of Israel for many years to come," he read off a piece of paper in a speech to the nation from his office in November 2005. He called this movement "Kadima." It was the big bang of Israeli politics.

On the way, Sharon shrugged off the irritating burden of his principles. In his resignation speech from the Likud, he did not supply even a single ideological reason to justify this dramatic move. He was not proposing a withdrawal, a constitution, war, or peace. He was not asking voters to embrace a new manifesto but to sign an irrevocable appointment letter: You can leave the state in my hands, and I'll do as I see fit with it. The polls, which forecasted over forty seats for Kadima, proved that the deal was acceptable to the other side. The Likud shrunk overnight to the size of the old Herut: just a dozen seats.

Polls and focus groups were Kadima's ideological superstructure— the reason for its birth and the secret of its fleeting success. Kadima was the political version of a fast-food fad: a 3D-printed hamburger without meat. It set out to be a party, but it was really an almost unprecedented invention of a list in the image of a single man. Thirty years in the Likud had brought Sharon to this point: He had outflanked and been outflanked, schemed and been schemed against, betrayed and been betrayed. He had run out of patience with bothersome activists, noisy party conferences, and members of the Knesset who did not know their place.

Sharon was too polite to sugarcoat this explicit deal for the voters. But Meir Sheetrit, one of Kadima's senior officials, was later asked at a parlor event what a Likudnik like him was doing running with Labor politicians like Shimon Peres and Haim Ramon. His answer was refreshingly honest and frustratingly vapid: "We have cut ourselves off from all ideologies. That's what's special about Kadima. You have here former members of Labor, former members of the Likud, and people who were never members of either party. We're no longer carrying kitbags with the heritage of Jabotinsky or Berl Katznelson. We're looking only at the future." In order to illustrate the benefits of joining the party, Sheetrit wanted to give out membership cards that were probably unlike anything in Israeli or world political history, giving new members discounts at certain business. Only a directive from the attorney general put an end to this initiative, which would have turned politics into a consumer club.

As mentioned earlier, Kadima, meaning "forward," was neither left nor right. When a movement prides itself on moving *forward*, it signals that *movement* is the most important thing, regardless of the direction of travel. Sharon's heir, Tzipi Livni, would later come up with an even more vacuous name: "the Movement" (Hatnua). Kadima was set up to take the place not of the Likud but of the old Mapai, which Sharon had joined nearly fifty years earlier as a condition for getting promoted to lieutenant colonel: a centrist party that would not be at the mercy of tiny coalition partners and their blackmail, but on the contrary—it would form a government that everyone would be desperate to join and beg to enter.

Sharon was correct in his diagnosis but wrong in his prognosis. His diagnosis was that after the implosion of the right's dream of a Greater Israel and the collapse of the left's dream of peace, space had suddenly cleared up for a ruling party to govern from the center. But his prognosis was mistaken: No one-man list can outlive that one man. Kadima was born in his brain, and when his brain collapsed in the middle of an election campaign, so did his new party.

Without an ideology or its leader, Kadima stood no chance. It limped ahead to victory by force of inertia but failed to remain a centrist party, getting swept into the leadership of the left-wing bloc. Instead of getting weighed down by ideology, it got bogged down by criminal probes: The finance minister went to jail for theft, the justice minister was convicted for indecent assault, the prime minister was booted out of office because envelopes of cash were discovered in his safe, and amid all this, other party officials were investigated for corruption, rape, perjury, and harassment. At the moment that Kadima lost power, it also lost its raison d'être and vanished into oblivion. By the time Ariel Sharon died in 2014 after a long coma, and his body lay in state in the Knesset plaza, there was no trace of Kadima in the building behind him. He had outlived it.

Nevertheless, the shockwaves of this political bombshell can still be felt today. Kadima dealt a heavy blow to Israel's traditional parties, with their institutions and membership rolls. The voters, who at first loved internal party democracy, soon discovered the heavy costs of this system: The cynical mass registration of special interest groups (settlers, aerospace industry workers, even bikers) distorted the results in a way that completely disconnected the party's electorate from its list of candidates. Meanwhile, lawmakers hungry for self-promotion bombarded the Knesset with a monstrous number of pointless bills just to win media attention. Whereas in the First Knesset, lawmakers submitted fewer than two hundred private members' bills in total, in the Seventeenth Knesset, this quota skyrocketed to 4,200, setting a new world record.[7] Instead of fighting for their parties' positions, lawmakers increasingly fought their party colleagues.

In public opinion, internal elections became a byword for a disconnected political class, narrow interests, political bribery, and corruption. One member of the Knesset bribed party officials with a stay at a hotel in order to win their votes; another handed out sausages to voters. But the saddest story of all was that of Ariel Weinstein. He had served as a gray but diligent member of the Knesset for four terms, until the Likud first called party primaries in 1996. One evening, after another draining day of pathetic electioneering, he complained of chest pains, collapsed, and died. He was only sixty-three years old. "He was the first victim of party primaries," wrote one newspaper the following morning.[8]

Sharon, and many others after him, simply elected themselves: Instead of putting up with partisan infighting, they modeled brand-new parties in their own image. Take the Lapid family, for example. Tommy Lapid was not a particularly modest man. He loved the spotlight almost as much as he loved Hungarian cuisine and foreign trips. But when he wanted to join politics, he joined a veteran party: Shinui. He did not control the party list, and after two tempestuous terms, he was ousted in a palace coup by a clique of apparatchiks. On his deathbed, he instructed his son Yair, a popular, intelligent, and handsome media personality, to finish the job that he had failed to do and win power. Armed with the example of Sharon and Kadima, it did not even cross the young Lapid's mind to join an existing party. He made his own boutique, tailor-made party: Yesh Atid. Its charter stated that he would serve as its chairman for at least eight years, select its list, and fire its ministers at will. For added safety, and in order to prevent a *putsch*, he appointed to the party's central committee his mother, sister, children, and old school buddies.

One-man parties became the new standard, emptying Israeli politics even more of genuine personalities. Israel was rocked by a particularly alarming explosion of narcissism in the most recent elections. Instead of 120 lawmakers holding a mandate from the public or their movements, the Knesset came to contain only a small coterie of truly influential politicians, each leading a gaggle of flustered shadow politicians totally dependent on their party leader. Instead of a parliament, Israel has an assembly of ego trips disguised as political parties.

No less importantly, the Israeli center did not die with Kadima. At some point in the early 2010s, pundits started calling the left-wing bloc the "left-center." They later flipped the order to "center-left," and eventually party leaders dropped the word "left" altogether. At first, this looked like a simple rebranding exercise in an attempt to shake off the left's bad luck. But, in time, the center bloc started standing on its own two feet, cutting itself from both the right and the left. After General Ariel Sharon's Kadima came the journalist Yair Lapid's Yesh Atid, which offered, at least at first, an alternative to the old left-right divide. Instead of asking where Israel's future borders would run, Lapid asked, "Where's the money?" It was soon joined by Moshe Kahlon's Kulanu party, which focused on social issues and expressed no particular interest in matters of war or peace. Yisrael Beitenu also went from being a sectoral, anti-Arab, right-wing party to a secular, anti-Haredi centrist party.

In every election, the centrist party of the day wins a majority in Modi'in. Like the parties that it supports, this city was also planned from scratch on a piece of paper (incidentally during Sharon's period as housing minister) exactly at a midway point: between right wing, religious Jerusalem and left wing, secular Tel Aviv. The Israeli center is not a place but a state of mind, one located midway between Judaism and democracy, nationalism and liberalism. "Anyone looking for a rule of thumb about the Jewish-democratic balance will not find it in the center's worldview," said Lapid, explaining the rationale.

There are bus stops in the western Negev, near the Gaza Strip, spray-painted with both "Sharon is a murderer" and "Sharon is a traitor." The first is from the 1980s, when the left blamed Sharon for the bloodstained fool's errand of the Lebanon War and the massacre of innocents at Sabra and Shatila; the second is from the new millennium, when the right accused him of surrendering to terror and expelling Jews from their homes. Begin, Netanyahu, Ben-Gurion, and, of course, Rabin were all targets of nasty incitement, but no other Israeli leader has earned such ferocious vitriol from both sides of the political map, each in turn. Ariel Sharon's sons, Gilad and Omri, experienced this jeering twice in their lives: as children, from the left, and as adults, from the right. Nearly every Israeli of a certain age has both loved and hated Sharon, admired him and feared him, voted for him and voted against him.

That's another way to be in the center.

CHAPTER 9

Staying at the Wheel

Olmert's Decision—
Taking the Role of Acting Prime Minister

A SHORT AND STOUT MIDDLE-AGED MAN and a tall and thin fellow in his twenties walked down an empty street in Herzliya at 3:00 a.m. The older man spoke slowly; the younger man walked quickly. From up close, the frustration was unmistakable on the latter's face. Ehud Olmert was only twenty-eight years old, and he had just heard that his dreams of greatness were in mortal peril. The older gentleman, the chairman of the Free Center party, Shmuel Tamir, told him that he had decided to place him in the probably unrealistic fourth place that was reserved for his party in the electoral list of the fresh, united right-wing alliance: the Likud.

Tamir preferred to leapfrog into third place a songwriter who had just won fame as the only Israeli journalist to have landed an interview with John Lennon and Yoko Ono (incredibly, in bed in their Amsterdam hotel room). "You're more political than him; you'll go further in politics," Tamir tried to console Olmert. "What does it matter if it happens in four years?" But Olmert refused to take comfort. "And then something very strange happened," Tamir recounted years later. "We walked down the narrow street near my house, and Olmert walked along the sidewalk, constantly kicking it as he went. We walked, and he kept kicking and kicking. I told him, 'Ehud, chill, it's not the end of the world.'"[1]

Indeed, it was not the end of the world. When the last votes were counted, it turned out that Olmert had been elected to the Knesset, the first of the clique who would later be known as "princes": his father, Mordechai Olmert, had served as a member of the Knesset for Herut just a few years earlier. Revenge was served up cold to Tamir. A few months later, he woke up to discover that his party had been looted: Olmert had defected with a party colleague. Until his dying day, Tamir never exchanged another word with his former aide. As revenge, he told people about a conversation with Olmert a few years earlier: "Your father, may he have good health, is not an easy man," Tamir had complained to him, and Olmert stunned him with his reply: "If you want to get rid of him, I can sort that out within twenty-four hours." He was twenty-four years old at the time. "He gave me the chills," Tamir recalled.[2]

He had no reason to be surprised. At Herut's 1966 party conference seven years earlier, Olmert, fresh out of the army, had launched into a speech unlike anything that anyone had ever heard, demanding that Menachem Begin resign. "You've lost six times—draw your conclusions!" he had hollered.[3] Never had the undisputed leader of this party heard such blunt rhetoric, nor would he again. The audience shouted at this impudent young man to get off the stage. But Begin instructed him to continue and even clapped at the end of his speech. The following day, to everyone's shock, Begin resigned—not just because of the affront, but because he was convinced that such a young man could not have articulated such a radical idea unless he had extremely powerful forces behind him.[4] Only with great difficulty was he convinced to return to his position.

In time, Olmert would learn to appreciate the sweet flavors of slowly ripened fruits: He acquired boundless patience, which allowed him to survive in politics and move up, step by step. Along the way, Israel changed and so did he: He went from being the youngest member of the Knesset to the most veteran; from renting an apartment to owning a multi-million property portfolio; from campaigning against corruption to being convicted of bribery; from being a pro-settlement hawk who spent Shabbat in Ofra and Beit El to a pure-white dove who, as prime minister, proposed evacuating one hundred thousand settlers and almost 100 percent of Judea and Samaria.[5] He jumped between five parties and countless roles, and slowly, very slowly, paved his way to the top. These were different days, when people seemed to have time for everything: Begin could lose eight times, and besides one young man, nobody could send him home. Olmert, still "Ehud from Binyamina," learned this the hard way: He served as a rank-and-file lawmaker for fifteen long years before he was sworn in, at long last, as a minister without a portfolio. This time, he did not kick the sidewalk. Even in 1993, as an already very experienced politician, he did not dare run for the leadership of the Likud, like fellow princes Dan Meridor and Roni Milo. After two decades in politics, he still felt that he was not quite ready to lead the party. Benjamin Netanyahu, a total newbie whose career had peaked at the rank of deputy minister, picked up the abandoned spoils and conquered the party.

For most of Israel's history, until recent decades, most members of the Knesset were not Netanyahus but Olmerts: politicians who climbed their way up patiently but diligently, from local branches to central committee, then to the Knesset, then to government, and from there, they hoped, to the prime minister's office. Most of the people who sat around Israel's wooden government table in Jerusalem reached it after slowly climbing up the stairs, not by rappelling down from the roof in a daring commando raid.

Political life is what happens when you are busy with other things, and Olmert was busy with many things. He perfected juggling two jobs into an artform: In 1980, at the age of thirty-five, he volunteered to go to officers' school. The lawmaker-cadet had to get a pass from his commanders to attend important Knesset votes. Even earlier, he spent some of his time on tasks that were of more financial than national importance. As a member of the Knesset, in an act that now sounds completely fantastical, he opened a law firm called "Olmert & Co.": in the morning, he received and advised clients, and in the evening, he voted in the Knesset. Reports at the time accused him of exploiting his proximity to government ministers to procure benefits for his clients. His office expanded: When he was in the Knesset, his devoted secretary, Shula Zaken, answered the phone and sent case files to his associate, Uri Messer. Years later, they would both star in the investigation that sent Olmert to jail.

This loophole was eventually closed when it was decided to double the salaries of members of the Knesset and, in exchange, ban them from undertaking additional work. But Olmert found another job to fill his afternoons: In 1993, as the Likud rotted away in the opposition, he was elected the mayor of Jerusalem in a stunning victory over the eternal incumbent, Teddy Kollek, leveraging the Haredi vote for the first time in Israel's history to advance a secular candidacy. For five years, he served as both a member of the Knesset and mayor of Jerusalem.

At this stage, after a quarter century in the Knesset, it is safe to assume that Olmert had little interest in submitting parliamentary questions and motions for the agenda. He was simply following, with great diligence, the number one rule that had defined Israeli politics for generations: staying at the wheel. This saying is often attributed to Ariel Sharon, who also explained the logic behind it: "It doesn't matter if you're up or you're down," he explained, "as long as you stay in the game." And Olmert was determined to keep playing the game, even as the political game changed. One day, he hoped, the great political Ferris wheel would stop when he was higher up, somehow, than everyone else.

But the winds of time threatened to throw him down to the ground. At the dawn of the millennium, he was an old and rather tired-looking politician. Ahead of the 2003 elections, Likud members relegated him to the thirty-second place on the party list, as if to hint that he should draw his own conclusions. And in order to survive, somehow, he was dependent on a man with whom his relationship had experienced its ups and downs, just without the ups: Prime Minister Ariel Sharon.

They had first met on the sand dunes of Sinai. Long-forgotten footage from the IDF Spokesperson's Unit shows Ehud Olmert, a young and bespectacled army reporter in the reserves, interviewing the division commander who had just finished saving the country en route to crossing the Suez Canal in the direction of Cairo. They would next cross paths in a different kind of war—one that they would fight against each other. In 1999, they vied for the leadership of the Likud after Netanyahu took "time out," a phrase that we will elaborate on soon. Olmert insinuated that Sharon was too old and sick and that he had hired private investigators against him. More bluntly, he said that "if anyone has symbolized untrustworthiness throughout his career, it's Sharon."[6] But the Likud's voters preferred the aging lion to the veteran fox.

Having just scraped into the new Knesset, Olmert was in no position to bargain for much. The bounty had already been divided between much more powerful politicians. The Foreign Ministry was taken, the Defense Ministry had been sold, and when he discovered that the

Finance Ministry had also been given away—to none other than his archnemesis Benjamin Netanyahu—Olmert quietly started considering whether he should just hop off the wheel if the prime minister did not offer him a suitable ministerial job.

The heavy snowfall allowed Olmert's car to reach the prime minister's office only with great difficulty on the day his fate was sealed. It was just as chilly indoors. Sharon informed Olmert that he would serve as minister of industry, trade, and labor—a middling portfolio that did not satisfy his aspirations. He protested the snub and made one last request, which would change the course of his life and Israel's history: to be acting prime minister.

* * *

Olmert was not the first person to ask to serve as the most senior minister after the prime minister. David Levy beat him to it in the 1980s, demanding from Shamir the title "deputy prime minister." In time, there came to be as many deputy prime ministers as grains of sand on the beach. Eventually, the odd title "vice prime minister" was invented especially for Shimon Peres, conferring on him nothing but dubious honor and the air of a pharaonic court.

But unlike these other pursuits of prestige, "acting prime minister" was not another vapid title to embellish gold-embossed letterheads. It was a lottery ticket, offering its holder a very small chance of winning the jackpot. A recent law called "Basic Law: The Government" stated: "Should the prime minister be temporarily unable to discharge his duties, his place will be filled by the acting prime minister." The prime minister might be incapacitated because of a sudden health event, his murder, or criminal entanglements. Sharon at the time was suspected of bribery in a serious police investigation, the Greek island affair. He was also, as Olmert had observed years earlier, old and overweight—and he had just become the oldest person to become prime minister in Israeli history.

What Olmert was requesting, or rather insisting on, was to build his career prospects on the possibility of a disaster that might strike the man who was supposed to grant his request. This was bold, to the point of real chutzpah. There was a very good reason why, until then, there had only ever been two full-time substitutes: Shamir under Peres and Peres under

Shamir during their rotation government. Nobody ever likes being able to see his successor.

"Will he be prime minister every time I'm at the dentist with a drill in my mouth and can't talk?" Sharon inquired suspiciously in a telephone call in a side room.[7] "No," replied his associate Reuven Rivlin over the phone, "only when you're ill." "I'm never ill," answered Sharon. "I plan on being here till 2017, and then I'll retire to my ranch and you can do whatever you want."

Sharon and Olmert stared each other down from the greatest distance in the world: the three feet between both sides of the prime minister's desk. The place where the buck stops. Sharon knew why Olmert wanted the role, and Olmert knew that he knew. "OK, fine," said Sharon. They shook on it.

From this point on, Olmert was, as Americans say, one heartbeat away from the toughest job in the world. The wheel continued spinning.

* * *

Twice in Israeli history have prime ministers died in office. When Levi Eshkol passed away in 1969, the government chose Yigal Allon to fill his seat for days, until Golda Meir formed a new cabinet. On the night of Yitzhak Rabin's murder in 1995, for an hour and a half, Israel had no prime minister at all. The shell-shocked ministers chose Shimon Peres to fill the role temporarily, until he succeeded in forming a permanent government a few days later.

On neither occasion did the "acting" prime minister have to act for long. The most that Olmert dared to hope for, therefore, was a few days in the role until some more powerful politician, of whom there were many, won the confidence of the Knesset. At this point, he could have hoped at most to become the answer to a trivia question on a daytime quiz show: Who served as prime minister for less than a month, besides Yigal Allon?

From his position, even that would have been an achievement.

* * *

The events that unfolded between that snowy morning in Jerusalem in January 2003 and a cold night on Ariel Sharon's ranch in January 2006 should prove that the cosmos really wanted to see Ehud Olmert serving as prime minister.

On December 18, 2005, after a meeting with Shimon Peres, Sharon's secretary, Marit Danon, noted that the prime minister seemed slightly confused. "I don't feel well," he grudgingly said. He was not the type to complain, and so after a quick consultation, he was whisked away to the hospital. When he was wheeled out of the ambulance, he was groggy and disoriented. The prime minister could not count fingers or tell the time. For sixteen hours, he was incapable of making any decisions.

Nothing like this had ever happened in Israel's history. Prime ministers had been discreetly hospitalized and had suffered various ailments, but Sharon was the first one to mess around with his doctors and make sure that anxious viewers at home were following the joke. Because these were no ordinary times. Just a few weeks earlier, Sharon had deserted the Likud, together with Olmert and another dozen colleagues, to form Kadima: a one-man party that was polling at nearly fifty seats. When he sneezed, the whole party caught pneumonia. If he got a stroke, it might die. He had just celebrated his seventy-eighth birthday; his newborn party, still in an incubator, was yet to reach its first month.

The doctors decided to take no chances. They wanted to catheterize Sharon in order to treat the heart defect that they believed had caused his first stroke. For the three hours when he was completely sedated, Olmert would finally wield the powers of the prime minister. The doctors penciled in January 5, 2006. The day before, the prime minister met his substitute. "You'll transfer the authorities back to me quickly, right?" Sharon joshed with Olmert. "There are lots of things I can do in three hours," replied Olmert. "Just don't touch Marit," said Sharon, and that was that.

Sharon's cardiac catheterization never happened. At 8:00 p.m., Olmert was dining at an Indian restaurant in Jerusalem. Sharon was sitting on a couch at his ranch and instructed IDF Chief of Staff Dan Halutz over the phone to bomb Gaza, in what would be a rousing finale after sixty years of thumping Arab terror organizations with his clunking fist. Halutz hung up with a strange feeling. "Something in his voice sounded off," he surmised. An ambulance was dispatched to Sharon's ranch, and Olmert went home with a single bodyguard. He started shaving, just in case the worst came to pass, exactly as the ambulance pulled into the forecourt of the Hadassah Ein Kerem Hospital in Jerusalem. "Is he still lucid?" the cabinet secretary tried to ascertain from a paramedic over the phone. "Yes, he's lucid," came the reply. "Who'd you just call lucid?" retorted Sharon, outraged at the suggestion. Those were his last words.

When the acting prime minister's phone rang, he still had shaving foam on his face. On the line were Attorney General Meni Mazuz and Cabinet Secretary Israel Maimon. "What I suggest is that we transfer the authorities without a time cap, until the treatment is over," said Maimon. The phone call ended. Olmert looked straight ahead. He could not see anything. The mirror was completely steamed up. "That was very symbolic," he told me later, "because I had no idea what was about to happen."

The acting prime minister was not alone: Nobody else in Israel had realized that the Sharon era was over. I still remember that after a week of live broadcasts, four floors under the prime minister's heavily guarded ward, the hospital's manager stepped out into the forecourt. The microphones all swiveled toward him. "Leave!" he said, shooing us away. "Our medical care doesn't move at the same pace as your bulletins!" Who knows, if not for that remark, the camera crews might have stayed in the hospital forecourt for another eight years, until Sharon finally passed from this world.

If Sharon had recovered quickly, Olmert would have been remembered as the man who led Israel for a single night. Had he died promptly, the government would have convened and almost certainly elected as prime minister Tzipi Livni or Shimon Peres, two much more powerful and popular ministers. Had Sharon not quit the Likud, there would have been primaries to elect his successor. If Israel were not in the middle of an election, Kadima would have had time to groom an heir. But this was the kind of coincidence that happens only once in history. It made Olmert acting prime minister when nobody in his party had the political power or will to launch an ugly succession battle and when the prime minister was still breathing "spontaneously," to use a medical term that Israelis learned together with the word "incapacitation."

For months, Olmert refused to enter the prime minister's bureau. During Sunday morning cabinet meetings, he deliberately left Sharon's padded chair empty and sat in the seat next to it. The 2006 elections were extremely odd: Kadima's election posters bore the image of Sharon, not of its actual candidate. The general feeling was that Sharon would be back soon. One day, Kadima announced that it would gladly place Sharon at the top of its list of candidates, if only he woke up and scrawled his signature on the nomination forms.

But he never did. Olmert limped his way to victory, losing one-third of the seats that Sharon had bequeathed him in the polls. Nevertheless, on a spring day in 2006, the wheel stopped turning with Olmert on top. He became the twelfth prime minister of the State of Israel.

And then Olmert's luck ran out. One month later, a soldier by the name of Gilad Shalit was abducted by Hamas and smuggled into the Gaza Strip. Two months later, the Second Lebanon War erupted while the prime minister was stuck in an interminably long press conference with his Japanese counterpart. Sharp-eyed reporters noticed that while the Japanese premier was talking, his Israeli opposite number was busy texting on the phone at his podium, getting updates about events in the north and praying for the press event to finish already so that he could rush to the IDF's underground command room in Tel Aviv known as "the Pit." During Olmert's premiership, the war was seen as a terrible failure against an inferior terrorist organization, but with the passage of time, its image has improved considerably. Olmert's defense minister was snapped looking at the battlefield through closed binoculars, his justice minister forcibly kissed a female soldier before the security cabinet meeting that launched the war, and his finance minister was caught embezzling money and was sent to prison. He headed one of the most despised governments in Israeli history. One hundred thousand Israelis, from settlers in Samaria to radical left-wing activists, gathered together in Rabin Square to cry "Go home!"

Olmert paid black market interest rates for the massive loan that he had received from the public, depleting all his support. He received no points from the daring bombing raid on Syria's nuclear reactor or the Hollywood-style assassination of Hezbollah's chief of staff in the heart of Damascus. Detectives and police officers started prying into his property portfolio, and private investigators followed him all around the world. There was never a hint of criminal wrongdoing in Olmert's activities as prime minister, but the public came to associate him, perhaps rightfully, with corruption. The public hated his government and had no love for him. During a Kadima party meeting one night, he read out the most surprising speech of his term: "The papers are always reminding the public that I am an unpopular prime minister; our friends in the opposition miss no opportunity to emphasize that I am an unpopular prime minister. I wake up every morning to a deluge of venom." His speech was written for him by a journalist who was actually very popular: his friend Yair Lapid.

The enthusiastic young activist who had once shouted at his party leader to go home was now the prime minister standing on the stage and hearing similar jeering from the crowd. The member of the Knesset who had once urged the police to open corruption investigations was now at the center of eleven police investigations. The man who had managed to become the acting prime minister now felt his own substitute, Tzipi Livni, breathing down his neck. She called on him to resign, spoke out against him, and paved her way to succeed him. And unlike him, she had no intention of standing in front of a mirror and waiting for a phone call. Under pressure from the public, the party, the police, and his colleagues, Olmert was forced to announce his resignation.

He would never return to the Knesset or the government.

* * *

Is it possible to reach power just because you happened to be around, by chance, without planning on it? This question, the legacy of Olmert's term, depends on the answer to the question of whether politics is still what it was during the twelfth prime minister's time. All indications suggest that the answer is no.

How did modern politics even begin? The British House of Commons contains 650 members of Parliament but only enough space on its long green benches for two-thirds of them. It was not land scarcity that made the chamber's architects scrimp on seating but a belief that sounds quite odd nowadays: that being a parliamentarian is not a profession. This was not a snub but a statement of fact. In the past, nobody expected elected officials to show up every day at a place that was not their place of work. They were all politicians, but they were also lawyers, businessmen, and even vicars at the same time. Voters did not blame politicians who did not show up in Parliament but lauded those who found time to do so. That is why governments frequently allow ministers to vote remotely, by phone or by proxy, while—until COVID-19 at least—parliaments required members to be physically present in order to vote. Showing up is a statement of seriousness.

In the first United States Congress in Washington and the First Knesset in Jerusalem, lawmakers were not paid a salary, because they were expected, like Olmert, to earn a living elsewhere and then to hop to committees or the plenary after finishing their honest morning's work. The First Knesset's accountant doled out a few liras here and there to lawmakers who went into overdraft. After all, the Knesset is not a company or a factory: You can get in without an entrance exam and get fired without regard to the quality of your work. Knesset membership is a tool. The state gives you a salary, a driver, a phone, two aides, and a budget for keeping in contact with the voters but not an instruction manual. What are you supposed to do with them? That is up to you.

In time, politics evolved from a hobby into a profession, producing a series of specialized professions. In Israel, there emerged several different types of lawmakers: public speakers, whose power was based on their scathing words in the plenary, in committees, and on TV; legislators, who saw the core of their work as updating the statute book in the spirit of the times; supervisors, who focused on uncompromising criticism of the government when it acted out of stupidity or malice; sectoral leaders, who represented and embodied specific population groups owing to their biography, appearance, or power of expression; and, worst of all, ministers, for whom the Knesset is like the "Jail" space on the Monopoly board—an unfortunate but inevitable stepping stone on the road to the biggest prize of all: ministerial office.

But in recent decades, the combination of Israel's antiquated electoral system and a generation of publicity-seeking celebrity politicians created a new phenomenon: politics without politicians. The voters saw parliamentary experience no longer as an asset but as a liability: Politicians who had entered the Knesset the hard way through their parties were seen as boring apparatchiks, as if some secret sauce in the Knesset canteen had colored them all gray. The public kept voting for outsiders—people who would come from the outside to shake up this despised institution, only for it to chuck them out again after a single term, when they themselves had become the despised establishment.

Lapid set a new record in the 2013 elections: He promised that his new party, Yesh Atid, would not field a single incumbent politician.

According to this logic, in the subsequent elections two years later, he should have fired himself, because now he too was an incumbent politician!

This hunger for change, for something new and refreshing, turned the Knesset into a railway station: In the last decade, there was a turnover of over 40 percent of members of the Knesset in each election. In the 1970s, the average member of the Knesset had two thousand days of experience. In 2015, that number had been cut in half, and by 2021, it had collapsed even further.[8] As in the British Parliament in the nineteenth century, politics stopped being a profession and turned into what young Israeli backpackers look for during long treks in the Far East: a carefree year or two of refreshing experiences. Israeli politics was gradually ruined, emptied out of its organizational memory and veteran parties. The constant turnover also reduced the quality of the incoming star talent. Why should anyone sacrifice a respectable salary and a good reputation just for the title of "former member of the Knesset" a few years later?

Ministers and lawmakers with prime ministerial ambitions no longer wanted to stay at the wheel, like Olmert, but the opposite: to jump off and wait on the sidelines, so that the voters would not have time to sour on them. Moshe Kahlon took time out from the Likud and returned with a bang and ten seats for his new party. Gideon Sa'ar announced a time out in order to "watch my son David starting to walk," and then returned to run for the Likud's leadership. Livni, Barak, and even Netanyahu himself—all left politics and then returned with a new lease on life. The only one who did not benefit from a time out was Olmert himself. Despite wanting and planning a comeback, he never returned.

Even the title of "acting prime minister" is no longer what it used to be. When Benjamin Netanyahu succeeded Olmert as prime minister in 2009, he took this lesson to heart. His most forceful decision was to prevent anyone else's name from appearing in the same sentence as "prime minister," even if separated by the words "deputy," "acting," or "vice." He refused to appoint a substitute in his new government. His aim was twofold: to make "Benjamin Netanyahu" and "prime minister" synonymous in the public's mind and to thwart any subversion within his own party. Even when he flew abroad, he was careful to appoint a different minister as his stand-in each time, preferably someone junior who would not acquire a taste for the job, even for a day or two.

Netanyahu had plenty more plans to transform Israeli politics forever.

CHAPTER 10

Versus the Whole Left

Netanyahu's Decision—
Sticking to the Right at Any Cost

ONE EVENING, IN THE FALL OF 2005, I knocked on the door of an old, one-story house in the square at the end of HaPortsim Street in Jerusalem. I had been sent to persuade a certain author to grant me an interview about his new book. This is usually a simple task, but not when the author is ninety-five-year-old Professor Benzion Netanyahu, father of Benjamin Netanyahu.

The elderly professor shot me an icy look, at once ironic and suspicious. Like his son, he too was distrustful of journalists and did not enjoy being interviewed. He had just finished writing his biography of the late medieval Jewish statesman and philosopher Don Isaac Abarbanel, the most famous of the Jews expelled from Spain. We spoke for a whole hour, after which I invited him to grant me an interview and share a thought or two about current affairs.

I have a hunch that Netanyahu Sr. suspected that I was less interested in the finance minister of late fifteenth-century Portugal than the finance minister of early twenty-first century Israel. At the end of our long conversation, therefore, he straightened up and said firmly: "My friend, you wanted to talk about Don Isaac Abarbanel. But you cannot understand Abarbanel without understanding the Inquisition. Have you read my book on the subject?" I shook my head, and within seconds, a six hundred–page English paperback landed into my open hands: his monumental study of the origins of the Inquisition. "Come back on Saturday night after you've read this, and we'll talk about the possibility of an interview." It was a Thursday evening; what followed was a black Sabbath.

Forty-eight hours later, when I rang the doorbell again like a determined inquisitor, the door opened as little as its chain allowed. "Regarding your request," he said, cutting to the chase, "I have decided not to be interviewed." And he closed the door. I did not get an interview, but I did gain an important insight. Mr. Netanyahu was like his son not just in his aversion to unnecessary interviews: In his tough academic tome, he gave voice to the intransigent and extremely gloomy belief that also characterizes his son's view of the world.

Israeli children who study the Spanish Inquisition at school are told the following story: Once upon a time, there were Jews in a tolerant Muslim Spain. They prospered and gained great wealth, produced great writings and works of art, and enjoyed a golden age. Their hearts were in the east, but they would have stayed at the furthest reaches of the west if the Christians had not come along. The Jews' situation gradually deteriorated over centuries, until they were presented a cruel choice: to convert to Christianity—or to leave Spain. Some of them left Spain and others converted, but many Jews made the most tragic and heart-rending choice of all: They pretended to convert but secretly remained Jewish at home. They were known as "conversos."

The Inquisition was established as a religious police, with a mission to investigate, uncover, torture, and kill those who privately practiced Judaism while pretending to be Christians. Its cruel officials climbed the tower of the tallest church in Seville on the coldest Saturdays to spot the houses without smoke coming out of their chimneys—a telltale sign that their inhabitants were Jews, prohibited by their religion from lighting a fire on the holy day of rest. The accused were tortured, water was poured down their open throats until their bellies burst, they were given three hundred lashes, and some were burned at the stake, crying out the Shema prayer with their dying breaths. After reading accounts of such gruesome executions, it is hard to continue sitting and enjoying one's coffee in Madrid's sunlit Plaza Mayor, where so many Jews were burned alive.

This has been the conventional story about the Inquisition for centuries, but there was one scholar who reached totally different conclusions.

His name was Benzion Netanyahu. In his book, the conversos were not Jews determined to practice their faith and die a martyr's death. On the contrary, they had no problem assimilating into Spanish society, and they certainly had no intention to leave their native land. They did not see Ferdinand and Isabella's edict of expulsion as a threat but as a promise: Instead of living as second-class citizens, practicing a despised religion under restrictions and threat of torture, they might break the glass ceiling as members of the ruling faith. They did not leave Judaism for the sake of appearances, with a heavy heart; conversion came as a relief, and they embraced it wholeheartedly. Netanyahu shone a light on the leading rabbis' hostility toward the conversos and cited Abarbanel's own scathing denunciations of them, treating them as bona fide Christians.

And then, with other historians' jaws still on the floor, Professor Netanyahu flipped the standard theory on its head. The Inquisition did not cause mass conversions to Christianity; these mass conversions caused the Inquisition. It was the success of these "new Christians" that provoked an ugly wave of anti-Semitism against them, because now, freed from restrictions, they were able to claim influential positions in the hallways of power and wealth, completely disproportionate to their modest share of the population. The professor reserved his most lethal critique for Don Isaac Abarbanel himself and other high-ranking Jews, who, in their blindness and complacency, failed to see how their beloved country was turning against them and making them enemies of the nation.

Persecution on the grounds of ethnicity rather than religion, a murderous regime of terror against a minority group, and a Jewish community that wakes up to the dangers far too late—yes, in Professor Netanyahu's eyes, fifteenth-century Spain was twentieth-century Germany. The Inquisition was a prelude to the Holocaust. It certainly did not escape his curious eyes that convicted heretics were forced to wear a sanbenito, a special gown for those condemned to death, which was the same color as the Nazi badge: bright yellow.

One night, three days before the 2009 elections, I was invited again to the house on HaPortsim Street. Netanyahu Jr., worried that Tzipi Livni's Kadima had suddenly closed the gap that he had held over it for the whole campaign, spotted a vulnerability on his right flank and invited me for a one-off joint interview with his father, who was by then aged ninety-nine. "We are not only in existential peril, but in genuine danger of extermination!" declared the professor. "People think that the extermination, meaning the Holocaust, is over. It is not! It continues all the time!" His son nodded next to him and kept silent. The man painted by the media as a professional doom-monger turned out to be the most unabashed optimist in his family.

In the eyes of the Netanyahus, father and son, the Holocaust neither began in 1939 nor ended in 1945. It first emerged with the dawn of history and continued with varying levels of intensity, but it has not stopped for an instant. From time to time, like an active volcano, it erupts: with the banishment of the Jews from England, the expulsion of the Jews from Spain, the Farhud pogrom in Iraq, and the Great Arab Revolt of 1936. The Holocaust is still with us every time a Palestinian terrorist grabs a kitchen knife and sets out to kill a Jew; or when a Syrian officer conspires with a North Korean official at a Swiss hotel about the transfer of nuclear weapons technology; or when deep underground in Qom, in the reactors of Bushehr, centrifuges keep spinning. Netanyahu Sr. believed that Hitler was only the outlier when judged by results, not intentions.

The only thing that stands between the Jews and total annihilation is the IDF and the national instinct for survival, in Professor Netanyahu's analysis. But on the latter front, the professor was particularly confident. "Jews and Israelis also have a blind spot, just like on the eve of the expulsion from Spain, when they sat in their peaceful complacency and could not imagine what a calamity was about to befall them," he had prophesied in the 1990s.

From his father, Benjamin Netanyahu learned not only about the secret of cutting back on interviews but also about messaging. The differences between the two generations were more a matter of packaging than content. "Say something new," he used to urge his aides, "or at least something old dressed up as new." And what his father had written in academic English, he encapsulated in five-second TV soundbites: "The year is 1938 and [Mahmoud] Ahmadinejad is Hitler." In the Netanyahus' eyes, somewhere in the world, the year is always 1938.

The moment that he stepped into the Knesset, aged just thirty-eight, Benjamin Netanyahu shone brilliantly in the skies of Israeli politics:

He sprinkled stardust and prophecies of doom, and somehow, they both worked together. Within five years, he had crushed all the Likud's "princes" and taken control of the right. In his first meeting with the pollster Mina Tzemach, she showed him slides with data about voters who opposed him, along with some recommendations about how to win them over. Netanyahu cut her off impatiently. "There's no point wasting resources on people who disagree with me," he said. "Better to focus on my supporters." And thus, with one simple but revolutionary statement, Netanyahu rebelled against decades of political orthodoxy.

Netanyahu drew his inspiration from the same source as many of his imported ideas: America. This was around the time that the United States saw the launch of a new news network: Fox News. Its founder, Roger Ailes, proposed a revolution: Instead of appealing to all Americans, it would broadcast only to Republicans. Fox would offer them brash, provocative, right-wing, conservative news. America was big enough to make a lot of money from them.

Netanyahu knew Ailes very well. He was about to transform the Likud into the "Fox News Party": a party that would appeal to the right, not the center. But it would take time even for him to act on this principle. Because in the world of the 1990s, the most important voter was someone called the "median voter." Imagine Israel's millions of voters sorting themselves into a very long row, from the northernmost tip all the way to Eilat in the south. Now imagine the voter located perfectly in the middle of the Israeli political spectrum. Let's call him Shabtai.

Nobody in the country is less ideological than Shabtai. He is neither right wing nor left wing, neither Haredi nor secular, neither a socialist nor a capitalist. In the direct prime ministerial elections of 1996, Shabtai was like real estate on Tel Aviv's Rothschild Boulevard: a highly prized asset in the most central location imaginable. In a head-to-head contest between two candidates, whoever won Shabtai's vote would sweep the election. Why? Because if Netanyahu could convince Shabtai that Peres was dangerous for Israel, every other voter to Shabtai's right would automatically fall in line. It would be easier to persuade the voter to Shabtai's right, and the voter to *his* right, and so on, like dominoes falling one by one until the most extreme right-winger at the end.

Campaigns based on attempts to persuade the median voter have several features. First of all, they appeal less to the heart than the head.

Non-ideological voters are less interested in tribal belonging and more in tax plans and detailed manifestos. Second, they are more concerned about the future than the past. Campaigns that target centrist voters will struggle to persuade them to "return home," because these are precisely the voters who enjoy switching parties at every election. It is hard to play on the nostalgia of voters who plumped once for Begin and another time for Peres. These sorts of campaigns are more about promises than memories. And most importantly, they are about persuading voters that a particular leader is more moderate and less extreme than he seems.

In 1996, Netanyahu's slogan included the obviously left-wing term "peace" ("Making a Secure Peace!") while Peres used the right-wing buzzword "strong" ("Israel is Strong with Peres!"). Peres tried to convince voters that he was Netanyahu, and Netanyahu—that he was Peres. "Netanyahu's coronation as the angel of peace has succeeded," blared a Channel 2 headline a month before the elections when it became clear that using "peace" seven times in a single Likud broadcast had narrowed Peres's lead to just three percentage points.

In a world with one message targeted at the public from the same TV screen that everyone is watching at the same time, this strategy was the way to win. For ideologically right-wing voters, veterans of the protests against the Oslo Accords, the campaign caused an outbreak of hives. For three years, they had protested in the streets and been dragged by police officers at junctions, and when there was finally an opportunity at the ballot box to steer the country away from territorial withdrawals, they got white doves of peace on their TV screens and jingles that sounded like they came straight out of Aviv Geffen's songbook. But the campaign was not targeted at those who were already fired up and ready to go but at the swathe of voters in the middle who needed a kick. The ideological right already had some of the highest voter turnout rates in Israeli history. Like always until then, Israel's voter turnout rate was near 80 percent, and it was even higher in Haredi and national-religious areas. At 10:15 p.m., after the exit polls forecasted victory for Peres, the telephone rang at my parents' home in Ofra. On the line was a Haredi relative, who said that he had voted for Netanyahu but told the exit pollsters that he had voted for Peres. My parents hung up. On the screen, the celebrations at Labor HQ were in full swing.

One hour after sunrise the following morning, the president of the United States called the man who was still adjusting to the title of "prime minister–elect." In his southern drawl, Clinton told Netanyahu something supremely undiplomatic: "We tried to fuck you, but you have beaten us." It was an elegant hint at the Democratic administration's overt meddling in the Israeli elections against the Likud's candidate. Like the Israeli public, the people working in the White House had also gone to sleep with Peres and woken up with Netanyahu.

For the first time, the prime minister's office was occupied by someone born after the establishment of the State of Israel, a young man of only forty-seven years, who dyed his hair white in order to look more authoritative. Since then, for nearly thirty years, he has always looked sixty years old. In his first term, he maneuvered, quite clumsily, between his innately right-wing positions and the constraints of a world that still gave peace a chance. He flew to the United States for a summit with Yasser Arafat and gave him Hebron. One day, the Palestinian chairman sent him, through his adviser Ahmad Tibi, a large bouquet of flowers for his birthday. "It's Bibi or Tibi!" roared the Likud's billboards before the election, but afterward, it was both of them together. Two years later, at the Wye River plantation, Netanyahu signed another withdrawal agreement with Arafat.

When Netanyahu returned home, having committed to transfer 13 percent of Judea and Samaria to the Palestinian Authority, his coalition unraveled, and in the streets of Jerusalem, in a hallowed tradition, there appeared images of him wearing a keffiyeh. The prime minister tried to form a unity government: He invited opposition leader Ehud Barak for a conversation in the most discreet place imaginable, the headquarters of Mossad, at an undisclosed location in central Israel. It was no use: Netanyahu had nose-dived off a right-wing tower, but at the bottom, there was no left-wing safety net. He ended up imploding spectacularly, suffering a defeat on a scale that no prime minister had ever seen.

Netanyahu learned a lesson: Never pick a fight with the national-religious right. A few years later, in 2006, he would also learn not to mess with the Haredim and the Likud's own voters. These two angry power bases took revenge on him at the ballot box for his economic policies, which had been essential to saving Israel's economy but slashed the incomes of hundreds of thousands of his voters overnight. Rabbi Ovadia

Yosef refused to meet him for years. When he finally obliged, Netanyahu was smuggled into his home through the bicycle and stroller room in order to avoid igniting the rage of Shas voters who now had a hole in their bank accounts thanks to him. Netanyahu's conclusion from this decade was unequivocal: Don't mess with your base.

In the summer of 1999, after his defeat to Barak, Netanyahu was almost the only person who still bothered to go to work in the morning at the prime minister's office during the final days of his government. Everyone was convinced that Netanyahu, aged only forty-nine, had seen the end of his political career, and that, like a meteor, he too had fizzled out. Everyone, that is, besides Netanyahu himself. Packing his belongings, he was already planning a comeback. The first stage was to found a newspaper. If he returned one day, he told associates, it would be with a media outlet that would give him a tailwind against the hostile, liberal, secular, left-wing media in Tel Aviv that he blamed for his downfall. Eight years later, when he was leader of the opposition, the first edition of *Israel Hayom* went to print, flush with cash and copies of his speeches, and owned by the Jewish billionaire Sheldon Adelson from Nevada.

But until then, Netanyahu's salvation came from another, much younger Jewish billionaire, a Democrat rather than a Republican, who did not support him and who, as far as we know, had never met him before: Mark Zuckerberg. Facebook, the social media network that he created in 2004 as a way to connect students, quickly became the most powerful media outlet in the world, despite not employing a single journalist.

Netanyahu won the lottery without even buying a ticket. Years before he became Israel's ninth prime minister, Netanyahu was already dreaming about toppling the media wall separating him from the voters or finding a way around it. As Israel's ambassador to the United Nations, he had prided himself in 1985 on smashing the liberal media's hegemony in shaping the agenda of decision-makers. "Thanks to newspapers, pamphlets, faxes, and broadcasts, thanks to lobbies and email, which I have recommended using before, I have managed to place our concerns and arguments in the global mindset," he boasted.[1] Nobody else knew what an email was, but Netanyahu could already spot an opportunity to reach influential people directly, without an editor's meddling hand.

Social media allowed Netanyahu, finally, to reach his millions of voters directly without worrying that something would get cut out in editing, without annoying questions, without journalists. At first, even he struggled to adjust to the new reality: After all, Netanyahu was Israel's "Mr. Television," a wizard of camera angles and snappy messages, conscious of the power of one short clip to lift politicians up or destroy them.

One day, in 2008, I sat down with Netanyahu for a regular meeting in the opposition leader's office. "Tell me," he asked his spokesman, Ofir Akunis, pointing at me, "can I trust him?" "Sure," Akunis lied without blinking. Then Netanyahu opened a desk drawer. I was sure that he was about to give me the plans for an attack on Iran. But instead, he picked out a fat cigar, cut it, and lit it, shielded from the TV cameras that would have painted him as a hedonist. At another opportunity, when he spotted camera crews on their way to a government meeting that was about to impose painful cuts, he made a snap decision to pop a burning cigar in his pocket. "Mr. Netanyahu," came a radio reporter's unforgettable cry, "you seem to be on fire!" His suit was toast, but his career survived.

But the era of television as the undisputed king of media was about to end. In the 2013 elections, while Netanyahu still had a boring Facebook page that pumped out press statements to purchased followers from Indonesia, his young challengers, Naftali Bennett and Yair Lapid, reached impressive heights thanks to their cutting-edge messaging on Facebook. Netanyahu was still deeply invested in traditional media: One day, in a background conversation with Channel 2 reporters, he blasted his two senior coalition partners. "I don't like the country being run with Facebook statuses," he complained. On my way home, I remembered that similar things had been said about him, twenty years earlier. His rival, Shimon Peres, had said mockingly that "national policy isn't decided in short sentences on TV." The implication was that Netanyahu was passé. He was an analog man in a digital age. The countdown to his end had begun.

But then Netanyahu seized the advantages of this new technological medium. There is something odd about the fact that Israel's greatest social media whiz is in his seventies, has never performed a Google search or owned a smartphone, and still writes his speeches with felt-tip pens on pieces of card. In 2007, as the opposition leader, when his then-bureau chief, Naftali Bennett, brought to his office the first iPhone,

Netanyahu grilled him about its features but preferred not to use one, fearing eavesdropping. In his office at the prime minister's residence, he had a landline phone, over twenty years old, of the sort that is no longer manufactured, all because of his fears about eavesdropping.

Israel's ninth prime minister understood that the medium is the message—digging tunnels beneath the feet of the hostile established media. He hired genius social media advisers, brought himself down to ground level, and escalated his rhetoric. In the 2015 elections, he won a victory that no pollster or journalist had forecasted, thanks to his direct contact with the voters. What Facebook did not do, the eighteen million text messages that he sent straight to the back pockets of his voters' jeans certainly did. Ever since, he has physically blocked every initiative for internet regulation, from bills to censor online pornography to the oversight of extremist content or bans on hate speech. In his view, any regulation is a slippery slope that will eventually censor the right online.

Facebook's algorithm is not particularly tolerant of official, polished messages filmed behind mahogany desks. But it really does love extreme, surprising, buttoned-down messaging. Gradually, the "Mr. Prime Minister" of the TV studios evolved into the "Bibi" of the social networks. Fending off social media outrage in early 2016, Netanyahu flip-flopped in just two days from condemning the soldier who shot a wounded terrorist in Hebron to phoning his father in solidarity. The same week, with impeccably symbolic timing, Donald Trump and his rage-filled Twitter account conquered the Republican Party. "Be like Trump," the prime minister urged his aides. They followed his word. And then some.

Because what does Facebook's algorithm do? Its main objective is not to foster open dialogue or an exchange of views but to encourage users to spend more and more time on their feed. The way to do so is to avoid annoying them with contrary opinions. People who post about veganism quickly stop seeing photos of juicy steaks at Independence Day barbecues, avowed secularists do not see posts wishing them a "Kosher Passover," and right-wingers simply do not see left-wingers. Instead of making information accessible and broadening people's horizons, the internet has turned us all into your angry uncle sitting on his sofa in an undershirt and shouting obscenities at his television set. We have all become more confident in our beliefs, whatever they are.

Facebook and Netanyahu's base merged to strengthen his conviction from the 1990s: There is no point trying to persuade people, only to rally them to action. After all, what happened during the decades in which politicians appealed to the center? They took ideological voters for granted, assuming that they would vote for them anyway, for fear of the rival camp seizing power. But in time, it turned out that strategies that worked on the drawing board did not work in reality. In the United States, strategists color the map in Republican red and Democratic blue. But over time, as politicians appealed to the center, red states became pink and blue states became lighter blue, until finally, like in flavored water, it was only possible to detect the faintest shades of color.

The result was public despair with politics. For most of Israel's history, voter turnout was around 80 percent, which is really closer to 100 percent when you factor people who are ill or living abroad or just happen to be on vacation. But if the right flirts with the left and the left dresses up as the right, ideological voters no longer see a difference between the parties, at least not one that should keep them awake at night and make them waste their day off on something as dull as voting (in Israel, Election Day is a national holiday). Turnout plummeted to an all-time low. To borrow taxi drivers' five favorite words: "Politicians are all the same." Sometimes they change the ending to something less savory.

It has been ages since I last heard this from a taxi driver. Thanks to Facebook, voters doubled down on their opinions, and it became harder to shift votes between blocs. In the elections that Netanyahu has contested since 2009, very few voters wavered between the Likud and parties challenging it for power, whether it was Herzog's Zionist Union, Gantz's Blue and White, or Lapid's Yesh Atid. All the movement was within the defined blocs.

It therefore became clear that the same resources that could be used to persuade one person from the other side to switch to voting for Netanyahu could be used instead to get four or five sleepy and disgruntled right-wingers to go out to vote. And thus, from openly supporting the two-state solution, Netanyahu embraced annexation; from speeches supporting the Supreme Court, he pivoted to fierce attacks on it; from statesmanlike announcements, he switched to clips with pickle jars as a jibe against his "sour" left-wing opponents. Netanyahu 1.0, the television celebrity who signed agreements with Arafat, gave way to Netanyahu 2.0, the social media wizard who favored annexing settlements.

Ayelet Shaked, a well-known right-wing politician, was the first to experience this in the flesh. When she was appointed Netanyahu's bureau chief, during his period in opposition to Olmert's government, she entered the role with an organized handover. Netanyahu, her predecessor explained, was willing to speak to anyone from Israel and around the world. His door was open to everyone. But there were two exceptions, the previous bureau chief added, wagging her finger: two people who would never set foot in his office, whose faxes must be sent to the shredder, and who must be hung up on if they call—Avigdor Lieberman and the journalist Ben Caspit. When Ayelet Shaked joined politics, she discovered that a third name had been added to the list: hers.

Contrary to speculation and gossip, the reason that Netanyahu has spent the past decade fighting mainly against Ayelet Shaked and her party's leader, Naftali Bennett, has nothing to do with a personal obsession, accusations about leaks, or any other soap opera-style allegations. Because if Netanyahu were to blacklist everyone who has ever said something bad about him or briefed against him, there would be nobody in his coalition but his late dog, Kaya. The oxygen at these stratospheric heights of politics is too thin to waste on settling scores. Prime ministers, at least the most successful ones, live not in the past but completely in the present. If that is what it takes, they will do business with people who have tried to eliminate them politically, slandered their families, and hired private investigators against them.

Reuven Rivlin once gibed that in Africa, there was once born an elephant as thick-skinned as Netanyahu. And since most of Israel's prime ministers have such thick skin, one could say, who needs a backbone? The real reason for Netanyahu's war on Bennett and Shaked was that he had internalized the lessons of the implosion of his first term: Netanyahu vowed that he would never again let himself get outflanked on the right. That was why he adopted each and every one of Bennett and Shaked's positions, as right wing as they were. He has spent most of the past decade driving recklessly next to Bennett and Shaked's car, pressing against it on the right, and pushing even further, until their car flipped over the railings and plummeted beneath the electoral threshold. After that, they lurched left under the cover of the coronavirus pandemic.

Netanyahu's efforts to protect the right-wing bloc were a sign that he was about to act differently from all his predecessors. Seven men and one woman had served as prime minister before him, and each had headed the largest party in the Knesset. When Netanyahu was first elected, in 1996, his party was only the second largest, after the Labor Party. This was seen as an outlier, but it happened to him again in 2009: Once again, the Likud finished second, with one seat fewer than Tzipi Livni. There were parties at Kadima HQ all night long, but in the morning, Netanyahu received the mandate to form a government. In 2013, the Likud controlled fewer seats than Yesh Atid, but it was Yair Lapid who addressed Netanyahu as "Mr. Prime Minister," not vice versa. In the first of the two rounds of elections in 2019, Netanyahu celebrated a "stunning victory" despite reaching a tie with Benny Gantz's Blue and White party.

From the moment he had entered politics, Netanyahu decided on a new strategy. In basketball terms, he played the whole court. Instead of looking after his party, he looked after the whole right-wing bloc. He fully understood the implications of the Israeli electoral system: Whoever wins the support of sixty-one members of the Knesset, whatever parties they may come from, will form a government. In economics, this is called "pyramidal ownership": A businessman with a modest fortune of a few tens of millions of dollars can own the controlling share of a large company, which controls another company, which controls yet another—and suddenly he is sitting on top of a billion-dollar empire.

Netanyahu's long premiership was based on a similar principle. In the Likud, he has always had his fair share of opponents: David Levy once called himself an "anti-Bibiotic," Sharon called him names that he usually reserved only for Yasser Arafat, and the whole party top brass has always bad-mouthed him behind closed doors. But they have never managed to join forces and send him home.

The Likud, for most of the Netanyahu years, has not even won half of the right-wing electorate. Most right-wing votes went to other sectoral parties. But the Haredim did not want Lieberman as prime minister, Lieberman would not support Kahlon, Kahlon could not stand Bennett—and they all fell under the Likud's wings.

In fact, the right has not always won a majority of the electorate, either. In the 1996 elections, it won less than half of the votes, and of course, the same happened in the 2019–2021 elections. So how did Netanyahu cling onto power for so long? Because in Israel's electoral system, the only number that guarantees victory is sixty-one: a simple majority in the Knesset. But what result can force a candidate to deliver a concession speech? Indeed, Netanyahu's bloc shrank in 2019 to fifty-five seats, and he still went to sleep every night at the residence on Balfour Street and woke up there the next morning. This was possible because the Arab parties had always sat out the coalition-building game. In short: The right's fifty-something seats were enough for a tie, and since they were already in power, that was as good as victory.

The fate of the thirtieth or fortieth-placed candidate on the Likud list has therefore never particularly troubled Netanyahu. Perhaps he was even secretly happy when they did not make the cut. He remembered well that his first government was dismantled by anonymous backbenchers in his own party. Fewer seats for the Likud also meant fewer senior portfolios for his party, and this did not cause him anguish, either: In his first term, Netanyahu saved the top three jobs—foreign affairs, finance, and defense—for his own party, only for these three ministers (David Levy, Yitzhak Mordechai, and Dan Meridor) to resign from his government and his party and then topple him from power.

Netanyahu set about fortifying his bloc, not his party. This was a twenty-year effort, at the end of which he became the undisputed leader not only of the Likud but also of the Haredim, the religious Zionists, and voters in Israel's periphery. A Haredi journalist once told me that he could write almost anything about the greatest rabbis in the land, "but just touch the last hair on Bibi's head, and you'll get attacked for it in the streets and on Shabbat at synagogue." But this was true not just in the Haredi city of Bnei Brak, but also in the national-religious towns of Givat Shmuel and Efrat. From his first moment in politics, Netanyahu worked to cultivate the religious Zionist vote. The religious Zionists, who had been used to sitting in the kosher food supervisors' carriage in the train of Israeli politics, were suddenly upgraded to the driver's compartment. "I only work with people who wear a kippah, or used to wear a kippah, or will wear a kippah," Netanyahu has often joked at farewell events for retiring staff.[2] For the first time, the first floor of the prime minister's office started hosting afternoon prayer services.

Netanyahu saw the religious Zionists as his frontline defenders, the ultimate insurance policy against left-wing opinions and overly warm relations with journalists. Perhaps it helped that his wife, Sara, had grown up in a national-religious family. It is easy to understand, therefore, why it came as such a massive blow when four religious Zionists played a major role in the indictments against him: the attorney general he had appointed; the police chief he had promoted; and two of his most loyal and discrete aides, who turned state's witnesses against him—Ari Harow and Shlomo Filber.

Netanyahu's coalition with the religious Zionist community was one of shared but not identical interests, a matter of ideological compatibility, not full confluence. Netanyahu is an old-fashioned right-winger, who believes in the power of words, speeches, and international treaties, while the ideological arm of the religious Zionist community, Gush Emunim, was based on the old Mapai belief in facts on the ground. Netanyahu is a big believer in the power of diverse cities, while most of the ideological settlers live in small, homogeneous villages.

Like the religious Zionist community, Netanyahu also looks at Israel from a historical lens spanning millennia, but unlike them, he is painfully anti-messianic. He sees eye-to-eye with the religious Zionists about the dangers of the Palestinian national movement but is appalled by their vision of annexation, which includes the whole of Judea and Samaria; he completely shares their nationalist values but utterly disputes the religious values that they represent. One day, as the leader of the opposition in 2007, Netanyahu visited Judea and Samaria. "See these hills?" he told his bureau chief, Naftali Bennett, as his retinue observed the Tel Aviv skyline from a lookout point. "From here, you could fire rockets straight at Ben Gurion Airport." Bennett, a kippah on his head, replied: "See these hills? This is where our forefather Abraham walked."

The political implication of this dispute was that Netanyahu regarded the religious Zionists as menial workers fit for his government's drudgework: They would serve as loyal aides who would implement his vision, not as partners with views of their own; they would work in his shadow, not by his side; beneath him, not opposite him; beyond closed doors, not in the cabinet room.

For Netanyahu, there are good religious Zionists and bad religious Zionists. The good ones are discreet, deferential, and docile. The bad ones are ambitious and have dreams of grandeur. Netanyahu eagerly quotes his father's lethal four-word put-down of religious Zionists: "Big heart, small brain."

Absurdly, Netanyahu's Jewish coalition saw him not as the Messiah, as his naysayers claimed they did, but as Jesus Christ, whose personal agony brought atonement for his believers' sins. In their view, when he was defamed, it was a way to get at his apostles. When he was persecuted, it was because of his followers. When he was investigated, it was because of his principles.

And what was true of Mr. Netanyahu was also true of Mrs. Netanyahu. One day, after another maid quit the residence in tears, I mustered the courage to ask Netanyahu whether his wife, Sara, was an electoral liability. "Liability?" he scoffed. "She's worth two seats!" He might be right: His supporters see Sara as more Bibi than Bibi himself, suffering for the sake of the man who suffers for them. This might be the reason for an extraordinary political fact about Netanyahu: Like his chum across the sea, Donald Trump, his marital infidelity did not destroy his career, as it would have done for other politicians, and in fact, it did not damage him at all. Netanyahu did the physical equivalent of abolishing the laws of gravity. Thousands of miles above Israel and the United States floated two politicians who were not considered personally trustworthy but who did not pay for this untrustworthiness in public opinion.

Americans are diehard statistics fans. In the 2016 elections, it turned out that 78 percent of candidate Trump's statements were utter lies, an all-time high since records began. By the time he left office, *The Washington Post* had counted over twenty thousand presidential fibs. Nevertheless, if the COVID-19 pandemic had not happened, Trump would have easily sailed toward a second term.

One day, during the recording of our regular Friday night news show, the political analyst Amnon Abramovich spelled out the familiar list of Netanyahu's left-wing credentials: implementing the deal to give Hebron to the Palestinians, signing the Wye River Memorandum, voting for the Gaza disengagement, and backing the two-state solution. After the recording ended, I told my left-wing colleague, "Sounds like you've got the dream candidate, with an impeccably left-wing record. Why don't you vote for him?"

"Because I don't believe him," Amnon replied and then asked me: "But why don't you denounce him, as someone on the right?"

"Quite simple," I replied. "Because I don't believe him, either."

Netanyahu's voters believe that he is engaged in manipulation, but not against them—instead against annoying US administrations, a hypocritical international community, hostile interviewers, and left-wing challengers. They agree with what Winston Churchill said during the Second World War: "In wartime, truth is so precious that she should always be attended by a bodyguard of lies."

When it came to light that Ehud Olmert had been receiving envelopes full of cash from an American benefactor, the prime minister's career was quickly destroyed. But when his successor became implicated in three separate investigations into bribery, fraud, and breach of trust, support for him only grew. He was sitting in a meeting with Donald Trump when his media adviser turned state's witness. One year later, he announced Trump's peace plan in Washington just as severe charges were filed against him in a Jerusalem court. Just a few weeks later, he led his party to its most powerful performance in a generation, bringing over one million voters to the ballot boxes. Did they not care about corruption? Of course they did. But they were convinced by his arguments that he was being investigated and charged not because of the corruption of the accused but because of the political biases of his accusers.

The deeper undercurrents tell an even bigger story. The investigations, which grew into criminal charges and a trial in Jerusalem, amplified Netanyahu and his supporters' claim against Israel's elites: the same controversial story about the few against the many. The "few" in this case controlled the media, the universities, the military, and the justice system—and the "many" were the millions of voters. Who calls the shots in the country? The government, elected by the people, or the fifteen justices of the Supreme Court? Ministers or bureaucrats? Politicians or their legal advisers? The people in the news or the ones who are supposed to report it?

When the argument over the Palestinian issue gradually dissipated, therefore, Israel's two political camps realigned themselves around a new question: What is the core principle of democracy—majority rule or so-called substantive democracy? One side believes that other than in extreme exceptions—extreme like Nazi Germany—the majority should get to decide. The other side believes that the majority's power should be restricted because it tends to exploit it. Therefore, one side believes that a prime minister may stay in office until a final conviction, while the other side believes that the prime minister should recuse themselves as early as the investigation stage. One side believes that ministers should be able to govern, shrinking their advisers back to their natural size, while the other supports giving more power to ministers' legal advisers. One side dismisses civil servants as "functionaries"; the other side hails them as "gatekeepers." Here too, Benjamin Netanyahu was a symbol of a wider struggle: Before he entered office, no Israeli prime minister was investigated by the police, although none of them were saints. Since Netanyahu's first term, every prime minister has been investigated, although not all of them were corrupt. The left argued that this was a vital process to clean up politics; the right argued that extreme judicial-ization had made politics itself a criminal offense.

This battle has gradually pushed every other issue off the agenda, becoming the main bone of contention between the Israeli right and left. This—not conflict or economics—is the fault line. Netanyahu, who for most of his time in power protected the justice system and blocked legislation that would have affected it, suddenly changed his tune and positioned himself at the head of this offensive. The photograph of him standing at the Jerusalem District Court on the day when his indictment was filed, surrounded by senior Likud politicians wearing masks, will not be forgotten for many years. Netanyahu thus squeezed his crimi-nal lemon into political lemonade. In his second decade with his finger on the red button, Benjamin Netanyahu's supporters still saw him as a persecuted underdog, needing backup against his enemies from the old elites.

Like Trump, Netanyahu also thereby refuted the fashionable theory of identity politics, namely, the belief that the political arena is a boxing ring where groups clash on the basis of color, ethnicity, and sex, and the derivative theory that it is more natural for people to support politicians who share their skin color, religion, or gender. Benjamin Netanyahu does not wear a kippah, and yet he is the most popular politician among religious Zionists; he could not be more different from the Haredim, and yet he is the most revered figure in the Knesset among the Haredim—practically a point of consensus in a community riven with arguments and fissures; he is the son of a European Jewish family, who enjoys extraordinary levels of support among second-generation immigrants from North Africa; he is a millionaire, living in the upmarket neighborhood of Rehavia, and the knight in shining armor of Israel's poor and dispossessed.

The obsession in counting women, kippahs, and faces of color did not damage Netanyahu, just as it did no harm to Trump. The forty-fifth president of the United States is the richest man to have ever lived in the White House. He was a good friend of the Clintons, whom he even invited as personal guests to his wedding with Melania. Gold is the dominant theme in the design of his palatial penthouse on the eighty-ninth floor of Trump Tower, and, as I can personally attest, even the toilets are made of gold. Donald Trump was the first person in history to receive an airplane from work and to see it as a downgrade in his conditions, compared to his much more luxurious private jet. Yet, when he ran against Hillary Clinton in 2016, *she* was seen as the disconnected candidate of the superrich, while he was seen as the envoy of the poor. Trump won the votes of millions of blue-collar Americans, including many women who were not particularly impressed by claims of chauvinism and misogyny on his part.

Similarly, Netanyahu—like Begin before him—did not lose out on the votes of Israel's cultural and social periphery on account of his personal identity. This American-style leader, who was initially seen as somewhat artificial, cold, and uninspiring, quickly became a focal point of love and hatred at levels that Israel had never seen since Begin and Ben-Gurion, if at all. Amos Oz, the brilliant novelist celebrated for his wit and wholesomeness, once told a Meretz conference that in his childhood, his parents used to take him for afternoon tea at synagogue on Shabbat. "Young Bibi, aged three, had a habit of crawling under the table and untying the guests' shoelaces. Once, I had enough of this and gave him a kick. I am still consumed by feelings of guilt: Either I kicked him too hard, and this is all my fault, or I didn't kick him hard enough, and so this is still all my fault." His cultured audience burst into laughter.[3]

This is a good place for a discussion about chickens and eggs: Does the left despise Netanyahu because he lurched right? Or did Netanyahu lurch right for want of a choice, because the left despised him? It is probably impossible to give an answer from the distance of a mere quarter century, but we can try. Perhaps it was the ferocity of the campaign against the Oslo Accords, Rabin's murder, his victory over Peres half a year after the assassination, or all of these together. But the fact is that at the dawn of his political career, Netanyahu ran into the enmity of the media and the elites, and he decided back then to place all his eggs, if we are already talking about chickens, in one right-wing basket.

Without deciding which came first, the result was that Netanyahu became the most despised and revered leader that Israel has ever known. Right-wing stalwarts such as Benny Begin and Gideon Sa'ar were denounced and smeared as leftists just for daring to come out against the Likud's leader. On the other hand, anyone who dared to collaborate with Netanyahu, however fleetingly, was politically eviscerated in the rival camp. Benny Gantz was treated as the Messiah by the center-left and scored electoral achievements that nobody had won since Rabin, but none of this helped him the day he decided, in the middle of a once-in-a-century pandemic, to enter a unity government. The statistics are brutal: Every politician from the rival camp who entered a Netanyahu-led government was swiftly obliterated by the court of public opinion.

Israeli officials used to warn during the Second Intifada that if the conflict with the Palestinians were not resolved, it would evolve from a bitter national struggle into an unsolvable religious war. Perhaps what happened was that, in front of our eyes, the fierce but conventional political dispute over Netanyahu's suitability for the premiership morphed into a religious war.

Once, not so long ago, all politicians wanted was a share of power. As old-fashioned and dogmatic as it sounds, their aim in elections was to win. Faced with the choice of being wiped out or entering the government, most politicians therefore preferred to enter the government; and parties, as simplistic as it sounds, chose leaders who were best placed to win as many votes as possible at the ballot box. By the third decade of the twenty-first century, this was no longer the case. Israeli politics had become a war between two religions: "Only Bibi" and "Anyone but Bibi."

The most sacred ritual in the Only Bibi religion is to vote for Netanyahu, even if hundreds of polls and four consecutive elections show that doing so will not lead to the establishment of a government. If Only Bibi, the cult of Benjamin Netanyahu, is a religion, then can we understand why its adherents kept voting to disperse the Knesset when Netanyahu was unable to form a government? This means that, faced with a choice between their leader and a right-wing government formed by someone other than Netanyahu, their leader came out on top. The biggest sin in the "Bibista religion" is to deny the truth of the divine connection between Netanyahu and the prime minister's office.

No less zealous, if not more so, are the high priests of the Church of Anyone but Bibi. While whispered hints of heresy can sometimes be heard on the right, no such thing exists in the center and on the left. Their leading church, with over one million devotees, was founded quite recently as the result of religious reform: It abandoned the old beliefs in the two-state solution and secular reforms in favor of just one mission—sending Netanyahu home. It thus managed to bring under its wings Israelis of different faiths, from hardline adherents of annexation to the white doves of territorial withdrawals. When Amir Peretz was asked to swear that he would not join Netanyahu's government, he did so with an act that monks used to perform when making a vow to God: He shaved off his mustache in the presence of witnesses.

On the day when the Twenty-First Knesset was sworn in, in April 2019, Netanyahu was convinced that he had finally won the battle against his rivals. The right had won a clear majority, and he was about to pass a series of laws that would block the indictments against him. When he entered the Knesset for the festive ceremony, a white plastic rosette was pinned to his lapel, for the last time, he was sure, in the next four years. But something interrupted his bliss: A terrifying swarm of millions of black flying beetles suddenly descended on Jerusalem at the exact time that the new members of the Knesset took their oaths.

As in a Hitchcock horror movie, masses of beetles invaded every corner of the Knesset building, from the salad counter in the canteen to the prime minister's suite. Something momentous was about to happen. Also as in a Hitchcock movie, this foreshadowed the nightmare that was about to plague Netanyahu—and Israel—over the next few years. The country wanted stability? It got chaos. Lieberman bolted from Netanyahu's coalition, the new Knesset was dissolved the same month, and after that, Netanyahu failed time and again to build a stable government and enjoy a Knesset majority.

The hatred and love for Netanyahu, which paralyzed Israeli politics and propelled it into a nightmare sequence of elections, showed just how far cause and effect had been reversed: With all due respect to Netanyahu's personality, his opponents wanted to get rid of him first and foremost because his government was steering the ship of state into what they saw as dangerous waters, giving immense influence to the Haredim and the settlers and torpedoing a political solution to the conflict with the Palestinians based on a territorial division along the 1967 lines. But at the moment of truth, when they had a chance, Netanyahu's opponents offered the Haredim everything and were ready to crown any other right-winger, no matter how radical, just to evict the Netanyahu family from the residence on Balfour Street. And although the charges against Netanyahu are as severe as white-collar charges get, this is not the core reason for the resistance to Netanyahu. After all, he was despised even before the police started investigating him, and at one point, his critics were open to him receiving a pardon, just as long as he went away. A few years earlier, the same people had tried to mollycoddle Ariel Sharon when he was accused of corruption and had urged Ehud Olmert to run for prime minister even after he was convicted on four counts of fraud and breach of trust.

By the same token, over the past few years, the Israeli right has agreed to massive concessions on its core beliefs just in order to strengthen Netanyahu's rule. The Justice Ministry was given to an avid supporter of judicial activism, the Economy Ministry was handed to a socialist, the annexation plan was shredded, and the clear right-wing majority that had taken hold in the Knesset was wasted time and again. Even the idea of forming a "right-wing" government propped up by anti-Zionist Arab lawmakers, something that was previously inconceivable, was at one point floated as a serious option.

Together, Israel's two rival camps sacrificed what was dearest to them—the stability of the State of Israel—in order to keep throwing the dice, producing an endless cycle of elections that each ended, again, with results that offered escape from paralysis, political stability, or a functioning government. The right legitimized the far-right Kahanists and anti-Arab racism, and the left sold its soul to anti-Zionist parties, some of whose members support terrorism. Future historians who examine Benjamin Netanyahu's last years in power will summarize them thus: Millions of good Israelis discarded almost all of their principles because of their fierce attitudes toward one man, and they did so, absurdly, in the name of a war for those exact same values. When Israelis look back at this period in the future, they will not believe how their opinions about Netanyahu led them to support things that they considered totally abhorrent.

It is doubtful whether any Israeli prime minister, even in fifty years, will ever overtake Netanyahu's record time in power. Babies born when Netanyahu was first elected prime minister in 1996 are now parents. High school students have not yet realized that "prime minister" and "Benjamin Netanyahu" are not synonyms. The man who pitched himself when he first ran for office as a young alternative to a tired leadership then ran, a quarter of a century later, on a ticket of experienced leadership, warning of the dangers of gambling on neophytes.

What will happen in the post-Netanyahu era? His opponents are sure that he is the main obstacle to the historic triumph of the right. After all, the large majority of Israelis no longer believe in the old fantasies about peace. And still, Netanyahu kept struggling to form a stable government. When thirty years' worth of personal hatreds and bad blood eventually subside, the thinking goes, a new right-wing leadership will come along and cruise toward victory.

There is also another possibility: Someone might step into Netanyahu's shoes when there are no longer shoes to fill. On the face of it, this is a paradox. We have already seen that the Likud survived Begin, and even thrived, defying gloomy forecasts. Labor collapsed after the public soured of its two flagship causes: peace and socialism. But the same public warmly embraced the Likud's positions in two main fields: the free market and skepticism about the notion of land for peace.

The issue is that sometimes political parties collapse when they succeed, not just when they fail. Nowadays, almost no party offers an ideological alternative to the Likud, but as with cell phones, most people do not mind having an imitation instead of the real thing. This is definitely true when the alternative to Netanyahu is a much less charismatic leader. After decades of defections, the Likud now looks like *Fifty Shades of Grey*. Just as more attractive alternatives to Labor emerged on the center-left, the same could happen on the center-right.

How will politics remember Benjamin Netanyahu? As the man who resurrected the Israeli right or the one who liquidated it? As the man who led Israel to new heights of international diplomacy or as someone whose trial changed the country forever? Will he be remembered for shaking hands on the White House lawn or for standing when the usher said, "Please rise"? As a historian's son, the man who held office for longer than anyone else in Israel knows that only history will judge.

CHAPTER 11

The Last Exit

Bennett's Decision—
Breaking All the Rules

THE NEEDLE JERKED ANGRILY across the white paper; one end rolled up in a scroll. It was connected with a long wire to a lie detector. And this lie detector was connected to an anxious young man, aged thirty-seven, called Naftali Bennett. His professional career, he knew, depended on the polygraph answers to a very important question. Bennett wanted to be the director general of a new ministry in a government set to be formed in the next few days in the spring of 2009. But the prime minister-designate had vetoed him, and everyone knew why.

"Did you ever leak any secret documents from Benjamin Netanyahu's office to journalists?" asked the polygraph examiner.

"No," replied Bennett.

"Thank you," said the examiner. "I'll get back to you with answers."

An hour later, the fax machine beeped in the incoming prime minister's office: The test showed that Bennett was not responsible for the embarrassing reports about the Netanyahu couple's wasteful foreign trips and free perks, which had tantalized the Israeli media one year earlier, mortifying the Likud chairman. But it was no use. Not even the lie detector could convince Netanyahu that Bennett had not lied. His path to a position of influence was blocked.

Instead of proving his honesty to Netanyahu, Bennett thought to himself, he would bring Netanyahu to heel. And if Netanyahu were unwilling to advance his career out of the goodness of his heart, then he, Bennett, would promote himself against the prime minister's wishes. He would do it even if he had to go against a leader he admired, after whose late brother, the war hero Yoni Netanyahu, he had named his eldest son. He would inherit his seat one day, with or without his agreement.

From the outset, it was clear why the opposition leader picked Bennett as his bureau chief immediately after the Second Lebanon War. He was religious, a veteran of the elite Sayeret Matkal commando unit, a fluent English speaker, and a high-tech millionaire—in short, the kind of human material that Netanyahu greatly valued. They had both experienced the frustration, futility, and lack of leadership of that war in 2006: Netanyahu, as the opposition leader, in his regular briefings with Prime Minister Olmert and Bennett, as a reserves officer in the Lebanese village of Qouzah, fruitlessly pursuing Hezbollah rocket launchers.

By the end, it also became clear why they had parted ways so quickly: Bennett was no ordinary religious Zionist. At the age of eighteen, he was the only member of his high school yeshiva class to enlist straight into the army, without first going to higher religious studies. He had removed his kippah at officers' school, only to put it back on after the assassination of Rabin. In his high-tech business, he worked alongside left-wing partners, and he built a family with a secular woman, Gilat. His father, Jim, was arrested twice in his life in a political context on both sides of the ocean: once in the 1960s, when he staged a sit-in in the lobby of a San Francisco hotel that refused to employ black people, and the second time in the 1990s at a protest against the Oslo Accords in Israel.

A well-known venture capitalist told me once that there are no religious Zionists in his profession because they are too risk averse. Their whole lives they are taught never to go "all in" but always to be a bit of everything: to be the hyphen connecting religiosity and Zionism, Judaism and democracy, religion and state. But Israel's first religious Zionist prime minister has swung from risk to risk with panache: from serially eliminating terrorists in the elite Maglan IDF unit to making exit after exit in the cash-rich New York of the early millennium.

The religious Zionist community, a former minister once observed, suffers from a combination of two personality disorders: an inferiority complex and delusions of grandeur. Bennett has never suffered from problems of the first kind. Netanyahu promptly fired him after whiffing a scent he knew all too well: the smell of almost insatiable ambition. In their conversations over the years, all in English of course, they argued about Julius Caesar's Gallic Wars, Ulysses Grant's memoirs, and what exactly Milton Friedman got wrong after all. But most of the time, Netanyahu suspected that his former aide was vying to succeed him. It would be hard to say that his suspicions were misplaced.

Bennett's road back into politics, this time not as somebody's aide but as a figure in his own right, also involved a series of start-ups. He was a flighty and jumpy kind of politician: After a brief term as the head of the settlers' council, which gave him a certain degree of exposure, he showed up one day at the office of the strategic consultant Moshe Klughaft in order to plan the rest of his political career. On his way, when he stopped at a cash machine, someone approached him and said, "Hey, I know you!" Bennett responded with a bashful but gratified look. "You're our computer technician, right?" asked the man. It was the summer of 2011. Less than a decade later, this "computer technician" would swear an oath of allegiance as the thirteenth prime minister of the State of Israel.

Bennett reestablished contact with Ayelet Shaked, the young secular engineer who had brought him into Netanyahu's office. They promised voters a new political bargain: two for the price of one. They established a party called The Israelis, which did not last long, and then they plotted a takeover of the religious Zionist community's shelf company, which appeared to be taking its dying breaths: the NRP, then known as the Jewish Home.

On November 6, 2012, the world held its breath for the results of two critical elections. In the United States, millions of Americans marched to the polls in a race between incumbent President Barack Obama and his Republican challenger, Mitt Romney. Meanwhile, in synagogues across Israel, several thousand religious Zionists were voting for the next leader of their movement's party, in a race between the veteran Zevulun Orlev and a young Naftali Bennett, thirty years his junior. Netanyahu was rooting for Romney and Orlev, but at dawn, it was Obama and Bennett who delivered victory speeches.

Looking back, it is unclear which race mattered more. Overnight, the Jewish Home party went from being the Likud's very junior partner to a strategic threat—a party with big ambitions, which accused the Likud of being left wing and angled for votes outside its core constituency.

Netanyahu already suspected Bennett of wanting to take his seat, and Bennett suspected Netanyahu of seeking to eliminate him at any price. In 2013, half of the Likud's election budget was earmarked for a surgical intervention to treat to the party that was exhilarating the right-wing youth and seizing another seat with every poll. Not for the first time, the surgery was successful, but it nearly killed the surgeon: Netanyahu made such a convincing case that Bennett and Shaked's party was too extreme that hundreds of thousands of voters deserted it—straight into the arms of Yair Lapid's new centrist party—leaving the entire right-wing bloc with just sixty-one seats, just a few thousand votes away from losing power.

After the elections, there emerged another phenomenon that would define the Netanyahu-Bennett relationship over the following decade: The prime minister did his best to try to shrink his former aide to more modest proportions, and if he could push him into the opposition— even better. But Bennett proved, as he would prove again years later, that while he always disappoints at the ballot box, nobody is more cunning than he is in the negotiating room.

While Netanyahu was preparing to bring the left's top politicians, Tzipi Livni and Shelly Yachimovich, into his coalition, a new alliance emerged under his nose, one that would transform Israeli politics. Yair Lapid, a second-generation TV personality and politician, met every night in the basement of his Tel Aviv home with Naftali Bennett, the heir of the religious right. They called the collaboration between Yesh Atid and the Jewish Home the "alliance of brothers."

For anyone looking at Israeli politics through the lens that Netanyahu used—that of left and right, friend or predator—this was an extremely odd alliance. Previously, the only place where former Shin Bet director Yaakov Peri and Hebron settler Orit Strock might have met was a Shin Bet interrogation facility, with him interrogating her. Yet suddenly, a powerful political alliance emerged to force Netanyahu to part from his natural partners, the Haredim, in favor of a government that he loathed from the first moment.

This alliance was born out of self-interested reasons, as a mutual insurance policy against getting thrown into opposition, but it soon developed into a much more meaningful development: the disman-tling of the old fortification lines dividing Israel's two historic camps.

Bennett and Lapid pitched a new paradigm for Israeli politics, instead of the familiar argument about territories and peace: a free market, Haredi enlistment, conversion reform, and a more welcoming rabbinate. If secular and religious Zionist Israelis slept in the same tents in the army and sat in the same lecture halls at university, why should they not also share power? In the religious Bnei Akiva youth movement, one standard activity involves asking participants whether they feel closer to Haredim or secular people. Bennett's answer was unequivocal: secular people.

This was the last exercise, a wet run, ahead of the much more ambitious operation that would lie ahead, but it was a resounding failure. The bromance gave way to a messy divorce: Bennett's conservative flank and Lapid's liberal flank did not stop bickering, and in less than two years, both men returned to their respective camps, their tails between their legs, and collapsed at the polls. They both swore to themselves and to their voters that it would never happen again.

But it gradually dawned on both Bennett and Lapid that without forming an unconventional alliance, neither of them would be able to reach his target of the prime minister's office. For center-left voters, Lapid lacked the experience and gravitas to be prime minister, while for right-wing voters, the Likud would always be more attractive than the Jewish Home as the party of government.

Ahead of the April 2019 elections, both Bennett and Lapid drew their conclusions: Lapid agreed to play second fiddle to three retired military chiefs in the hope of somehow defeating Netanyahu, while Bennett had long gotten fed up with the party that he had taken over— his dreams of greatness far surpassed the modest, sectoral aspirations of his religious Zionist peers. He coveted the Defense Ministry; they wanted the Education Ministry. He courted secular votes; they promoted a religious agenda. He scorned their narrow-mindedness; they were alarmed by the breadth of his ambition. On the night when his party had crashed in the 2015 elections, Bennett called his father, Jim, to update him about the results. "We won only eight seats," he said, dejected. But his father was interested in something else: "Forget about that, Naftali, how many seats did the bloc win?" As a former officer in an elite commando unit, Bennett was finding it hard to adapt to the role of someone else's backup.

His separation from the Jewish Home party became inevitable.

On the first Saturday night of the 2019 election campaign, Bennett bolted from the Jewish Home in favor of another ambitious start-up: the New Right. It would be a party in which, he hoped, he would no longer be shackled to the rabbis and political operatives who were so easily swayed by Netanyahu or to a conservative agenda on matters of religion and state. His co-leader, Ayelet Shaked, still had serious doubts the moment he switched his phone off as Shabbat came in. He charged secular emissaries with texting her messages of reinforcement for the whole day, while he observed the Jewish day of rest.

It was no use. On Saturday afternoon, Shaked knocked on the door of Bennett's home in Raanana for several more hours of indecisive deliberations. When Shabbat ended, Bennett made Shaked an offer: to drive to their press conference, where reporters were already waiting, and continue their discussion there. That conversation never happened. Nobody who knows Bennett from the high-tech world was surprised: As the CEO of Cyota, he had scrapped the cybersecurity product that the firm had worked on for two years and invented a brand-new product that everyone thought was a fool's errand.

This was in one sense typical of their decade-long stormy partnership: He had the mentality of an entrepreneur, and she, of a salaried employee. He was the gas, and she was the brakes; he was in a rush, and she was cautious; he jumped in headfirst, and she was hesitant. It is often said that opposites attract, but from the side, it often looked like Bennett and Shaked's car was always recklessly speeding, suddenly stopping, and constantly weaving between lanes.

Three months later, in April 2019, when the last ballot slip was emptied from the last ballot box, it turned out that this time she was right, and he was wrong. Only 1,451 votes stood between their new party and the electoral threshold. The Likud's brutally effective campaign had hoovered up their voters at the last minute. Once again, Netanyahu had been too successful. For long, sleepless nights, hundreds of volunteers, together with Bennett and Shaked, scoured for missing votes. In a historic irony, if missing votes had somehow been found in an unopened ballot box, Bennett would have ended his political career as the culture minister and would not have settled, two years later, into the prime minister's office. Had he succeeded then, it would have been the end of him. But since he failed, he eventually succeeded. Netanyahu won a Pyrrhic victory and Bennett—whatever the opposite is. It was such an unlikely kind of victory that nobody has ever come up with the right literary expression for it.

At the age of forty-seven, Bennett found himself in early retirement. The security booth outside his house in Raanana was dismantled; his diplomatic passport was voided. He had plans to establish a high-tech corporation. Shaked received an offer to head a cannabis company and the promise of another coveted role: a regular right-wing talking head on a Friday night news show.

But then Bennett and Shaked discovered that, like in the song "Hotel California," they could check out of politics, but they could never leave. By failing to win any seats, the New Right deprived Netanyahu of the right-wing votes that he needed to form a government when Yisrael Beitenu bolted his coalition, plunging Israel into another election, then another, and then another. Bennett turned out to be the Bitcoin of politics: skyrocketing one day, crashing the next, and fluctuating wildly—not for the faint-hearted. He lurched from the security cabinet to the underside of the electoral threshold and from there, thanks to a genius negotiating maneuver against Netanyahu, to the role of defense minister, despite belonging to a faction with only three seats. This time, Netanyahu's hostility and suspicion were an asset: He was so afraid that Bennett might defect and join a coalition headed by opposition chief Benny Gantz that he quickly promoted him to the second-most important role in the government.

This same suspiciousness meant that half a year later, when Netanyahu formed a unity government with Gantz's center-left party, he banished Bennett from the Defense Ministry to the opposition at the first opportunity. Bennett seemed to be toast again: What more could he offer the Israeli public now that such a broad coalition had been formed and COVID-19 was rampaging outside?

But the deadliest pandemic in a century brought Bennett's political career back to life. His scathing criticism of the government's handling of the crisis sent his popularity soaring to previously unknown heights. The book that he wrote—*How to Beat a Pandemic*—was passed around from hand to hand, although a more appropriate title might have been: *How to Win an Election*. Instead of talking about annexation and security, Bennett pivoted to talking about epidemiological investigations reducing unemployment. He was not the only person whose life was transformed by the coronavirus pandemic, but he was probably one of the few whose lives it changed for the better.

The year 1973 was the year zero of modern Israeli politics. The fiasco of the Yom Kippur War led to the fall of Labor and the rise of the Likud, the end of the hegemony of the working class and the rise of the traditionalists, the decline of the Ashkenazim and rise of the Mizrahim, the end of the debate about the economy and the start of an argument about territories and peace, and the collapse of the historic alliance between Labor and the NRP and the birth of the natural alliance between the Likud and religious parties.

During the coronavirus pandemic, I found myself wondering: Was 2020 the new 1973? Would the worst pandemic of the past century transform Israel just as momentously as the worst war in its history had done?

On the face of it, why should these be linked? How can a security fiasco on Israel's borders be compared to a public health crisis? Or an armed enemy to a virus? But they definitely are linked. In 1973, Israelis' sense of national security was irrevocably shaken. Beforehand, they had felt invincible, and then suddenly they discovered that all that stood between them and columns of Syrian artillery were the Sea of Galilee and a handful of national heroes in broken tanks, that the IDF's generals were not all-powerful after all, and that their government was blind.

In 2020, Israelis' sense of economic, employment, and health security was similarly shaken. They had previously felt in complete control of their lives, but suddenly, even El Al pilots found their jobs disappearing. Venue owners sat at home, desperate for compensation. Families that had felt safe, surrounded by grandparents and friends, had to self-isolate at home without seeing anyone else. Because when the enemy is faceless, every face becomes the enemy.

A well-known British professor who specializes in the study of political aftershocks in the wake of pandemics recently admitted that only during the coronavirus pandemic did he fully understand what he had been writing about his whole life, at an academic distance: When a virus destroys your whole world, you have nobody to blame. The virus itself is indifferent to people's feelings. Their frustration, distress, and anxieties get directed at the government. Throughout history, pandemics have led to wars and the fall of royal dynasties. The major pandemic of the twenty-first century has led to political upheavals instead.

Seven countries held elections during the pandemic. Only in New Zealand did the incumbent government survive, thanks to a hardline policy that contained transmissions. In every other country, the ruling party was dealt a devastating blow. When the Netanyahu-Gantz government collapsed, Israel became the first country in the world to enter its third lockdown. "If my rivals think that COVID[-19] will eliminate me," Netanyahu said at the time, "they're about to discover that I'm going to eliminate COVID." In practice, they wiped each other out.

In the week when Israelis voted in their fourth consecutive election, in March 2021, the economy was almost completely open thanks to the fastest and most efficient inoculation campaign in the world. Public disappointment with Netanyahu was compensated for by his obsessive insistence on getting the vaccines before any other country. Having discovered that COVID-19 had evaporated from the public consciousness, Bennett had to settle for just seven seats for his Yamina party, which he won in large part by swearing an oath of allegiance to the right-wing bloc on live television and promising that he would never, ever serve in a government with Lapid, the left, or the Arabs.

Israel's first mass gatherings after a year of lockdowns were at the party headquarters, with the broadcast of the exit polls. But when the last absentee votes were counted (including those of citizens in quarantine), it turned out that Israel had said goodbye to COVID-19—but not to political paralysis. The right-wing bloc gained a seat, its opponents lost a seat, but otherwise Israel's fourth consecutive election ended just like the first three: indecisively.

Or did it?

COVID-19 is dangerous *not only* for people with preexisting conditions. Everyone knows of a neighborhood café that was slowly languishing until COVID-19 gave it a kiss of death or of a store that was struggling to adjust to the digital age and collapsed as soon as shops were ordered to close. And this pandemic, it turned out, was also lethal for parties with comorbidities.

If the Likud had been admitted to a COVID-19 ward, what would a doctor have diagnosed? First, its advanced age put it in a high-risk category. Israel's main right-wing party had governed the country for thirty-three years with only minor interruptions, longer than the Alignment at the time of the 1977 upheaval. Netanyahu was the only world leader to have been in power in the previous millennium, besides Queen Elizabeth. Under him had served both David Levy and his daughter; he had worked with a President Clinton and a Secretary of State Clinton; and he had dominated the ages of both television and Facebook.

Only a handful of Netanyahu's coalition colleagues remembered the taste of opposition. At some point, every political party should experience not just the pleasures of power but also the grief of opposition, and for the Likud, this would have happened in a year or two anyway. Netanyahu had amassed enemies by the score, inside and outside the political system. His trial, rivals, and many years in power were like a millstone around his neck, preventing him from taking off toward another term. Most Israelis had voted for the right, but most of them had voted against the leader of the right. Like a ninety-year-old man, the Likud had its life expectancy cut by COVID-19 by a couple of years, no more.

The second illness ailing the Likud was chronic internal bleeding. In 2019, the right-wing camp lost a large chunk of the Russian vote because of a personal dispute with Lieberman and a wider dispute about religion and state. In 2020, with the formation of the COVID-19 unity government, the Religious Zionist Party was belched out of the coalition. In 2021, many liberal right-wingers defected to Gideon Sa'ar's New Hope party. Without fresh blood, the Likud started growing pale, hemorrhaging both its voters and its vitality.

COVID-19 also seriously impaired the motor skills of the right-wing camp's most important organ: the Haredi population. For a whole year, the general public was outraged by what it saw as ridiculous celebrity discounts given exclusively to the Haredim: their schools remained open even when regular schools were shut, mass funerals were held, weddings were celebrated, and morbidity in Haredi communities skyrocketed because of cramped living conditions, turning Bnei Brak and similar towns into massive COVID-19 incubators. When the pandemic seemed to have been stamped out, the criticism appeared to subside, but energy, as everyone knows, never disappears; it only changes form. When Bennett and Lapid's "change government" started taking shape behind closed doors, the change that it had in mind was to surgically separate Haredi politicians from the levers of power.

No less importantly, the negotiations spanning several weeks to form a government encompassing nearly the entire Israeli ideological spectrum, between people who had called each other "fascist thugs" and "terror supporters," pointed to a much more substantive shift in Israeli society. In the first two decades of the millennium, Israelis had discovered three times that their state, which they love and pay for, was not there for them when they truly needed it.

In 2006, war erupted in Lebanon and thousands of rockets rained on population centers in northern Israel. This was a time before the Iron Dome missile defense system, when rocket shelters were old and moldy after many years of quiet, and dozens of Israelis were killed trying to sneak out for a few minutes to fetch diapers, water, or a fresh breath of air. The government decided to build a temporary tent city for residents of northern Israel in the center of the country. It did so with a small delay: The war lasted thirty-four days, and the tent city was inaugurated on day thirty-five. That was when Israelis discovered the disappearance of local government.

In 2010, two young men were smoking hookah in their yard in Usfiye when a hot, dry wind blowing at 50 mph swept the fire from their coals to the nearby forest. The whole world watched in horror as Israel's greatest natural asset, the Carmel Forest, went up in flames. It turned out that the whole of Israel's northern district had only a few forty-year-old fire engines. That was when Israelis discovered the miserable state of their fire services.

In 2021, two hair-raising events took place in the same week: An Israeli car without a roof, according to foreign reports, pulled up by the side of a road not far from Tehran. It used artificial intelligence to identify the vehicle of Iran's top nuclear scientist, Mohsen Fakhrizadeh, assassinated him with machine-gun fire, and then self-destructed, but not before images of the event were broadcast to Mossad's headquarters. That same week, the same State of Israel scored a dubious record and became the first country in the world to enter a third COVID-19 lockdown, even before Iran, because it was not able to treat more than one thousand seriously ill patients simultaneously. That was when Israeli citizens discovered the hard-pressed conditions of their healthcare system. Their conclusion was that it was time to revise their contract with the state.

Israel's new government, which nobody could have imagined on the eve of the election, not least because of the vigorous denials of the person who would lead it, reflected this hidden shift in public opinion. The coalition's charter made no reference to diplomatic or security issues. Instead, the government promised to focus on matters of "consensus," those that are actually fiercely contested everywhere else in the world: healthcare and taxation, economy and transportation, environment and welfare. Israel is in the Middle East, but its government arranged itself around a Scandinavian agenda.

Had the public mood not shifted, nobody would have dared to conceive of a coalition stretching from the settlers' council to the Islamic Shura Council. Without the tremendous pent-up energy against Netanyahu, nobody could possibly have pulled off this maneuver. The combination of the two produced the upheaval of 2021. There is something ironic about the fact that the last event in Israel where masks were compulsory (until they were reinstated) was the Knesset vote in which, by a single vote, Bennett replaced Netanyahu. The pandemic that had helped to wipe out Netanyahu's rule was wiped out by him on the same day as this political upheaval. In more than one sense, the masks came off. Four elections and one pandemic had come to an end.

When Israel's new government, sworn in by the slimmest margin in history, swore its oath of allegiance, it broke a pile of other oaths, vows, and election pledges: As mentioned, the incoming prime minister had repeatedly promised that he would not serve in a government with Lapid, or the left, and definitely not the anti-Zionist Arab parties. The day after the election, having won just seven seats, when he was offered to be prime minister, Bennett jettisoned all his promises. In this sense, the student truly surpassed his teacher. Peres sacrificed the premiership in 1986 in order to protect his credibility, and thirty-five years later, Bennett sacrificed his credibility in order to become prime minister.

The Bennett-Lapid government looks like a strange creature from an alien planet: a two-headed beast with a single tail, in the form of an Arab party, and many tongues. None of its members planned for it or wanted it until the moment it was formed. It was a product of necessity. No doubt, each of its constituent parties was convinced at the moment of its birth that this would be a temporary improvisation, which would endure until someone amassed enough power to establish a more conventional government.

But things don't work that way. Just as the direct prime ministerial elections of 1996 gravely undermined the major parties' power to this day, even though the system was long abolished, and just as the Netanyahu-Gantz rotation government was born as a temporary solution but its rotation format was adopted again—by its biggest critics, no less—so too will the ramifications of Israel's thirty-sixth government stay with it for many years to come.

The structure of Israeli politics was based for many years on two large camps, each of which was headed by a large party: the Likud on the right, Labor on the left. Surrounding each of them, like weeds in the shadow of a tall tree, bloomed a field of sectoral parties: on the right, an Ashkenazi Haredi party, a Sephardi Haredi party, a religious Zionist party, and a Russian émigré party; on the left, the party of the kibbutzim and the Arab parties.

The first tree fell in the left's forest. The ideological collapse of the Labor Party left a vacuum in the camp that has not been filled to this day. Nowadays, the left also has many short bushes: many parties vying for precedence and switching over every term or two. It is possible that something similar has happened on the right: The Likud, with its institutions and voter rolls, still commands a significant lead, but it is becoming clear that the small parties no longer want to remain in the shadow of this mighty tree. Avigdor Lieberman was the first to declare that although he was right wing, he was unwilling to accept the Likud's leadership, thereby triggering the rolling nightmare of back-to-back elections. Instead of wilting, he flourished. Lieberman was the teacher, and Bennett and Sa'ar, who both peeled away from Netanyahu, were his star pupils.

This might not be just about left and right but also part of a global trend. The internet has obliterated most middleman jobs: Our parents needed travel agents in order to plan a weekend city break, while we can book hotels online, without paying commission. The ability to advertise one's home online has seriously hurt realtors, and we no longer receive most of our information from journalists on TV but rather from friends on WhatsApp and Facebook. By the same token, those who want to enter politics on the basis of personal popularity no longer see any point in sucking up to primary voters and local bigwigs but rather prefer to set up their own personal parties, tailored to their own measurements.

The implications might be much more dramatic than anyone can predict. The moment the center of political gravity is lost, there is no reason why the next Knesset should not contain twenty microfactions or the role of prime minister should not be split between three or even four politicians. If everyone can serve in a government with anyone else and what matters is not public support in the streets but bargaining power at the plenary, then Israeli politics will become what Israelis have always suspected it of being: a Turkish bazaar.

The Israeli political system struggled to translate the will of the people into a functioning government, but the precedent that Bennett set—a minor party taking the reins of power thanks to political maneuvering—threatens to totally sever any connection between the will of the people and the identity of the prime minister. Bennett volunteered himself for the job after 95 percent of the public had not voted for him, and yet he still took the oath as prime minister.

Israel is a very young country, which loves making things up as it goes along and has little respect for political traditions. But even by local standards, the thirty-sixth government has blown all the rules of the game to smithereens. In a single vote, it smashed no fewer than six fundamental principles of Israeli politics.

First, power is no longer held by one of two major parties but by a parliamentary fragment representing just 5 percent of the voters. Twenty years earlier, Benjamin Netanyahu had refused the premiership when it was presented to him practically on a silver platter, because the Likud had only nineteen seats. He believed that he would not be able to govern effectively with such a small party. One generation later, Naftali Bennett became prime minister as the leader of the smallest Zionist party in the Knesset, with just six seats. Yamina is probably the first ruling party in the world whose lawmakers can all fit into a single minivan and still leave a seat empty next to the driver. Ben-Gurion bitterly regretted his choice of electoral system because he warned of the prospect of small parties extorting the big ones, but even he could not have imagined the small parties ruling over the big ones. The kingmaker became the king himself, or in the case of a rotation government: lord of half the kingdom.

Second, for the first time since Israel's independence, a non-Zionist Arab party joined the coalition. The historic agreement to bring Ra'am, also known as the United Arab List, into the government, holding the balance of power no less, is perhaps the most important historical development of the upheaval of 2021. It cast in leading roles actors who had always been extras since Israel's independence. Suddenly, the votes of the Arab lawmakers became legal tender. Rabin used the Arab parties as his government's mistress in 1992; Netanyahu enjoyed a passionate romance with them. Bennett and Lapid married them.

Third, for the first time since the upheaval of 1977, a government was formed without either the Haredim or the Likud. Menachem Begin established the natural partnership that later conquered Israeli politics. From a fairly loose association based on a love of Jewish tradition and generous budgets, it evolved into a tight ideological alliance, even at the cost of losing power. Bennett decreed that this natural partnership would continue, but from a much less natural place, from its own perspective: the opposition benches.

Fourth, for the first time, Israel has a prime minister who wears a kippah. But this is happening in one of the most secular coalitions that Israel has seen.

Fifth, for the first time since its establishment in 1973, the Likud lost power to another right-wing party. Ariel Sharon founded the Likud as a government-in-waiting, around which all the other parties in the bloc coalesced. When Bennett took the oath of office, he smashed the axiomatic belief that only the head of the right-wing camp could be prime minister and that in order to head the right-wing camp, one had to head the Likud. Sharon built the Likud and dismantled it. Bennett outdid him: He simply bypassed it.

Sixth, for the first time since the Six-Day War, a coalition has come together without a position on diplomatic or security affairs. In her failings, Golda Meir made security and peace the top issue in the eyes of Israeli voters. The eight parties comprising the government of 2021 chose, for want of a better choice and because of fierce disputes between them, to ignore the elephant in the room. This ability to turn a blind eye allowed the party that had promised annexation to bring Meretz back into the government after a generation in exile.

The cult classic *Fight Club* is about a secret boxing club. Brad Pitt's character shouts at the club's new members its eight rules: only one fight at a time, for example, and no wearing a shirt or shouting. Only at the end of the movie do viewers understand that there is a ninth rule: There are no rules. Everything is allowed.

In the fight club called Israeli politics, one can try to describe the rules and conventions. That was the purpose of this book. But Israel's thirteenth prime minister reminded Israelis of something that they might have preferred to repress: The most important rule of the fight club in Jerusalem is that there are no rules. That too is part of the story of Israeli politics.

The Decision That Was Never Made

I T WAS THE THIRD DAY of the catastrophic war that had erupted on the Jewish holiday of Simchat Torah, on October 7, 2023. In the south, IDF soldiers were still battling the last holdout terrorists. The bodies of the elderly, women, and children lay unrecovered in the kibbutzim. In the north, the well-trained and heavily armed forces of Hezbollah's terror army were perched at the border, seriously contemplating whether they too should invade Israel. Israel was stunned and bleeding.

And for the first time, so was Prime Minister Benjamin Netanyahu. He called me that day, the first conversation after the largest slaughter of Jews since the Holocaust. He, long crowned "Mr. Security" by the public, who took pride in his famous ability to spot danger in advance, had learned about the war from a dawn phone call that jolted him awake on the holiday morning. He probably hadn't slept since. The eternally confident, decisive man, the one who always had a plan, now sounded hesitant.

That week brought many unimaginable events, but my conversation with Netanyahu was still the most astounding of all. Netanyahu told me one thing that I never imagined would cross his lips: "Listen to me and listen well. Never go into politics."

Hearing this from Netanyahu, the Western Hemisphere's gold medalist of politics, was like hearing Trump extol the virtues of humility or Margaret Thatcher denounce female ambition. The man whose shadow had dominated Israeli politics for half its years as a state, who had led the country longer than all five of his predecessors combined, was suddenly confronted by the ruthless nature of politics. This wasn't the first time sharks had circled him while he was wounded. But he had never faced such a ravenous pack of sharks, never been so gravely wounded.

Every Israeli leader experiences this moment, when the ground slips beneath their feet, and they plunge into an abyss from which there is no return.

The American Constitution limits presidents to two terms, for a maximum of eight years. This is especially important for voters: Those who detest the commander-in-chief can at least hold onto the hope that change is on the horizon, even if that horizon is still far off. No less important is that even the president's most ardent admirers understand that all good things must come to an end and, more importantly, that even the best president has a successor. Americans, like NBA talent scouts, are constantly on the lookout for the next presidential prospect.

Therefore, in US presidential elections, the best candidate wins. This sounds almost banal but far from it. In a long, expensive, and meticulously orchestrated process that begins with knocking on doors in snowy Iowa and ends with the oath of office on chilly Capitol Hill, America sifts through its candidates until it elects the one it considers most suitable. Even today, Americans know exactly when the New Hampshire primaries, the presidential debates, Election Day, and the handover will take place during the 2076 elections. That's America.

And in Israel? It is all upside down. The last attempt to limit prime ministerial terms was in the 1990s and was reversed at the first opportunity by the eleventh prime minister, Ariel Sharon. Opposition leaders tend to support term limits and then forget their promises as soon as they sit behind the prime minister's desk.

Other countries may also lack term limits, but they also have a political culture that does not give politicians countless opportunities. You break it; you own it. You lose; you're gone. In Israel, as an American journalist once discovered, politicians have three ranks: dead, dead and buried, and dead and buried and never coming back. And even from beyond the grave, some still contemplate a comeback. In Israel, unlike the United States, elections are never won, only lost. The winner's identity rarely has anything to do with his personality, the quality of his election messaging, or the composition of his list, but mainly with his fortunate timing of running just as the weight of the incumbent's failures and fatigue tips the scales against his achievements and experience.

Does the prime minister get replaced at the ballot box? Not in Israel. Only five times in Israel's history, four of them between 1992–2001, did the premiership change hands because of an election.

I was a young reporter at IDF Army Radio in the fall of 2000, still too young to be allowed on the airwaves. But Ariel Sharon's secretary invited me one day to sit with him in the members of the Knesset's canteen. No more-senior journalist wanted to waste his precious time in the canteen with a backbencher who was already considered a dead horse, a "bulldozer with a bust engine," as one newspaper called him. A few months later, he was elected prime minister by the biggest margin in Israel's history. But he did not win; rather, Prime Minister Ehud Barak lost because of the bloody intifada raging under the watch of his helpless government. Nor did Ehud Olmert imagine on the afternoon of January 4, 2006, that he would be the prime minister by nightfall. He was a veteran and not especially a popular minister. By the evening, he was entrusted with Israel's biggest secrets. When he opened the windows of his Jerusalem home, he suddenly discovered dozens of guards outside. He was not elected prime minister; Sharon had suffered a stroke, and he was given power over the phone.

Benjamin Netanyahu considered quitting and going into business in the summer of 2006. He headed a battered faction of just twelve members, his best years in politics behind him. A month and a half later, he was already ahead in the polls, cruising all the way to his second term. The public had no particular love for him; it simply punished Olmert and Livni's Kadima for the disastrous Second Lebanon War and corruption scandals. Naftali Bennett can also tell himself nice stories about his clever political ruse. But the truth is that he was not the winner. As always, the incumbent lost. That's how it works in Israel.

The fact is that it is not so easy to lose the prime minister's seat. In Israel, unlike the United States, the date of elections is like traffic lights for pedestrians: only a recommendation. Nobody knows whether the Knesset will live out its full term or whether snap elections will be called tomorrow morning. This noisy circus is held together only by improvisations. The last time that Israel held elections on time was in 1988, and the last time that a government served out its full term was when IDF soldiers could still paddle in the Suez Canal.

The prime minister holds almost absolute power to set the date of the next elections. The prime minister usually commands a majority in the Knesset, which is legally empowered to dissolve itself in a manner that is usually irreversible. The Knesset's ability to call snap elections is like the comedy skit about Beitar Jerusalem soccer fans who threaten to burn down the stadium if they are not allowed to pick the players, the coaches, the weather, and the score.

Timing is nearly everything in life, and certainly in politics. Israeli prime ministers already wield massive control over the agenda: They are privy to diplomatic agreements secretly being negotiated as well as clandestine operations the IDF is planning. They have access to economic data before publication and sensational political news that will soon become public knowledge but is still top secret. Besides being able to manipulate the election date, prime ministers have a secret weapon: They can set elections for the week after a dramatic diplomatic summit or, alternatively, a month before unflattering growth figures are published. And, of course, prime ministers who can call elections at the most convenient time triumph more easily than their counterparts overseas. The last sitting premier in Israeli history to suffer an unambiguous electoral defeat was Ehud Barak, over twenty years ago. The best springboard to the role of prime minister is the role of prime minister itself.

US President Donald Trump could not postpone or bring forward the 2020 presidential elections by a single day. Had he been Israeli, he would have delayed them by just a month, until the start of the COVID-19 vaccination campaign, and won in a landslide. But he is American, and therefore elections were held on time, and he lost the presidency because of a few thousand votes in swing states.

The combination of an absence of term limits with near-guaranteed reelection has produced quite an illogical result: Almost all the men (and the one woman) who have sat in the seat of the Israeli prime minister became convinced that they would stay there forever. They, of course, recognized their mortality, yet their actions betrayed a mindset of immortality. Like Winston Churchill, Margaret Thatcher, and other world leaders who lingered too long in power, they convinced themselves that their departure would imperil the nation's very existence. And if that were true, how could they dare relinquish power?

In Tom Clancy's novel *The Sum of All Fears*, a thriller about nuclear terrorism, the Israeli prime minister informs the defense minister that he has appointed him his heir. It is the least believable moment in the book, even more ridiculous than the claim that the Golan Heights is full of sand dunes, with an atomic bomb lurking under one of them. There is no sand in the Golan Heights, and Israeli prime ministers do not groom heirs. There is a good reason why none of them have done so. Why designate an heir if you plan to rule forever? But nobody lives or governs forever. The head-on collision between this natural law and Israeli prime ministers' supernatural thirst for power can end only one way in an endless cycle: tragedy.

David Ben-Gurion was a seventy-seven-year-old pensioner in 1963, at a time when the life expectancy for Israeli men was a mere sixty-eight. Yet he persisted in running again and again, launching one unsuccessful party after another, the last at age eighty-four. The most iconic political cartoon in Israel's history shows a diminutive Ben-Gurion whacking his own stone statue, which is towering over him, with a heavy hammer. "In the second decade of his rule," cartoonist Dosh later explained, "only one man could have defeated him, the man himself—and he succeeded!"[i]

Levi Eshkol, the Yiddish-accented civilian leader, masterfully prepared the IDF and the country for the Six-Day War. But the credit was snatched from him by Moshe Dayan, whom he had reluctantly appointed defense minister just a few days before the war, due to heavy public pressure. The ailing and kindhearted prime minister is remembered mainly for stuttering his way through a speech on the eve of the war, an incident that would haunt him for the rest of his life. Israel's third prime minister never read the commentaries vindicating him. They were written only after he died at home in Jerusalem. While heart disease was listed as the official cause of Eshkol's death, the more likely reason was heartbreak. Eshkol took to heart the chasm between how history would flatteringly remember him and how Israelis perceived him during his lifetime. Readers of *Maariv* learned of his death after a delay: The

---

i   Kariel Gardosh (Dosh), "Ben-Gurion," The Official Website, available at: srulik.co.il [Hebrew]

political correspondent who called Eshkol's office and was told, "Eshkol is not with us," mistakenly assumed that he was merely away from the office. The rival paper, *Yediot*, got the scoop on the premier's death.

Golda Meir was a popular prime minister in 1973 but an ailing and solitary woman. She wrestled with doubts about seeking a third term. Not long earlier, her cancer had returned, prompting daily trips to "visit an ill friend" at Hadassah Ein Kerem Hospital, as the official cover story went. "It's exhausting," she admitted, "sometimes deadly so. But that's all we need right now: a prime minister with cancer." Had she quit then, the most famous disaster in Israel's history would have happened on someone else's watch, and she would have been remembered as the stalwart leader who led Israel during a golden age. But like her predecessors and successors, not even she knew when it was time to call it a day. Even after the war, she insisted on running again, only to depart shamefaced. Google would forever complete searches of her name with the phrase "Yom Kippur War."

Menachem Begin reached the premiership long past his prime. His 1977 victory came while still recuperating from a devastating heart attack that had sidelined him through most of the campaign, and when he first appeared in an election broadcast, viewers were shocked by his pallid and haggard appearance. Four years later, in 1981, after the historic peace treaty with Egypt, a Nobel Prize, and the bombing of Iraq's nuclear reactor, he could have gracefully announced his early retirement, having notched up enough achievements. He too never considered this. His last two years were agonizing. He launched a war that he did not want, his wife died, and he frequently arrived at work in a wheelchair and under the influence of hormone treatment that impaired his performance and emotional stability. One day, disoriented, he entered the Knesset confused and sat in the opposition leader's seat, which he had occupied for years. In his final months in the prime minister's office, he showed little interest in the role that he had coveted for so long. This revered leader barely left his home from the day he resigned until the day he died.

Yitzhak Rabin endured a miserable and unpopular first term, paying for his Alignment predecessors' sins. Nevertheless, he insisted on seeking reelection in 1977. But even this was denied: He was forced to step down because of a criminal scandal implicating him, his wife, and an illegal bank account holding enough money to buy a Tel Aviv apartment.

The curse of Israel's prime ministers struck Rabin too, and with him the nation, in the horrific end to his second term: felled by the bullets of a despicable Jewish assassin in Kings of Israel Square.

In August 2005, Ariel Sharon summoned his secretary. "Marit," he said in a fluster, "I had a terrible dream last night. I dreamed I was abseiling [rappelling] down into a well, and the rope snapped." The eagle-eyed secretary had noticed in the last months of the prime minister's term that something was amiss. He was exhibiting "growing signs of physical decline" and struggling to walk. When invited to events, his bodyguards carefully measured how far he could walk. During his last foreign trip to the United Nations General Assembly in September 2005, they counted his steps between the meeting rooms where he conferred with world leaders. For dinner one night with the British ambassador, he walked exactly sixty-four meters, according to his bodyguards' measurements, and arrived "gasping and barely breathing." He dozed off in meetings. There was a visible decline in his ability to function, later recalled the chairman of the Knesset Foreign Affairs and Defense Committee, Yuval Steinitz.

Yet Sharon firmly believed that he would govern for many years to come. "Why not share your medical records?" I asked him in a radio interview. "It would be thin on content," he said, shrugging off the question. When Knesset Speaker Reuven Rivlin asked why Sharon had appointed an air force officer with no experience in activating ground forces as the chief of the military, he replied with three words: "But I'm here." After a few weeks, he suffered what his doctors termed a minor stroke. "Sharon is healthy," his personal physicians lied. A few days later, he succumbed to a second stroke, never to regain consciousness. In his final years, confined to a hospital ward, he no longer knew that he had once served as Israel's prime minister.

Ehud Olmert, Sharon's successor, clung to power even after the Second Lebanon War debacle, defying all predictions and against all odds. "You'll get used to me eventually," he boasted in an interview, when his approval ratings appeared to briefly stabilize. And then the "envelopes of cash" affair exploded. Olmert made history as the first person to go from the prime minister's residence to a prison cell.

Yitzhak Shamir, Shimon Peres, and Ehud Barak could have each chosen not to run again and step aside for a more electable candidate.

They all had envious achievements: Shamir had brought one million Jews to Israel from the Soviet Union and was a tough prime minister whom even his ideological opponents admired; Peres restrained Israel's hyperinflation; and Barak kept his word and pulled IDF forces out of Lebanon. But they insisted on running for reelection, only to deliver humiliating concession speeches the day after.

The only Israeli prime minister who left office in good health and of his own free will was Moshe Sharett, and even he did so with a heavy heart. "It is not for me to govern this country, which is probably impossible to govern without relying on adventurism and deceit," he said. "Of these, I am incapable."

Given this dismal legacy, it is hardly surprising, albeit regrettable, that the current Israeli prime minister's tenure will also end badly. Benjamin Netanyahu's appetite for power, to put it delicately, rivals that of his predecessors, and he too has no thoughts of retirement. In his eyes, Israel's paramount strategic asset is, simply put, himself. For years, a criminal conviction seemed the looming tragedy. Instead, it was eclipsed by a security failure and disaster unmatched since the Holocaust.

In 2022, he could have eluded the fate of all his predecessors: The attorney general offered to dismiss his criminal cases in exchange for retirement. But the negotiations collapsed. A few months later, he clinched a brilliant electoral victory. How bitterly he would come to rue that triumph.

Netanyahu returned to power after only a year and a half, blind to the fact that he was taking control of the state during the most precarious period in a nation's life: its eighth decade. Midlife crises don't just afflict people; republics face them too. The first generation is the one that fought. It had no time for existential dilemmas because it was preoccupied with surviving. The second generation focused on developing the state, too busy with state-building to entertain such questions. "When will we finally finish establishing the state and be able to rest?" Prime Minister Levi Eshkol once mused. But the third and fourth generations— my generation—are those for whom the state is a birthright, already built, paved, and functioning. All the profound existential dilemmas that our grandparents tucked away in the attic have come knocking on our national door. A nation's eighth and ninth decades almost invariably mark the moment when it tears itself apart over the ultimate question: identity.

The United States in its ninth decade of existence emerged as a won-derland unlike any other ever seen. The pursuit of happiness swept across the country, ultimately reaching California. Then, with two oceans safe-guarding what would evolve into the world's greatest empire, Americans found themselves confronting an unsettling question. Their Declaration of Independence contains words never before articulated in human his-tory: "All men are created equal." How then, Americans pondered, is it possible that Thomas Jefferson, the author of those very words, owns six hundred black slaves on his Monticello estate in Virginia?

The answer: It is not possible. In the United States, two values col-lided with devastating force: the right to liberty and the right to property. To us in the twenty-first century, it seems self-evident that America is the birthplace of freedom, epitomized by the Statue of Liberty. Yet, had the South emerged victorious, a "Statue of Property" might have stood at the entrance to New York's harbor. The American Civil War resolved this clash of two values through bloodshed, claiming over six hundred thousand American lives, including that of the president.

We all know the Soviet Union's fate in its eighth decade. Countries do not always survive their identity wars.

Against this backdrop, Israel's five successive elections and then Netanyahu's return to power suddenly come into focus: This was the Israeli civil war.

It ignited with a proposal for a judicial reform that addressed the Israeli courts' power to overturn government decisions through the application of what is known as the "reasonableness doctrine" and the composition of the Judicial Appointments Committee—topics that had previously concerned only a handful of legal experts. But the streets erupted in protest. The Ayalon highway, bisecting Tel Aviv as Israel's main traffic artery, was paralyzed almost nightly. Thousands threatened to abandon military service. Business leaders withdrew their capital from Israel. The country became a battleground of protests and equally furious counterprotests.

Seventy-five years after the state's founding, many Israelis questioned whether it was feasible to remain united as one country. What fueled this outburst of mutual hatred? Not just between proponents and opponents of the judicial reform, but between religious and secular, right and left, Jerusalem and Tel Aviv?

The answer is that Israel's identity conflict centers on two core values of the State of Israel: Jewish and democratic. While no one advocates for either a Jewish dictatorship or a Greek Orthodox democracy, the struggle centers on the proper balance and mix of these values.

The right-wing camp essentially says this: Israel is undeniably democratic, but democracy is merely the operating system. The critical question is content. The answer is almost a cliché—Israel is the world's only Jewish state. That is why the Jewish people came here, to the land of the Bible, rather than establish a state in Uganda or an autonomy in Argentina, both once considered alternatives.

If we dare forget this, cautions the right, and are tempted to dilute the Jewish identity of the state even slightly—say, by permitting public transportation on Shabbat, as many desire—just to become yet another liberal Western democracy like Austria, Sweden, and Finland, we risk the fate of the Crusaders. They preceded us by a millennium; their leadership too, like ours, arrived here in the Holy Land from Europe, driven by religious zeal. They too faced Islamic terrorism and violence. Jews have battled terrorism for 150 years; the Crusaders valiantly resisted for two centuries, before ultimately faltering, breaking, and retreating to Europe. The crucial difference between us and them, the right warns, is that should we fail, no continent awaits our return.

Convincing? Certainly. But so is the opposing view.

We are undeniably Jewish, counters the left. Every Jewish kindergarten child comes home Fridays bearing a challah after Kabbalat Shabbat. The state's emblem is the Temple's seven-branched menorah, and the national flag is essentially a prayer shawl. But that is merely the state culture. The state's raison d'être, however clichéd, is being the only democracy in the Middle East.

And if we are tempted to compromise the democracy of the state even slightly—say, by eliminating the reasonableness doctrine—to become yet another Middle Eastern country where religion predominantly shapes identity, we won't share the Crusaders' fate. We'll end up like Lebanon, Israel's neighbor to the north once hailed as the "Switzerland of the Middle East." It boasted excellent restaurants, the finest ski resorts, and a thriving tourism sector at a time when Israel was still just transit camps and camels. But then it veered toward fundamentalism, and the rest is history.

And Netanyahu found himself ensnared in this culture war during a term he had hoped would be crowned by a peace agreement with Saudi Arabia. His government plummeted in the polls and was on the brink of collapse. The IDF faced losing its operational readiness amid a massive wave of refusal to serve from reservists, spearheaded by over a thousand pilots. Observing these developments not far from Israel's borders was seasoned murderer Yahya Sinwar. The Jewish people have faced many sworn enemies, but none spoke flawless Hebrew quite like Gaza's Hamas leader. After twenty years in an Israeli prison, he expertly followed Israeli TV news in its original language. Years earlier, in a prison interview, he suggested in Hebrew that a ceasefire might be an option because, "We know that Israel has the most sophisticated and aggressive air force in the region. We know that we can't defeat Israel." But after watching pilots declare that they would abandon their cockpit night after night, perhaps he changed his mind? For years, he had methodically planned the lethal assault aimed at overrunning southern Israel and igniting a general offensive against the Zionist state until its annihilation. He interpreted the disintegration of Israel's air force as a sign from above—from the cockpit—that Allah stood with him.

It was not the rift that caused the war. The murder and rape gangs that attacked Israel on the Jewish holiday of Simchat Torah had been training for the raid for nearly two years. But the rift blinded Israel from taking preemptive measures to ward off this devastating assault. The Israeli civil war played out over five successive election campaigns, culminating in 2023 with violent clashes in the streets, the Knesset, and courts. Every Israeli contributed about a thousand dollars in taxes to fund this celebration of democracy, aimed at recruiting the finest minds and talents in media and advertising to outmaneuver the opposition and secure the crucial sixty-first Knesset seat—the one that would ultimately determine the outcome of the conflict. Meanwhile, every Hamas member and Iranian citizen contributed, albeit a lesser amount, to the finest minds and talents in terror and murder, recruited to kill as many Israelis as possible.

Tragically, the latter proved more successful. While Israel tore itself apart on Simchat Torah over whether Orthodox Jews should be allowed to dance in gender-segregated areas in Tel Aviv's Dizengoff Square in the name of religious freedom or be prohibited from doing so in the name of gender equality, media crews and extremists from both sides prepared to document this impending religious conflict set for October 7 at six thirty in the evening.

By nightfall, Dizengoff Square already overflowed with aid packages for the stunned kibbutznikim barricading themselves and their children against Hamas murderers. Horrific videos of the murder, rape, burning, and looting inundated the internet, most filmed by the terrorists themselves to celebrate the slaughter of 1,200 innocent Israelis, from a ten-month-old baby to a ninety-seven-year-old senior.

The most chilling video contained no graphic images. It captured the voices of two terrorists racing toward Kibbutz Be'eri. Kibbutzim in Israel are long-standing leftist strongholds, and Be'eri was one of the most notable among them. The collective socialism that has vanished elsewhere still thrives within these landscaped communities, with shared property, equal incomes, and communal dining rooms. Nevertheless, as the terrorists raced with death through the fields, they shouted to one another ecstatically: "There's the settlement! There are the settlers!" It is hard to imagine a greater insult for a kibbutznik than to be called a "settler," and vice versa. Another example? When Iranian political cartoons depict a cruel Zionist soldier, they draw him as they imagine Jews: wearing a kippah, a thick beard, and curly sidelocks—in other words, as a Haredi. Try explaining to them that Israel's fiercest internal conflict stems from the Haredi community's refusal to serve in the military.

So if a raging hostile mob a mile from our borders perceives a kibbutznik and a settler, a leftist and a rightist, a Haredi and a secularist as indistinguishable from one another, what does this reveal about the fierce debate of recent years, which occasionally devolved into violence, chaos, and the feeling that burning the country down might be preferable to letting it fall into the other side's hands? It reveals that while very important, this debate should be addressed at a much lower temperature and decibel level—and perhaps shelved for another generation or two.

Nations, I contend, experience a midlife crisis. They are born, grow, and then after establishing themselves, ask themselves—where to from here? But Israel stands unique. Like Benjamin Button, it occasionally regresses in age. In our case, we have regressed from middle age to draft age. We now realize that the war for our survival never ended.

On October 7, an earthquake struck Israel. As we learned in geography, seismic events occur when tectonic plates collide. One plate shifts rapidly from left to right, carrying hundreds of thousands of well-intentioned Israelis. They believed in coexistence, the two-state solution, and land for peace until that holiday morning's monstrous wave of evil crashing into peaceful communities shattered their belief in compromises. The coast is not to blame for the tsunami; it is the sea.

Conversely, a massive tectonic plate is shifting from right to left, carrying even more Israelis. For years, they cast their votes for right-wing parties that pledged to take a firm stance on terrorism. October 7 forced them to confront the terrible cost of long-term policies that fed the monster with cash-filled suitcases and supply-laden trucks. They refuse to even consider supporting the previous leadership.

The result of such collisions, after a few million years, is that a mountain may form at the center. This mountain consists of countless voters who are sick and tired of the old, toxic debate that has drained the state's strength. They recognize that 80 percent of the public can cooperate on 80 percent of the issues they agree on. In terms of security, the public has pivoted to the right, meaning that they have become convinced that the most effective way to address threats is not through agreements, treaties, impassioned speeches from the president of the United States, or withdrawals but by deploying IDF soldiers to the danger point, and swiftly and decisively identifying and eliminating the threat. However, on domestic issues, the public has moved to the center, meaning that it prefers to agree on what is possible rather than to quarrel over what is not.

Politics is like an accordion. Sometimes it is closed, the hands holding it very close together. Such periods are characterized by governments of technocrats, political apathy, and low voter turnout. And then the accordion gradually expands, producing a discordant sound as the ends move further apart. That is when identity trumps meaning, populism eclipses substance, friendships fracture over ideological differences, voter turnout soars, and temperatures approach the boiling point. Good people begin to fear that the accordion—pardon the metaphor—may tear apart.

But this is also the stage when states often begin to heal and reconcile, with calm gradually restored.

This kind of political transformation is almost always accompanied by a change in personnel. As described earlier in the book, leaders typically fall into two distinct types. The first is the cilantro type: You either love it or hate it. Cilantro's distinctive flavor, so prevalent in Middle

Eastern dishes, elicits strong reactions, and there's no middle ground, no convincing someone to change their mind. No cilantro opponent has ever granted it a second chance. David Ben-Gurion inspired both love and hatred; so did Menachem Begin. Some loathe Netanyahu, while others cannot envision life without him. Such leaders typically form narrow governments, face a contentious opposition, and exhibit a confrontational nature. We need such leaders. Establishing a state, signing dramatic agreements, or making painful cuts rarely achieves broad consensus.

But then it ends. The great Ben-Gurion, who established the state but also ordered the Shin Bet to target his political adversaries, was succeeded by Levi Eshkol, who formed Israel's first unity government. Begin, renowned for his eloquence and occasional incitement against rivals, was followed by Yitzhak Shamir, a man about whom it was joked that he avoided speaking on the phone until the day he died, fearing that British police were still listening.

I cannot predict who will lead Israel through the long healing process needed after the trauma of October 7, the long war, and the societal rift. But like in police work, I can try to sketch a profile: This leader will be unremarkable, devoid of charisma, and boring. More radish than cilantro. They will lean right on security, hold capitalist economic views, practice traditional Judaism, embrace a liberal civic outlook, and enthusiastically support broad governments. They will lead a center-right or right-center government where minority shareholders cannot seize control of the corporation.

I haven't wagered too much here. Most Israelis share these traits, as will the overwhelming majority of their leadership. And most importantly, that is how history works.

End, with the verse "Merry Christmas Maggie Thatcher / We all celebrate today / 'Cause it's one day closer to your death." Thatcher was succeeded by John Major, who was portrayed as uniformly gray in every television satire show.

In France, the gaffe-prone and controversy-stricken Nicolas Sarkozy was followed by the pallid François Hollande. Fed up with scandals, the French warmly embraced him as "Monsieur Normale." Donald Trump made as much noise as an out-of-control jackhammer for four whole years, until he lost to Joe Biden, a professional politician with nearly fifty years' of experience. Biden's presidential schedule included, instead of angry tweeting, tea with his wife in the morning and fireside cuddles with her in the Oval Office. An American journalist wisely identified the reason for Biden's victory: "I want to spend two weeks of my life without having to think about my president even once."

Franklin D. Roosevelt steered the United States into the Second World War by force of charisma. When he died in office, he was succeeded by Harry Truman, an obscure politician with modest oratorical skills. Yet it was Truman, of all people, who dropped two atomic bombs on Japan, spearheaded the Marshall Plan for the reconstruction of Europe, and now ranks among America's finest presidents. Truman garnered far more respect from historians than contemporaries: Not daring to seek reelection, he quit politics. It is no coincidence that he was among the American presidents whom Yitzhak Shamir most admired. That's politics: Sometimes it's like *The Truman Show*, and sometimes it's just like Harry Truman.

This book has chronicled fateful decisions of twelve Israeli prime ministers who forged Israeli politics. But one decision evaded them all: to say, "Enough." To retire with dignity, depart in good health, and walk away with a reasonable reputation, a clean criminal record, and a legacy untarnished by shortcomings. This eluded Israel's first fourteen prime ministers. Who knows, perhaps the next one will break this pattern.

Timeline of Important Israeli Political Events

January 25, 1949—Elections for the Constituent Assembly, which becomes the First Knesset, using proportional representation.

1948–1954—David Ben-Gurion

October 30, 1950—Ben-Gurion resigns in the wake of political difficulties, the first of seven resignations.

1954–1955—Moshe Sharrett

November 3, 1955—Sharrett leaves office after losing control over his government.

1955–1966—David Ben-Gurion

June 16, 1963—Ben-Gurion resigns as prime minister for the last time.

May 29, 1965—Ben-Gurion quits Mapai and forms Rafi.

1963–1969—Levi Eshkol

June 1, 1967—Establishment of the first unity government: Begin is appointed a minister in anticipation of the Six-Day War.

January 21, 1968—Formation of the Labor Party, a union of three workers' parties.

February 26, 1969—Levi Eshkol dies of heart failure; Yigal Allon briefly serves as acting prime minister.

1969–1974—Golda Meir

September 13, 1973—Formation of the Likud, a union of five right-wing and centrist parties.

October 6, 1973—The outbreak of the Yom Kippur War causes the postponement of Knesset elections for the first time, by two months. Golda Meir's Alignment wins but loses strength and for the first time loses to the Likud in the soldiers' vote.

April 11, 1974—Golda Meir resigns in the wake of the Yom Kippur War.

1975–1977—Yitzhak Rabin

December 14, 1976—The "Sabbath desecration" crisis over the late arrival of fighter jets brings down Rabin's government.

May 17, 1977—The "upheaval": The Likud wins power for the first time in Israel's history.

1977–1983—Menachem Begin

January 12, 1981—The first murder of a member of the Knesset: Hamad Abu Rabia is shot dead by the sons of the man next in line on his Knesset list.

August 28, 1983—Begin resigns as prime minister, saying, "I cannot continue to fulfill this role."

1983–1984—Yitzhak Shamir

July 23, 1984—Shas first enters the Knesset, with four seats.

September 13, 1984—Formation of the Peres-Shamir rotation government; the last Knesset to date to have completed its full term.

1984–1986—Shimon Peres

October 20, 1986—Peres honors the rotation agreement and hands power to Shamir.

1986–1992—Yitzhak Shamir

March 15–June 11, 1990—The stinking maneuver: Peres topples Shamir's government but fails to swear in his own government. Shamir returns and forms a government.

1992–1995—Yitzhak Rabin

June 23, 1992—Labor under Rabin returns to power and forms a government with Shas, with the support of the Arab parties.

September 13, 1993—Rabin signs the Oslo Accords, just a few days after Deri resigns from his government.

November 4, 1995—Prime Minister Rabin is murdered in Kings of Israel Square in Tel Aviv by a Jewish assassin.

1995–1996—Shimon Peres

May 29, 199X—Netanyahu beats Peres in direct elections and the Likud returns to power.

1996–1999—Benjamin Netanyahu

December 13, 1998—Netanyahu's government falls because of the agreement with Arafat to transfer to him 13 percent of Judea and Samaria.

1999–2001—Ehud Barak

May 17, 1999—Barak beats Netanyahu and forms a government with Shas.

July 25, 2000—The Camp David Summit, attended by Barak, Arafat, and Clinton, ends in failure.

2001–2006—Ariel Sharon

February 6, 2001—Sharon beats Barak in direct elections. Labor has never since returned to government.

February 28, 2003—For the first time since the upheaval of 1977, a coalition is formed without the Haredim: Sharon forms a government with Tommy Lapid's Shinui.

November 21, 2005—Sharon dismantles the Likud and forms Kadima.

2006–2009—Ehud Olmert

January 4, 2006—Sharon suffers a serious stroke and is declared incapacitated. Ehud Olmert becomes acting prime minister.

May 28, 2008—Businessman Morris Talansky testifies in court about the transfer of envelopes of cash to the prime minister. Olmert is forced to announce his resignation as prime minister.

2009–2021—Benjamin Netanyahu

March 31, 2009—Netanyahu returns to power after a decade in opposition.

January 28, 2013—Yair Lapid and Naftali Bennett first enter the Knesset.

May 29, 2019—The Twenty-First Knesset is dissolved after just a month because of Netanyahu's failure to form a government.

July 20, 2019—Netanyahu overtakes Ben-Gurion and becomes the longest-serving prime minister in Israeli history.

January 28, 2020—For the first time in Israel's history, an indictment is served against a prime minister: Netanyahu is charged with bribery, fraud, and breach of trust.

May 15, 2020—The Knesset approves the establishment of the rotation government between Netanyahu and Gantz, but the agreement collapses after a few months. Gantz swears an oath as prime minister, but the Knesset is dispersed before he enters the role.

2021—Naftali Bennett

June 13, 2021—The Bennett-Lapid government wins the Knesset's confidence.

Endnotes

Chapter 1

1 Yossi Sarid, "Israel's first kibbutz-free Knesset," *Haaretz* (25 December 2012), available at https://www.haaretz.com/. premium-israel-s-first-kibbutz-free-knesset-1.5281076.

2 Gil Littman, *Yitzhak Shamir's Political Career, 1970-1992: From His Entry into Politics until his Resignation as Prime Minister* (PhD. diss., Haifa University), 123 [Hebrew].

3 *Yediot Aharonot*, 1 March 2020 [Hebrew].

4 Meron Medzini, *Golda: A Political Biography* (Tel Aviv: Yediot Books, 2008), 476 [Hebrew].

5 Meir Ariel, "Schism" (*Pilug*) [Hebrew], excerpt courtesy of Shahar Ariel.

6 Yoram Taharlev, "Herzl," excerpt courtesy of the author.

7 Gideon Rahat, "The Electoral System 1948-1959: From Default to an Entrenched System," *Iyyunim Bitkumat Israel* 11 (2001), 369-446 [Hebrew].

8 Nir Atmor, *Regional Elections, Pros and Cons* (Jerusalem: Israel Democracy Institute, 2008).

9 Rahat, "The Electoral System 1948-1959," 391 [Hebrew].

10 Rahat, ibid., 380 [Hebrew].

11 Boaz Shapira, "Electoral Reforms in Israel, 1949-1996," in Gideon Doron, ed., *The Electoral Revolution* (Tel Aviv: Hakibbutz Hameuchad, 1996), 19 [Hebrew].

12 Littman, *Yitzhak Shamir's Political Career*, 187 [Hebrew].

13 Vico Atooan, "Thirty Years of Netanyahu: Chapter 1," Channel 11, 23 April 2018 [Hebrew], available at: https://www.youtube.com/watch?v=F8j6ltbGMSU.

14 Bina Barzel, "Modai Will Demand Guarantees from Likud Worth $10 Million," *Yediot Aharonot*, 23 April 1992 [Hebrew].

Chapter 2

1 Nahman Tamir, ed., *Golda: Anthology in Her Memory* (1981), 37 [Hebrew].

2 Medzini, *Golda*, 132 [Hebrew].

3 Medzini, *Golda,* 117 [Hebrew].

4 Daphna Aviram-Nitzan, Assaf Shapira, *Voting Security* (Jerusalem: Israel Democracy Institute, 2019) [Hebrew].

5 *Yediot Aharonot*, 5 October 1973 [Hebrew].
6 Medzini, *Golda*, 536 [Hebrew].
7 Ronen Bergman, "An Officer and a Gentleman: In Memory of Amos Gilboa," *Yediot Aharonot*, 13 December 2020 [Hebrew].
8 Medzini, *Golda*, 486 [Hebrew].
9 Yossi Goldstein, *Golda—A Biography* (Beersheba: Ben-Gurion University of the Negev, 2012).
10 *A History of the Yom Kippur War* (IDF, 2019) [Hebrew].
11 *Yediot Aharonot*, 17 November 1973 [Hebrew].
12 *Haaretz*, 21 October 1969 [Hebrew].
13 Avi Shilon, *Begin: 1913-1992* (Tel Aviv: Am Oved, 2007), 247 [Hebrew].
14 Moshe Arens, "Why the Likud Remains in Power," *Haaretz*, 23 March 2016 [Hebrew].
15 "What's Burning with Razi Barkai," IDF Army Radio, 17 June 2005 [Hebrew].
16 Ari Shavit, *Haaretz*, 30 April 2014 [Hebrew].
17 Nachum Barnea, *Yediot Aharonot*, 29 March 2006 [Hebrew].
18 Michal Shamir, ed., *Israel's 2013 Elections* (Jerusalem: Israel Democracy Institute).
19 Medzini, *Golda*, 656 [Hebrew]; *Yediot Aharonot*, 10 December 1978 [Hebrew]. There are conflicting accounts of whether she shouted "Eli" or "Eddy."

Chapter 3

1 Ze'ev Jabotinsky, *Story of My Life: Part I—Autobiographical Writings*, 18 [Hebrew].
2 Ofer Grosbard, *Menachem Begin: Portrait of a Leader* (Jerusalem: Resling, 2006), 145.
3 Haaretz, 2 June 1949 [Hebrew].
4 Eliezer Don Yehiya, "Between Nationalism and Religion: Shifts in Jabotinsky's Position Toward Religious Tradition," in Avi Bareli and Pinhas Ginossar, eds., *Man in a Storm: Essays and Studies about Ze'ev Jabotinsky* (Beersheba: Ben-Gurion University, 2004), 164 [Hebrew].
5 Haggai Segal, *Land for Dreams* (Tel Aviv: Yediot Books, 2013), 67 [Hebrew].
6 Don Yehiya, "Between Nationalism and Religion," 169 [Hebrew].
7 Grosbard, *Menachem Begin*, 115 [Hebrew].
8 Shilon, *Begin*, 122 [Hebrew].
9 Alex Ansky, *The Sale of the Likud* (Modan: 1978), 47 [Hebrew].
10 Shilon, *Begin*, 194 [Hebrew].
11 Ibid., 244 [Hebrew].
12 Ibid., 151 [Hebrew].
13 Grosbard, *Menachem Begin*, 124 [Hebrew].
14 Shalom Ratzabi, *Jabotinsky and Religion* (2004) [Hebrew].
15 Shilon, *Begin*, 257 [Hebrew].
16 Carolina Landsmann, "The Real Reason Mizrahim Vote for Netanyahu, and Why the Left Can't Win Them Over," *Haaretz*, 11 January 2020, available at: https://www.haaretz.com/israel-news/elections/.premium.MAGAZINE-the-real-reason-mizrahim-vote-for-netanyahu-and-why-the-left-can-t-win-them-over-1.8378189.
17 Littman, *Yitzhak Shamir's Political Career*, 273 [Hebrew].
18 *Yediot Aharonot*, 28 September 1997 [Hebrew].

19 Kave Shafran, *Master of Influence: Benjamin Netanyahu's 10 Secrets of Power, Rhetoric, and Charisma* (eBookPro, 2021).
20 Shilon, *Begin*, 241 [Hebrew].
21 Ibid., 274 [Hebrew].

Chapter 4

1   Littman, *Yitzhak Shamir's Political Career*, 97 [Hebrew].
2   Ibid., 73 [Hebrew].
3   Ansky, *The Sale of the Likud* [Hebrew].
4   Haim Misgav, *Conversations with Yitzhak Shamir* (1997) [Hebrew].
5   Littman, *Yitzhak Shamir's Political Career*, 73 [Hebrew].
6   Nahum Barnea, "The Prime Minister-Designate," *Davar HaShavua*, 9 June 1978 [Hebrew].
7   Misgav, *Conversations with Yitzhak Shamir*, 174 [Hebrew].
8   Ilan Kfir, *Maariv*, 29 August 1983 [Hebrew].
9   Arieh Avneri, *The Defeat: The Crumbling of Likud Rule* (Tel Aviv: Midot, 1993), 235 [Hebrew].
10 Misgav, *Conversations with Yitzhak Shamir*, 122 [Hebrew].
11 Yitzhak Shamir, *In Summary* (Tel Aviv: Yediot Books, 1998) [Hebrew].
12 Arnon Lammfromm, *Levi Eshkol: The Biography* (Tel Aviv: Resling, 2014), 22 [Hebrew].
13 Eshkol's letter to members of Kibbutz Afikim, 14 December 1965 [Hebrew].
14 Shilon, *Begin*, 177 [Hebrew].
15 Yehiam Weitz and Ofira Gruweis-Kovalsky, "The Reburial of Ze'ev Jabotinsky in the Discussions of Israel's Cabinet," *Cathedra* 155 (2015) [Hebrew].
16 Lammfromm, *Levi Eshkol*, 335 [Hebrew].
17 *Levi Eshkol: Collection of Official Documents*, 489 [Hebrew].
18 Avi Shilon, *Ben-Gurion: Epilogue* (Tel Aviv: Am Oved, 2013), 58 [Hebrew].
19 Lammfromm, *Levi Eshkol*, 483 [Hebrew].
20 Broadcast to the nation on Kol Israel, Jerusalem, 21 February 1966 [Hebrew].
21 Lammfromm, *Levi Eshkol*, 274 [Hebrew].
22 Telegram to Moshe Dayan, 4 June 1967 [Hebrew].
23 Littman, *Yitzhak Shamir's Political Career*, 313 [Hebrew].
24 Misgav, *Conversations with Yitzhak Shamir*, 205 [Hebrew].
25 Shilon, *Ben-Gurion: Epilogue*, 90-91 [Hebrew].

Chapter 5

1   Babylonian Talmud, Sanhedrin 102b.
2   Michael Bar-Zohar, *Shimon Peres: The Biography* (New York: Random House, 2007), 389.
3   Ibid., 389.
4   Ibid., 436.
5   Keren Neubach, *The Race: The 1996 Elections* (Tel Aviv: Yediot Books, 1996), 7 [Hebrew].
6   Bar-Zohar, *Shimon Peres*, 387.
7   Ibid., 505.
8   Ibid., 505.

Chapter 6

1 Yosef Tamir, *The MK Who Filmed Everything*, Channel 2, 11 January 2007 [Hebrew].
2 From author's conversation with pollster Manu Geva.
3 "Uproar After Recording of Rabbi Ovadia Against Aloni," *Yediot Aharonot*, 22 September 1992 [Hebrew].
4 Haim Ramon, *Against the Wind* (Tel Aviv: Yediot Books, 2020), 290 [Hebrew].
5 Shimon Shiffer, *Yediot Aharonot*, 5 August 1992 [Hebrew].
6 *Maariv*, 21 August 1979 [Hebrew].
7 *Aryeh Deri: The Movie*, HaMakor, Channel 10, 22 October 2012 [Hebrew].
8 Tzvi Alush and Yossi Eliyatuv, *Ben Porat Yosef: The Life, Teachings, and Politics of Rabbi Ovadia Yosef* (Or Yehuda: Kinneret, 2004), 257 [Hebrew].
9 Ramon, *Against the Wind*, 288 [Hebrew].
10 Ibid., 301 [Hebrew].
11 Shimon Sheves, *Friend* (Tel Aviv: Yediot Books), 143 [Hebrew].
12 Yonatan Reguer, *When Rabin Said 'Gush Emunim is a Cancer,'* Channel 2, 24 September 2015 [Hebrew].
13 Sheves, *Friend*, 125 [Hebrew].
14 Alush and Eliyatuv, *Ben Porat Yosef*, 25 [Hebrew].
15 Nahum Barnea, "Behind Their Backs," *Yediot Aharonot*, 1 January 1999 [Hebrew].
16 *Yediot Aharonot*, 13 June 1993 [Hebrew].
17 Shimon Shiffer, "Rabin Will Warn Aloni: Another Out-of-Line Statement and You're Out," *Yediot Aharonot*, 27 September 1992 [Hebrew].
18 *Yediot Aharonot*, 7 September 1993 [Hebrew].
19 Full list of laws struck down by the Supreme Court: https://en.idi.org.il/articles/31874
20 Nitzan Chen and Anshel Pfeffer, *Maran: Ovadia Yosef—The Biography* (Jerusalem: Keter, 2004) [Hebrew].
21 Interview with Ehud Barak, *Yediot Aharonot*, 11 December 2020 [Hebrew].
22 Tzvi Alush, *Yediot Aharonot*, 19 March 2000 [Hebrew].

Chapter 7

1 Amit Segal, "At Any Price?" *Haaretz*, 25 June 2010, available at: https://www.haaretz.com/1.5139405.
2 Haggai Segal, *Blood and Champagne*, 19 August 2018 [Hebrew].
3 Sheves, *Friend*, 43 [Hebrew].
4 *Yediot Aharonot*, 7 August 1990 [Hebrew].
5 *Haaretz*, 17 August 1990, 31 January 1991 [Hebrew].
6 *Yediot Aharonot*, 11 September 1993 [Hebrew].
7 From data collected by Dr. Or Anavi of the Israel Democracy Institute.
8 Raviv Drucker, *Harikari: Ehud Barak Put to the Test* (Tel Aviv: Yediot Books, 2002) [Hebrew].
9 Ibid.
10 Ibid.
11 Nahum Barnea, "Dancing with Arafat," *Seventh Eye*, 1 January 2002 [Hebrew].
12 Gidi Weitz, "Shelly Yachimovich: Miss Mainstream," *Haaretz*, 19 August 2011 [Hebrew].

Chapter 8

1 Eitan Glickman, "Sharon: Evacuation of Yamit Was a Mistake," *Yediot Aharonot*, 30 January 2011 [Hebrew].
2 Yossi Sarid, *Haaretz*, 10 January 2014 [Hebrew].
3 Levi Zini, *Sharon: The First Chapter*, Kan 11, 2020 [Hebrew].
4 Dov Weisglass, *Arik Sharon: Prime Minister* (Tel Aviv: Yediot Books, 2012), 117 [Hebrew].
5 Ibid., 278 [Hebrew].
6 Ibid., 141 [Hebrew].
7 Chen Friedberg, "Improving the Legislative Process in the Knesset," *Israel Democracy Institute* [Hebrew].
8 Nahum Barnea, "Beauty Queen," *Yediot Aharonot*, 25 March 1996 [Hebrew].

Chapter 9

1 Shmuel Tamir, *Son of This Land: A Biography* (Lod: Zemora Bitan, 2002), 430 [Hebrew].
2 Ibid., 431 [Hebrew].
3 Ibid., 322 [Hebrew]
4 Ibid., [Hebrew].
5 Gil Samsonov, *The Princes* (Tel Aviv: Dvir, 2015), 48 [Hebrew].
6 Samsonov, *The Princes*, 333 [Hebrew].
7 Weisglass, *Arik Sharon*, 101 [Hebrew].
8 Amichai Cohen, *The Supreme Court Wars: The Constitutional Revolution and Counterrevolution* (Tel Aviv: Kinneret Zemora Bitan, 2020) [Hebrew].

Chapter 10

1 Shafran, *Master of Influence*.
2 Ibid.
3 *Haaretz*, 14 February 2015 [Hebrew].

Acknowledgments

THANK YOU TO EVERYONE who read this book and shared comments: to Professor Reuven Hazan and Gideon Rahat, world experts in political and electoral systems, for your important corrections concerning Ben-Gurion; to Dr. Avi Shilon, an expert Beginologist; and to Kobi Arieli, Naomi Kandel-Toledano, Lior Friedman, Yehudit Damari-Agassi, Hani Weiser, Yoram Cohen, Aluf Benn, Nadav Perry, Amos Harel, Shelly Yachimovich, and especially Yaron Dekel for your new insights and stories from decades of covering Israel's politics.

Thank you to my editors and managers: Avi Weiss and Guy Sudri of Channel 2 and Netta Livne from *Yediot Aharonot*, who wished me well, read drafts, shared comments, and for years served as my focus group for ideas that I have elaborated on here.

Thank you to Shmuel Rosner, who advised me long ago to focus on the politicians' decisions as a way to tell a more rounded story about Israeli politics and generously contributed his good advice. Thank you to Hanoch and Efrat Daum, whose experience and insights helped me self-publish the Hebrew edition of this book. Thank you to Noga Goldfinger Haran and the whole team of the Israel Democracy Institute.

Thank you to the editor of this book, Hagai Segal, with whom I have a certain prior acquaintance. Thank you to Rina Nakonechny for proof-reading. Thank you to Keren and Golan Gafni from the Keren & Golan Graphic Design Studio, who turned this manuscript into the product you are holding now.

Thank you to Reut, who is not only my wife and my best friend for the past decade but also a one-woman marketing, development, and sales

Acknowledgments

department. She was the one who turned an amorphous idea into the book that you are holding and who reminds me every day that there are more important things in life than politics. Three of them are the adorable Ivri, Aner, and Eliana, who have had to hear far more conversations about coalitions than is advisable for children their age. I wish them calmer years to come, God willing.

About the Author

Amit Segal is Israel's most influential journalist, known for his sharp analysis and insider access to the country's power corridors. As the chief political correspondent for Channel 12 News and a columnist for Yedioth Ahronoth, he has covered Israeli politics since the early 2000s.

Segal holds a master's degree in political science from University College London and a law degree from the Hebrew University of Jerusalem. His bestselling book, *A Phone Call at 4 AM* (originally *The Story of Israeli Politics*), became Israel's top-selling book of 2021 and has been translated into Arabic and Russian.